Hamlyn all-colour paperbacks

Flower Arranging

Violet Stevenson

illustrated by George Thompson
June Baker and Elsie Wrigley

Hamlyn Paperbacks

FOREWORD

Flowers can be used for every occasion – to enhance your furnishings, decorate your table and inspire your party. They can become the talking piece at a social function breaking the ice between awkward guests or be the object of much attention in a competition. Advice on each is contained in this book. Whichever way you like flowers, simplicity should be the keynote to good flower arranging and the best results have usually been easy to arrange. Everything is given here from when to pick flowers and how to transport them, to drying them and creating them into actual arrangements. Oriental arrangements are dealt with too. Colour harmony is important, and it is essential for a beginner to understand this. The colour wheel and chart help to explain it.

Different flowers ask for different types of arrangements and different containers. It is surprising just how many varied utensils can be employed when searching for holders – tea caddys, ashtrays, all can be suitably used. And most plant material arranges well, fruit, leaves, vegetables and seed heads – even wood can be used effectively. Explanations are given in this book.

With this book as a guide, even a beginner can find a worthwhile hobby that's bound to bring hours of enjoyment, and plenty of praise. And it's beautifully illustrated throughout with colour drawings that help to clarify the text.

Published by Hamlyn Paperbacks
The Hamlyn Publishing Group Limited
Astronaut House, Feltham, Middlesex, England

Copyright © The Hamlyn Publishing Group Limited 1969
Eleventh printing 1979
ISBN 0 600 00125 3

Phototypeset by BAS Printers Limited, Wallop, Hampshire
Colour separations by Schwitter Limited, Zurich
Printed in Spain by Mateu Cromo, Madrid

CONTENTS

INTRODUCTION

Quite the best way of teacning is by example and in the past I have been fortunate in having been given the opportunity to show my kind of flower arranging, and so through the medium of both words and pictures to pass on my experience to others. However, this is the first time I have been given the opportunity to teach in a book which is completely in colour. What a wonderful advantage this is! One can write for ever about colour harmonies, contrasts and analogies; one can try to explain the subtleties of tinge and shade of tone and hue, but words are not enough. How much better to be able to say what I mean by showing my flower arrangements entirely in colour.

If flowers are to be arranged both attractively and skilfully it follows that one must know and understand what lies behind the skill of the art of flower arrangement. There are certain rules which can be followed, though perhaps these are more properly described as guide lines rather than rigid laws. There are also many tricks of the trade which can be used to save time and materials. Some can be used to make

Flower arrangement means value for money. By placing a few blooms in a simple pattern you display each one to its full advantage.

Even in large, glorious decorations each flower should have room to breathe. There are simple, easy to follow rules, that aid the arranger.

cut flowers live as long as possible; others help us to preserve and keep them and so enable us to enjoy their beauty for a little longer.

It is a firm maxim of mine that besides being aesthetically beneficial, flower arrangement is also absolutely practical, for it is value for money! If you understand it you can display as little as one flower and make a decoration of it. And yet, should your garden be full of bloom, you can fill your house with flowers in the shortest possible time in such a way that they will enhance their surroundings and reward you with that wonderful sense of achievement. Flower arrangement is really worthwhile!

GOOD BEGINNINGS

If you want your flowers to live for many days after you have brought them home from the shop you must see that they are in the best condition when you buy them. When I see lovely flowers on sale I am always reminded of a market wholesaler who told me that a grower had just telephoned him to say that he had a greenhouse full of flowers which at that moment were looking as beautiful as he, the grower, had ever seen them. 'If that's the case, you keep them!' my friend told him. 'They are no good to me if they look absolutely beautiful to you! I want them looking that way after they reach the customers!'

There are many flowers which ought to be only sold in bud: all narcissi, including daffodils, irises, tulips, most lilies and many other bulb flowers, all of which will mature in water. Not only will these flowers travel better in bud and become less damaged but they will live longer indoors and you will have the extra pleasure of watching them open into full-grown blooms and change daily before your eyes.

A flower's true function is either to fertilize another or to become fertilized itself, or maybe both. Once this happens and the flower reaches maturity it will begin to fade and nothing will prevent it. Some flowers take longer to reach

this point but obviously, the younger a flower is, the better. Ripe and/or spilled pollen is an indication that a flower has reached or even passed maturity.

Double and full-petalled flowers like chrysanthemums, that show no central cluster of stamens, should show instead a central zone of young petals, still tight enough to make a dimple in the flower's centre. If you see a curled, thread-like anther rising above the petals of a double flower, such as a carnation, it is likely to be much too old for you to buy. and you should avoid doing so. The stem ends should look wholesome, with no signs of slime, decomposing foliage or brown stains.

(*Left*) All narcissi should be bought in bud. Supplement week-old blooms with new buds, either together in a vase or apart, as they are in this little brass balance.
(*Right*) Young chrysanthemums have a central dimple of young often green petals. Anemones have immature sepals and no spilled pollen on the base of the petals. Gladiolis should have only the lower floret opening. Narcissi should be in bud. Tulip petals should still be curled under.

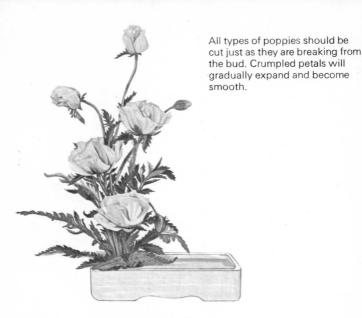

All types of poppies should be cut just as they are breaking from the bud. Crumpled petals will gradually expand and become smooth.

How to gather flowers and when

If you go into the garden early to gather flowers, you are more likely to catch them just as they are breaking bud and before the bees have visited and pollinated them. After a long cool night, stems should be turgid and cells well charged with water.

Roses are said to last longest in sunny weather if they are cut at midday.

If roses are picked too tight in bud the petals will never expand properly. The calyx of sepals, which covers the petals and protects them when young, should be growing outwards and downwards. It is safest to wait until at least one of the petals has begun to grow away from the mass.

Many of the daisy tribe will not take water well after cutting unless the flowers are at the right stage. The ray florets should have fully expanded, although the disc florets, those which form the centre 'eye', should still be immature.

Almost all bulb flowers can be picked in bud when the colour of the bloom is beginning to show. If you want the bulb to produce flowers the following year, either cut the

Where flowers grow several to a stem, wait until the first bloom is open and then cut. Then the younger flowers and buds will mature as the first one fades. Be sure to cut sweet peas with sharp secateurs. Do not try to pull them from the vine.

Rose buds can be cut too young in which case they will never open prettily in water. No matter what type, modern or old-fashioned, double or single, the calyx gives one a guide. Wait until the sepals begin to grow outward and downward.

stem as short as possible, or in the case of the leafless stems like narcissi, try to cut as few leaves as possible. Take one or two only from each plant. When narcissi buds crook to the 'gooseneck' stage, they are perfect for cutting.

Gladioli and other flowers which have a similar mode of growth should just be showing colour in the lowest floret.

Lilies should just be breaking bud. Reflexed petals should not yet have begun to turn back. Some people remove the pollen bearing anthers as soon as the petals open.

Rhododendrons may be cut as soon as the buds are sticky.

Blossom and early flowering shrubs may be cut after the turn of the year on a moist not freezing day.

To help stems take water quickly, split the ends upwards for an inch.

How to harden flowers

If flowers are to keep their first fresh appeal they must not be allowed to wilt. All flowers and foliage should be 'hardened' before being used in an arrangement by being given a long deep drink. Sometimes they will wilt inexplicably after having been arranged. A way to avoid this is always to use tepid water, not only for the first drink but also at the time of arrangement.

(*Left*) Cutting stems above the thick nodes. (*Below*) Removing alternate leaves from stocks. (*Right*) Covering hellebores cutting stem ends under water and stripping stem ends.

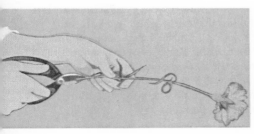

To put it in the simplest terms, a flower uses the same pores to give off moisture as it does to breathe. If, because of adverse conditions, it gives off water more quickly than it can be replaced, then the flower wilts. While any cut flower is out of water it still breathes but it is also losing essential moisture. It is not enough merely to stand the stem end in water, but if the stems and leaves can be covered no water can be lost and the stem cells will quickly conduct water to the flower.

This is why it is good to give most flowers and leaves a long, deep drink before arrangement. There are a few exceptions to this rule and these are dealt with later. However, before the stems are placed in water they need attention to ensure that they can function properly. One of the main causes of wilting is an air bubble which forms in the stem when the flower is cut preventing the flow of water from the stem end to the bloom. In most cases, all that is necessary to remedy this is to recut the stem a little higher up before placing it immediately in water.

Another method, good for hollow stems such as delphiniums, is to recut the stem under water. Both splitting the stem upwards and cutting it on a long slant are effective for many types of flowers.

Where there are many leaves, and especially if the blooms have soft petals, it may be necessary to remove some to cut down the area from which moisture will be lost. Stocks and many others are improved if every other leaf is carefully cut off. This retains the character of the flower which is lost if the stem is completely defoliated. Certainly all leaves on the part of stem to go under water should be removed. Leaves very near a bloom, where they are likely to hide the flower, as with roses, should be cut away.

Delicate flowers like gypsophila, fern fronds, young tender leaves or anything else of great frailty should be gently drawn through water.

Transporting flowers

If they have not been properly wrapped, many flowers fade on the way home. Usually, standing their stems in tepid water after recutting the ends is sufficient to help them become turgid again but sometimes a little first-aid is needed. Water is heavy and if these flowers or leaves are immersed in it, for even a minute they become bruised,

When you buy flowers in winter see that the florist envelops them entirely so that not only are the stem ends covered but also the blooms. In very cold weather a double layer of paper will keep out the cold.

damaged and discoloured. Instead, frail flowers and foliage should be gently drawn through a bowl of water so that some of the moisture is held on the petals like dew.

After this, gently shake them so that the surplus water is swished off, recut stem ends and stand them in tepid water to harden. Although this method is the salvation of some flowers, others spoil if allowed to remain wet, sweet peas and pansies are examples of these. Deterioration, however, can always be prevented by shaking flowers to dry them.

If flowers are to be transported, cut and pack them while they are dry. Do not give them a drink first. It is best to pack them in such a way that they lose little moisture. Remember that the best packing material for a flower is another flower. Those packed tightly in a box or plastic bag are less likely to come to as much harm as those in which moss or paper has been used to separate the flowers. If a box has to be lined with paper see that it is non-absorbent.

I find that the best way of all to transport flowers is to use strong, transparent plastic bags. They are best packed either according to their stem lengths or to their kind. Roses should not be packed with soft-petalled flowers in case the thorns damage them. Place the flowers upright, stem first, in the bag. There should be a good space between the top of the flowers and the opening of the bag for this cushion of air will protect them. Sappy flowers such as nasturtiums and soft velvety ones like pansies are best packed in a shallow tin or plastic food box with a well-fitting lid. Keep both bags and boxes out of sunshine. I transport flowers this way even in the height of summer.

A strong plastic bag is one of the best containers for transporting flowers from country to town. If the stem ends of roses are dethorned before they are packed and plenty of foliage is left on the stems, the plastic is not so likely to be torn. The bag should be made as airtight as possible so that no moisture is lost on the journey.

Violets must have humid conditions or they quickly die. One way to keep them is in wet gravel in a brandy balloon or glass bowl.

Helping flowers to live longer

Quite the most important factor in helping flowers to live longer is that both the containers and the water should be clean. Always wash vases after use. To keep the water clean and wholesome see that the portion of stem which is to go under water is stripped of foliage. Most leaves begin to decompose once they are immersed and this speeds up bacterial activity in the water. Worse offenders are members of the daisy family. Rose leaves are not likely to begin to decay before the flowers fade and, in fact, it is advisable to let some of these remain on the stem, even if they are under water, because they are known to feed the blooms. Evergreens also take a long time to decompose. But, generally speaking, it is best to take the lower leaves off.

Flowers respond to some form of plant food in the water. A teaspoonful of sugar or, alternatively, a saltspoonful of honey to a pint of water is appreciated by all.

When branches of blossom or evergreens are expected to stand for many days, a little soluble plant food helps to sustain them. Rose nutrients and other preservatives can be bought.

If these foods are to be added it is doubly important that the water does not become fouled. It is a fact that aspirin helps to keep water clean but only because it helps to delay bacterial activity. A copper coin has much the same effect and water keeps sweeter in metal containers but fouls quicker in glass. Some of the foamed plastic stem holders such as Florapak contain formaldehyde which acts as a deterrent to decay. A few small nuggets of charcoal help to keep water sweet. Rain water is better than tap water.

Some flowers live longest in shallow water; sweet peas are an example. Almost all bulb flowers last best this way, but forced tulips should be first stood in deep water to harden. The leafless kinds really do not need hardening.

If a flower, except a bulb one, has wilted very badly stand the stem in two inches of boiling water.

Flowers last longer if they are given certain easily assimilated foods. Sugar, glucose and proprietary nutrients can be added to the water.

It is not necessary to change the flower water daily but in shallow containers, best for bulb flowers, it evaporates and should be topped up.

Blossom lasts longest if it is undisturbed. A container with a narrow aperture prevents evaporation. Top up from time to time with a little soluble plant food. Water in metal containers keeps sweeter longer than in those of other materials.

Care and treatment of arranged flowers

Once flowers have been arranged it should not be necessary to disturb them again until the decoration is changed. If the water has become dirty, change it by taking the entire arrangement to the tap and let fresh water pour into some part of the container.

In hot rooms many flowers and leaves benefit by a light spray of clean room-temperature water. Flowers which grow in cool conditions, like violets, appreciate this. Chrysanthemums live longer if petals and leaves are sprayed once or twice a day. Full-petalled blooms like carnations seem to be prevented from becoming 'sleepy' too quickly.

Sometimes flowers wilt inexplicably. To revive them, remove them from the arrangement, recut the stems' ends and stand them in two inches of boiling water until the water cools. This method can be used on all flowers except those which grow from bulbs, because the boiling water will 'cook' the stems. However, few of these except tulips are likely to wilt. If tulips should wilt, recut the stems under water. If the stem end is much lighter than the rest cut all the pale portion away. Stand in deep tepid water to harden.

Lilac and other shrubs, garden fresh or forced, sometimes wilt badly after cutting. Cut away all leafy side stems, split these stem ends also and arrange them separately.

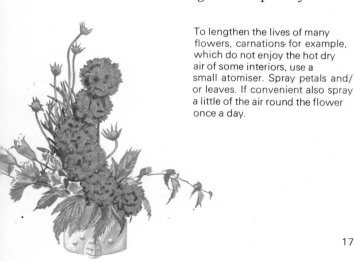

To lengthen the lives of many flowers, carnations for example, which do not enjoy the hot dry air of some interiors, use a small atomiser. Spray petals and/or leaves. If convenient also spray a little of the air round the flower once a day.

17

Every colour of the spectrum can be found in flowers. Foliage, stems, seeds and fruits bring a variety of hues, tones, tints and shades.

THE IMPORTANCE OF COLOUR

The colours of the rainbow are the only ones to be found throughout nature. These are known as the spectrum. Among them are three primary colours: red, yellow and blue. The secondary colours, orange, green and purple, are derived from combinations of primary colours. In a rainbow the primary colours appear to overlap to produce the secondary colours and we can see that blue and yellow give green, and yellow and red give orange. If we make the spectrum into a star we can see how red and blue overlap to give purple.

In a rainbow there always appears to be the same degree of light. Sometimes we see it more clearly when the colours seem more intense and we can say that they have a good tone but we do not see a dark rainbow or a very pale one. However, the colours round us vary much more. Dark ones which appear to have black in them are called shades.

Light colours that appear to have white or light added to them are known as 'tints'. 'Hues' describe those which lie between the true spectrum colours. A forest may appear green, but when you look more carefully you will see that it is composed of many kinds, or hues, of green.

If the spectrum colours are arranged in a star we can see that certain colours are opposite each other. It happens that these have a natural affinity and are known as complementaries. Thus, blue is complementary to orange, red to green and yellow to purple. When these are mixed we find that they make familiar 'safe' colours. Blue and orange make a grey, red and green make a brown, and purple and yellow make a tan. All of these are 'broken' colours.

Other colours may also be broken. It is worthwhile playing with a paint-box for an hour or two to discover what clear colours lie in any broken colour for these are found in many natural materials and are therefore useful.

If the rainbow colours are isolated and arranged in a star in their natural sequence, we can see that they have a natural affinity.

Colour harmony is important

As you become more familiar with flowers you will learn much about colour harmony from them, but in the meantime you can be guided by the colour wheel. The neighbouring colours, those which lie side by side, create natural analogous harmonies. Because we are dealing with flowers and not manufactured materials, it so happens that these harmonies are the easiest to create.

We can create two-colour analogous harmonies, but these are not always quite so satisfying nor so pretty as those in which three colours are used. Once again, because we are using flowers and not, say, fabrics, we are more likely to find that the three colours which we have chosen are of varying intensity.

Some colours are much more dominating than others. Red flowers in an arrangement tend to dominate the rest, but if this is not desirable one colour can always be toned down by using a greater proportion of some other colour to balance its stridency. You will find that broken colours are often helpful in this respect. And these broken colours should contain the true colour, by which I mean that to balance red, use brown, which contains red mixed with green.

Complementary harmonies, though natural are sometimes a little strong for some tastes. Orange and blue flowers, for example, in a large decoration might dominate a room but the same harmony made from tints of the same colours, in this case soft apricot and pale blue, might prove more pleasing. It all depends on the interior of the room or the setting in which the flowers are to be placed. Fortunately, in flower decoration lovely green is almost always present in the form of leaves or stems or other parts of the flower and this helps to form both a link or a buffer between one flower and another.

Colour can deepen in intensity from a tint, which is the colour with light or alternatively white added to it, to a shade which is the colour with shadow or black added. We speak of the variations in colour values as tones of a colour.

(*Left*) Many dried and preserved materials are in broken colours. Pleasant harmonies can be made by using them with one or more of the clear colours from which they are made. Here there are also tints of the brown made by mixing red and green.

Orange dahlias and gentians make a natural complementary harmony. The orange-hued ligularia leaves match the interior of the bowl ; the dahlias match its surface.

Harmonic themes

It is seldom possible to make colour harmonies of flowers in the same way that we could make them from paints or lengths of cloth. Flowers contain within their petals, stems, foliage and other parts, many colours, not all of which are evident from a casual glance. This means that if we want a two-colour harmony it is likely we shall find that other colours do creep in. A flower's stems, stamens, even leaves may be a bright green and although it is possible to defoliate a stem, it is not always desirable, for the sake of the flowers or even sometimes for their appearance. So we must compromise.

Quite often leaves coloured other than green can be used either to emphasise the floral colour or even to hide the existing green foliage and/or stems. This is one reason why it is wise, if you have a garden, to grow a good stock of plants which will produce leaves as well as or even instead of flowers. Sometimes you will find that the under-surface of leaves may be more colourful than the upper.

Flowers often point the way to analogous harmonies by the way that types of flower may vary in colour. Thus you

A blue glass and purple sweet peas set the theme for this analogous harmony. Anchusa, columbines, geranium, delphiniums and anemones contribute towards it.

will find that nasturtiums, for instance, all have colours and hues that can be arranged together in harmony. This cannot be taken as an infallible rule because Man has interfered with nature's colour plan and where once only two primary colours were ever present in a genus the hybridist has presented a third thus often taking us out of the analogous zone. For example, once sweet peas could be said to follow through from the reds to the purples but the hybridist is endeavouring to introduce yellow. However, in general the above rule stands and it is very helpful to the flower arranger who can take some flowers, say cornflowers, and arrange them together knowing that she is well on the way to creating a pleasant harmony. Her next step is to look for other flowers or plant materials that also carry the colours, perhaps in tints or shades, of the mixed cornflowers which she has chosen as the basis of her colour scheme.

Often the container in which the flowers are to be arranged will supply a missing colour. In analogous harmonies it is important that the container is considered part of the colour scheme, so enhancing the design.

Sprays of blackberries in varying degrees of ripeness suggested the colours for this arrangement. The container reminded me of blackberries and cream !

Learning about colour

As I said earlier, no flowers have one pure colour and by studying a flower an arranger can learn more about floral colour than by any other method. Quite often an idea for a lovely colour harmony is there in the heart of a tulip. Perhaps the petals are pink, at their bases you can see a zone of deep blue, the anthers are creamy, the stems and foliage a soft jade green. Here is your colour scheme ready to follow! Plan to use the colours in much the same proportion as you see them in the flower.

Take another lesson. Perhaps you do not want to use a particular flower, but it has just the colour that you have in your furnishings. If it is a flower that contains other colours at its centre, on the underside of its petals, foliage, or even buds and thorns, you can compare those colours not only with other self-coloured blooms but also with containers.

Since flower arrangement has become so popular I have met many people who have told me how 'doing the flowers' has taught them to see with new eyes.

It is fascinating to find that floral colours are not always what they seem. Take pink for example, I imagine that most of us think that we know that pink is a tint of red, but once we begin comparing floral colour we find, in fact that the pink we know most, that is the pink of cherry blossom, of sweet peas, peonies and carnations, is in fact a tint of spectrum purple! Salmon pink is a tint of red.

Earlier I recommended that one experimented with colours to find what lay behind the broken colours, but it is also well worth while spending some time diluting water colours to discover more about their tints. After this, spend a little time adding black to a colour so that you can make a mental colour scale of colours you know well.

Autumn leaves offer thrilling lessons in colour for their harmonies are gorgeous! If you want to make a special seasonal arrangement look for a multi-coloured leaf to be your guide!

The plush brown centres of the annual chrysanthemums seemed to ask for this container! It is also the 'broken colour' of the red and greens.

Monochromatic arrangements

If you have a piece of really dark glass which you would like to use as a container for your flowers, hold it up to the light and find its true colour and then arrange matching flowers in it. If you select some flowers which have a tint of the colour and others which have a full tone you will, in effect, have made a floral colour scale on one colour.

Your arrangement would be pleasing but it might not be obvious to everyone that you have taken just one colour as your theme as it would if you placed white flowers in white.

Monochromatic arrangements can be both beautiful and dramatic. Perhaps more than any others they can set the mood of an interior or even of an occasion. In my cottage home I have white walls and I find that there is an almost breathtaking beauty about a white arrangement against a white background. It is particularly tranquil. Yet for drama, the same arrangement seen against a contrasting background, would have the desired effect.

Some arrangers (I consider them over-zealous) become so obsessed with the idea of monochrome that they not only defoliate a stem to banish green if this is not required, but also remove parts of the flower should they be of another colour. Frankly, I do not take flower arrangement colour seriously enough ever to be likely to do this. Instead, even when I am planning monochromatic schemes, I accept the

All-green arrangements can be both lovely and enduring. Not only leaves are green. There are also green flowers, fruits, seed heads, calyces and, in this case, candles.

fact that a little green is likely to creep through and that some of my flowers are likely to have centres which contrast with or differ from the main colour. As a matter of fact, I like them best this way.

It seems to me inevitable that green is always with us and many would not prefer it otherwise. It never fails to fascinate me that while we all love flowers for their colour's sake and, one would assume, for the fact that these colours offer a contrast to the ubiquitous green, green flowers have a tremendous appeal to arrangers and gardeners alike. Many of them are of great beauty.

I think that I am right in thinking that there are more monochromatic arrangements made in green than in any other colour and they are interesting to assemble and plan.

Monochromatic arrangements in which container and flowers match can be very beautiful as well as practical. This is a good way to display bought flowers.

Fruit and leaves can play their own role in monochromatic arrangements. Contrasting croton leaves extend the colour of lemons and anemone-centred chrysanthemums in a long trough.

This arrangement was designed for my white-walled cottage bedroom. The colours of apple blossom, scillas and anemones and variegated kale match the patterned carpet.

Flowers as furnishings

If you grow your own flowers, plan to cultivate those which will suit your home. If you have to shop for your materials, buy those which will harmonize with your surroundings rather than those which happen to catch your eye.

Flower arrangements ought not to be dominant in your home. Instead they should fit into it like any other ornament you display. It is important that the container for the flowers should be well chosen. If your taste is for antique furniture then you may need to choose some vessel that will not detract from the beauty of the piece upon which it stands.

But not all homes can be classified so clearly. The flower decorations in most homes can be linked to the furnishings very simply, as I have already shown, by colour. Sometimes a definite theme is most effective, for example, an arrangement could be staged below or near a painting, the colours of which can be repeated by the flowers.

If your soft furnishings are patterned you may do best to

choose one of the colours represented and to use this as the main theme in the flower arrangements with perhaps just the lightest touch here and there of the other colours. But, I fear that if you place mixed arrangements near patterned material, neither will be shown to advantage.

If you treat a flower arrangement as a piece of furniture you are more likely to achieve success. Perhaps there are not many flat surfaces on which flowers can be placed and if this is the case, consider using a pedestal in a corner to display your flowers. There are many lovely torchères, once used to hold a candle or oil lamp, which can be used for this purpose.

A wall vase or a wall bracket are means of displaying flowers without encroaching on floor or table space.

Use flowers to create illusions! Place vivid, dramatic arrangements at the end of a too-long room. Conversely, arrange them on a wall opposite the door of a room which is too narrow. Use pastel tints and metal vessels to brighten dark interiors or to bring sunshine to dark corners.

Metal containers and white or yellow flowers, catch and reflect even the smallest amount of light — they are good for dark rooms.

SHAPES AND TEXTURES

The style of a decoration is bound to depend to a great extent on the flowers available. People who are dependent upon the florist shop for supplies almost inevitably become accustomed to arranging a quantity of the same kind of flower simply because so many of the commercially grown kinds are either marketed in bunches or sold by numbers. These flowers are usually so well grown that they are perfectly uniform. They are also usually very stiff stemmed and have such fine and healthy foliage that this can sometimes be an embarrassment. Because they are so well grown they are long lasting, but their very vigour, and certainly their uniformity, can cause some difficulty in arrangement!

A contrast of shapes and/or textures makes an arrangement more pleasing and sometimes much more distinctive than one of identical flowers. By studying this aspect of arrangement gardeners and those who buy their flowers can add interest both to the flowers and to their assembly.

Often some of the materials from a previous arrangement can be held over and used in the next simply for the purpose of contrast. I have in mind things like gladioli leaves which are long lasting and look well with other flowers. Even the stems of narcissi, cut on a slant after the faded blooms have been removed can be used.

A contrast of texture is often easier for the town dweller to provide than a contrast of form. A few tall daffodils in a slim vase can 'wear' a posy of violets tucked in at the rim. Chrysanthemum blooms look well in front of boughs of thick-textured leaves. They also look good with strong grasses and rushes. Roses go with almost anything for they are classic flowers! Try them with branches thick with grey-green lichen. Narcissi look perfect with a few of their own contrasting leaves but they are also in season with many lovely blossom boughs and young branches such as catkins and pussy willow. Soft-petalled poppy anemones borrow liveliness from glossy mahonia leaves. Ivy leaves particularly seem to suit the green centres of chincherinchees, while carnations seem to add glamour to any foliage whether it be simple laurel or exotic dracaena.

A mixture of flowers needs to contain a contrast of shapes as well as textures. Arrangers who grow their own have the advantage here !

Uniform flowers can be given individuality by originality of design and by choosing distinctive companions for them. The hosta leaves are extremely long lasting and can be used time and time again; even when they are fading they remain attractive.

31

Coalport china and *Cobaea scandens*; containers should not only be chosen with a room in mind they also need to suit the flowers they hold.

Mainly about textures

Flower arrangers need a variety of containers to suit all flowers and settings. I have some favourite containers which I use time and time again at all seasons of the year but even these do not suit all occasions! Large thick-textured blooms look ill at ease in fragile china just as flowers with a delicate air may not suit thick pottery.

Not only do all highly distinctive flowers need suitable containers, but their companions need choosing

carefully! One would not put fussy asparagus fern with arum lilies, but if no arum leaves were available, I would choose something of an equally strong character. Alternatively, I would rely on the design of the container and the style of the arrangement.

Where flowers have to be mixed you find that round flowers, chrysanthemums, carnations, zinnias, narcissi, for example, are enhanced by spicate forms. This means that containers used for short-stemmed, round flowers, if they are to be mixed with tall spicate forms, can be different from those employed if the flowers were arranged on their own. Spicate forms may be other flowers – gladioli, delphiniums, or ixias – but they can also be grasses, rushes, reeds, leaves, blossom-studded stems, berry sprays, seed heads and ivy trails.

Although we use the term 'flower' arrangement, in fact, any plant material that appeals to us can be used.

There is real enjoyment in discovering that a red cabbage is 'mighty like a rose', that the acid-yellow crinkly leaves of forced rhubarb have a coral-like texture and are much too lovely to throw away, that the rough skins of lychees accentuate the satin petals of white tulips.

(*Left*) The long bare stems of nerines and the delicacy of their blooms can stand strong contrasts. Thick-textured kale leaves anchor the stems to the modern glass dish.

(*Right*) Tall spikes of early-flowering gladioli bring height, contrast and grace to shorter, uniform stemmed, Super Star roses which they also match in hue. Pointed hosta leaves and ivy trails add contrasts of shapes and textures.

Decorations containing fruit and flowers can be quickly assembled. For this table decoration, hippeastrums, grapes, lychees, oak leaves and apples match the china.

Fruitful arrangements

Fruits are produced by flowers. Indeed, fruits are the whole purpose of flowers' existence so it is natural that they should look happy together! Sometimes you are able to use the flower and fruit from the same family; roses and hips, nigella and its seed vessels, early prunus and plums, but more often fruits are as varied and as mixed as the flowers themselves. I use the 'fruit' here in its full botanical sense meaning the product of a flower but for clarification let us now discuss the fruit we buy to eat.

All edible fruit is extremely attractive and can take part in home decoration. In fact, there are times when you are extra busy, when fruit will prove to be a great boon, for all you need are a few leaves, or other accessories, and a flower or two and you can make an arrangement in a minute.

Then there are the other 'fruits', many of which can be kept indefinitely – pine cones and large seed heads of many kinds such as lotus, poppy, magnolia. Some fruits last well but not indefinitely. These include gourds, berries, aubergines, peppers and fat, fresh, seed pods.

As you learn more about plants you will find that you will

come to appreciate lovely leaves as much as lovely flowers. I would find it hard to say if I loved one more than the other! Often a flower arranger begins by treating leaves merely as something to put with flowers, but there comes a time when foliage begins to be featured more and more for its own sake.

Leaves are certainly as varied as blooms. Like them there are some which can only be used fresh, but there are others which dry naturally or which may be preserved. When fresh leaves are to be used, some will need a little grooming. Evergreens, because of their long lives, need cleaning. If the leaves are large it is simple to wipe over the surface of them. If they are meant to be glossy a final wipe with a clean tissue will help. A touch of olive oil will make them gleam.

Often a whole plant can be used such as a small cabbage, a rosette of saxifraga, succulent verbascum or cryptanthus, or perhaps the centre of a plant such as the heart of the gorgeous ornamental kale.

Ornamental gourds and squashes of all kinds are highly decorative, and if gathered only when fully ripe and handled very carefully, long-lasting.

The delicate air of snowdrops belies their strength for no flower which blooms at their season could be anything but incredibly strong. The glass which holds these seems to me to reflect their character. Its shape reminds me of the bulbs from which they grow.

CHOOSING THE RIGHT VASE

On a previous page I said that it was important that a container should suit the flowers and that it should also fit the occasion and the setting. To me, this really is important. A badly designed modern vase looks sadly out of place on lovely pieces of furniture.

For our flowers we need something which will hold water to nurture them, therefore containers must be watertight or capable of being made so. Plastic bags and cooking foil can be used to line any container you suspect might leak. These

may also be used, when you want to protect a container from staining. I use them for metal and for some other containers I will describe later.

I find that newcomers to flower arrangement tend to choose vases which are really much too large on the assumption that the flowers must have plenty of water. But if all are properly hardened this really is not necessary. It is much more important, and certainly much easier and more economical eventually, to choose a container which looks in place even when empty. If arrangements are to be placed above eye level make quite sure that the container to be used is not so tall that it will be difficult to mask it. The wrong choice means that you see more vase than flowers.

When flowers are to be arranged on a dining-table, a similar point arises. Sit down at the table with the container in place and again make sure that it is not going to be too dominant and also that after the flowers are arranged they will not be too high.

The style of arrangement will also influence the choice of container. Long, low arrangements may be better in narrow troughs rather than in wide bowls, if you intend massing the flowers. A tall vase will give length to stems should this be necessary, because these will not have to reach the floor of the container.

(*Left*) Old-fashioned moss roses arranged in a brass tea-caddy. Many vessels originally designed for some other purpose are perfect for flower arrangements.

Bulb flowers like shallow water so this scoop-shaped dish is ideal for gladioli which are very quickly arranged in this style. The 'dessert spoons' repeat the shape of the dish.

The lovely smooth glaze of this modern vase is matched by many flowers but its pattern inspired the arrangement of hellebores.

Linking flowers with the container

All flower arrangers have favourite containers. They favour them for many reasons, but the most usual one is that the flowers seem to be arranged so much quicker and easier in them than in others. Quite a lot depends on how a stem holder can be fitted in. Sometimes a vase has an irritating shape to the rim and it is difficult to coax flowers to flow attractively over the edge. A tall vase with a fluted rim, on the other hand, often proves to be most agreeable. Many specially designed vases on sale seem hopeless and even a practised arranger like myself can experience great difficulty in making a two handled 'boat' vase, or an outsize egg-timer made of cut glass, look at all attractive. It is because potter-designed vases are often so inadequate that arrangers generally have turned to other vessels.

Metal containers usually look good filled with flowers. Glass needs careful attention so that stems seen through the water look attractive and not messy. Patterned vases can be very difficult to use because the pattern really ought to harmonize with the flowers.

Generally speaking, plain colours are best. White and black are always safe; after all, they represent shade and light and your flowers also will be shaded or tinted. Any of the broken colours and their tints and shades also look good. Metal vases, also, can be classified as colours, brass as yellow, copper as orange, silver as white and pewter as grey.

Textures are important, but I think that these are more likely to be influenced by personal tastes. Choice of textures is usually the result of experiment and of practice, for after a time you will find yourself reaching automatically for a vase to suit say, arums, cow parsley, rose hips or daffodils.

A container should be perfectly watertight otherwise furniture will become damaged. Some pottery needs a mat below it which can be a nuisance. Alternatively, a sealing paint on the base of the container can be used.

Make sure that any containers you select will stand perfectly firm as it is possible for them to overbalance when very tall stems are used. If they are opaque, this fault can be remedied by pouring sand in to weight the vessel.

Originally made as a glove box for a hall, the little drawer below this mirror now holds two gingerbread tins for use as flower containers.

Traditional flower containers

The reason why traditional containers are used less than they were is mainly because they are so difficult to use. The old method was merely to stand the flowers in the vessels with their stems reaching down to the bottom if possible. If we want to use any of these containers in the modern manner then we have to resort to modern means to do so. Church vases, for example, usually flute at the top and become narrow towards the waist. Flowers, therefore, need to be arranged mainly in the top wide portion.

Arrangements in any vase of this type can be made to be high, wide and handsome by arranging the centre upright stem vertically. If this is also branched but flat, like beech for example, or if several stems can be mounted and fanned from a central stem like cycas fronds, a large area of the arrangement is then filled. Other flowers or stems can then be arranged before this background.

The way that branch stems are cut or pruned can also ease arrangement in any tall narrow vase. If side stems are cut in such a way that a little of the main stem is retained this main portion can go into the vase and the side stem will still flow away from it, often at a right angle to it.

Pitchers have been used for centuries as flower containers but always for the bunch rather than an arrangement. I think

Carnations and nigella are arranged with silver-grey senecio foliage and phacelia; a bowl arrangement is still one of the most popular designs for decorating a table centre.

(*Below*) Church vases are notoriously difficult to fill. One way of easing the task is to fill in the background with a flat vertical but well branching stem in front of which a few flowers can be arranged.

(*Above*) The simple pitcher is usually reserved for the un-sophisticated bunch of flowers yet it can also be used for arrangements in a more modern style as this one here.

that jugs of all kinds are attractive, but if they are to be used for an arrangement certain points need to be explained. The handle of a jug is an important part of the design and I feel that it ought also to be part of the flower arrangement and should not be hidden. It helps, I find, if the contents are arranged in such a way that they appear to flow away from the handle. This means that curved stems will follow its curve – or roughly so. This rule applies to mugs, many of which make charming containers.

Extremely popular among flower arrangers are vases made in the style of the silver wine-coolers. I have used them for the humble yet graceful hedge parsley as well as for great blowsy old-fashioned roses – no flower seems ever to be ill at ease in them. If you are lucky enough to own a silver cooler then do use it for flowers!

Modern containers

The present interest in flower decoration has meant that all aspects of the art have been under examination. The Japanese have practised flower arrangement for centuries, so long in fact that it is not the simple domestic but pleasant art that it is here. It is instead a highly sophisticated and ritualistic pastime. While the classic manner of oriental flower arrangement might not fit into our Western ways, certain aspects of it have a tremendous appeal and have influenced our own attitudes. One influence which has been most strongly felt is the oriental approach to the importance of the flower container. Eastern types are often very beautiful. Another aspect is the successful way in which only very few flowers are used in these containers. Western flower arrangers have been quick to learn the fundamentals of oriental design and have applied them to their own flowers. At the same time, a universal 'oriental' style, Ikebana, has captured a great deal

Cherry blossom and a Chinese bowl arrangement inspired by the Orient depends upon the beauty of a few stems in a lovely container.

of attention and this also has brought into popularity the shallow container.

This means that suitable containers abound but, once again, not all of them were intended as flower holders. Some of my own favourites are oven dishes, others are outsize ashtrays. And not all of them are modern. Some are deep plates, pewter as well as china. Small but deep trays are ideal for some purposes especially when an arrangement of fruit is to be assembled. There are lidless china boxes. Anything deep enough to hold water or another supplementary vessel for water is pressed into service.

To use these particular containers effectively we have to realize that it is not intended that they should be filled with flowers in the manner of a traditional bowl but instead that they should provide an anchorage for them. The shallow container when used in an oriental style of arrangement is intended to be admired. It is as much a part of the arrangement as the flowers. The effectiveness of one is entirely dependent on the other. Invest in one or two well-designed dishes and there will be many times when you will find two, three, or four flowers enough for a decoration.

Peonies and copper beech : well-designed shallow dishes help you to make three flowers and a few leaves play the part of many.

43

Black Wedgwood bowl is filled with marguerites, wheat, golden privet and wild vetch ; the vase is modern and formal like the flowers and their arrangement.

Modern containers have exciting shapes

The container often calls the tune! Modern glass, ceramics and metal vessels have clear lines and exciting shapes. They cry out for distinctive flower arrangements. Some people are so influenced by them that they have developed what I can only describe as 'pop' floral art in which the designs are either interpretive or abstract. I prefer to follow the style of the clean lines and to bring to these containers, flowers which either reflect their style or emphasise it.

When flowers are to be arranged in a mass, the container is of little importance. In most cases it is not intended that it should show, but when a beautifully designed vessel is used it seems a great pity to hide it.

Take glass for example. I love to see stems through water when they become magnified and seem to take on a new meaning and importance. However, stripped stems, on the other hand, are not pretty and if the outer skin of the stem has been damaged the water soon becomes cloudy. When I am using glass for roses I do not remove the thorns from the stems because they are a gorgeous red under water.

Tall slim containers, providing that they stand firmly, are useful to the busy. An arrangement can be made in them from one gladioli spike and a posy of leaves at rim level. Or tie a few flowers in the hand, their blooms at different levels and wedge in a vase with a few leaves.

Contrasting textures are effective. Leaves with rough textures look well against smooth but solid ceramics. So do the woolly-leaved plants such as verbascum and stachys. I like to see narcissi arranged in a crescent, backed by their own leaves, and rising up either from a thick circular dish or a narrow, slightly bulb-shaped vase.

(*Top*) Driftwood and 'ribbon' loops made from their leaves supplement and support narcissi in a Scandinavian glass jar. Stem ends cut from shortened blooms are also included.

(*Bottom*) A tall glass cylinder holds three nerines elegantly yet sufficiently. Their stems were tied together before arrangement, the arum leaves hide the tie at rim level. Leafless stems look lovely through glass.

45

Flower arrangements that tell a story

Arranging flowers is very much like painting, embroidery and sculpture. The flowers are our raw materials, our paints, thread or clay. Once we have learned a few fundamental rules about handling materials, the way we present them is not only a matter of skill and artistic merit but also personality. We can let flower arrangements speak for us.

If we are prepared to think of flowers as paints, it follows that we should be able to paint a picture with them. Some pictures will just be lovely to look at, like any flower painting, but others can tell a story, represent a theme, give a message, make a joke or even interpret an idea. Many people enjoy making arrangements of this kind but most of these arrangements are more suited to a flower show. However, if we are to tell a good story we need to use extra materials or accessories.

So far in this book the emphasis has been on flowers with passing mention of leaves and fruits, but the flower arranger should learn that there are many other materials which can be used. Anything which originates from a plant is acceptable. We have seen that leaves, stems and fruits can look lovely with flowers, but at times so can roots, bark, pith, husks and driftwood.

When we want to compose a picture or describe a scene sometimes, it is necessary to bring into it something which is not from a plant. This may also be natural in origin such as a shell or stone but often a statue or some other little figure, a bird or butterfly perhaps, or even glasses, bottles, hats, boxes – any kind of object that has some relation to the subject, is used.

As I said earlier, this subject is to be dealt with more fully later but the reason it is mentioned here is because shallow containers are ideal for pictorial or scenic arrangements. In late winter you can lift many hearts by taking a prettily shaped branch and arranging it to represent a tree. Lay moss below it, stud this with the first tiny flowers to make a meadow in miniature. Or, in hot summer, cool the atmosphere with a low dish and an expanse of clear water, shell-strewn below; let a group of rushes rise from it and nearby let fresh green ferns lean out from mossy rocks.

(*Top*) Spring in Somerset: Alder catkin 'tree' towers above widow iris, primroses, daisies and toadstools 'growing' on a mossy bank below.

(*Bottom*) A Christmas scene: Madonna and child with pine, holly, hyacinths and daffodils 'growing' from rocks arranged in a deep copper tray.

Brass bound tea-caddy, anemones, spindle berry, fuchsias and canary creeper — many boxes make delightful containers for unusual arrangements. Containers must be made watertight.

Wooden containers

It is not surprising that flower arrangements made in wooden containers look so delightful because wood is just one more of the many things which originate from plants. In recent years 'treen' – objects made from tree – have become extremely popular among flower arrangers in many parts of the world.

Technically, treen is manufactured, but occasionally you see a delightful arrangement held in a rough coconut shell or an outsize nut husk. On the other hand most treen objects are beautifully made, you can find tea-caddys, bible-boxes, skilfully turned bowls and occasionally a little vase. Many of these are from another century and because of this they need to be cared for very well if they are to be used for arranging flowers.

Water will ruin any of these containers and so precautions must be taken. Many tea-caddys also contain little bowls which were once used to blend the tea and these are quite suitable for water but, even so, I would still line the caddy with metal foil in case any of the water should be spilled over the rim of the bowls.

A little vase made by a wood-turner and found in a junk shop holds a mixture of perpetuelles, cones, beechmast and leaves, pussy willow, honesty and grevillea.

If no container exists then the piece of treen must be carefully lined with a double thickness of foil or plastic. It is also wise to use a soft foamed water-absorbent plastic stem holder such as Florapak or Oasis and not wire netting which might pierce the lining. Take care also to insert stems gently to avoid piercing.

Where the container has a lid, like the little tea-caddy illustrated, it is easier to prop this open first before arranging the flowers. I usually take two pieces of stem, one on each side, to keep the lid lifted. You can then open the lid wide while the flowers are arranged and later lower it back on to the props.

I like to use a wooden container for a perpetuelle arrangement. These are described in a later chapter. In this case risk of damage to the container is far less because the stem-holding material is dry.

Certain flowers seem to look lovelier in well-polished wood than others, old-fashioned roses, velvety wallflowers, pansies, gloxinias and anemones please me a lot. A plywood cylindrical bath salts' container looks lovely with daisies!

49

Baskets are 'natural' containers

Like treen, most baskets are made from materials which have an affinity with flowers. Of course, I accept that modern baskets may be woven from man-made materials, but even then they follow traditional patterns which evoke rural atmosphere. As containers for flower arrangements, baskets have never gone out of fashion, and they have been used since mankind first began to pick and offer up flowers to the gods and even now they are used mostly for celebrations.

The reason for this is mainly because flowers for special occasions usually have to be transported to the person or people who are celebrating a certain event. And the special thing about a basket arrangement is that it can easily be carried without being disturbed.

This being the case it really is most important that the handle should be left free enough to be held comfortably and in such a way that flowers arranged near it are not beheaded or damaged in some other way. When the flowers are being assembled the handle should be considered part of the design. I usually treat it as a centre stem. This subject is discussed in the chapter on styles of arrangement.

Like treen and other containers which may not be water-tight, baskets need some kind of lining. Some are sold ready lined with a movable tin container. Otherwise a lining must be improvised. If you use baskets for home flower decoration, (and incidentally a basket of flowers is really useful in a place where the decoration has to be moved, often I use one

An Easter basket of chick yellow mimosa, daffodils, and tulips is arranged round a 'nest' of gaily painted eggs. The basket is lined with a tin. This is essential when a container is not water-tight.

on my dining table) you can use any vessel which happens to fit conveniently and fill it with water in the usual way. If the basket has to be transported, water which is easily spilled is not practical and in such cases it is best to use a well-soaked foamed plastic stem holder and to line the basket either with foil or sheet plastic.

Roses, candytuft, petunias and everlasting peas in a low basket make a pretty yet practical kind of decoration for a place where the arrangement must be moved from time to time.

For Mothering Sunday, violets, snowdrops and early viburnum blossom are arranged in a little basket lined with kitchen foil and packed with crumbled damp Florapak to hold and nurture the frail stems.

An antique sweet box is filled with cineraria blooms. Often a little assortment of flowers can be cut from a few plants without robbing them to provide a splash of colour when flowers are scarce.

A copper jelly mould with pinks, pansies, ornamental kale foliage and flowers and bunches of small red tomatoes makes a pretty and wholesome decoration for a kitchen. The lovely old mould is too attractive to hide away. The warm glow of the well-polished metal goes well with the gleam of the flowers and fruits.

Chincherinchees with magnolia and ivy leaves are in a glass bottle. Bottles come in all shapes and are often too lovely to throw away! Use them for flowers. The narrow neck is no problem if you first arrange the flowers in the hand and tie them in a slim bunch which is then easily wedged in place but don't forget to keep the water level topped up.

Parrot tulips, pansies and cabbage leaves are arranged in a copper skillet. The kitchen cupboard contains many vessels which are ideal for using in flower arrangement so why not borrow them from time to time?

A vase is filled with cornflowers, larkspurs, marguerites and Sweet Williams. You need never be at a loss for containers for there are many things around one that can be pressed into service with charming and attractive results. It is often surprising just what can be used.

Red anemones, a candle and pussy willow are arranged in a candlestick. Try a pair of these on the mantelpiece or arrange one at each end of a side table. Candlesticks make good pedestal vases and lift the flowers well out of harm's way.

Many flowers look well in shells. Not only is there a pleasant contrast of textures but often it is possible to colour-link blooms and the container. In this picture, the conch is a tint of some of the mixed ranunculus it holds.

Here a modern china swan is arranged with narcissi. There are many pieces of bric-a-brac which make delightful containers for flowers. There seems to be an abundance of swans to be found among Victoriana and they are worth collecting. Try a fleet of them as a table decoration. Flowers need to be heaped like ruffled feathers to achieve the most effective result.

53

Build your own containers

Ingenuity plays an important part in flower arrangement and not least where containers are concerned. Often you have a plan for an arrangement in your mind but the essential container is missing. There is usually a simple solution: build or make it yourself! It is surprisingly easy to marry one other object with another to achieve the effect you want. Take a very simple example; take two matching egg-cups of the traditional style, turn one upside down and place the other on it – result, a pedestal vase. Wrought iron can be fastened to a metal base and used as a pedestal. Two metal goblets can be joined in the way described for the egg-cups. A bottle, or if you are planning a buffet table, a pair of them, can be supplied with a candle-cup and used to hold flowers. Even an ordinary plate can be used as a base for flowers and fruit if it is first elevated in some way, but make sure that it is well-anchored. A well-covered tin filled with sand, the same size as the vase will make a pedestal.

White tulips, *cornus mas* blossom, ivy and deep-hued beetroot leaves in a fruit dish from the table china. Wine glasses hold more tulips.

Late Victorian clock sets do not seem to have much to do with flower arrangement, but parts of them are often to be seen both in flower shows and homes. The set usually consisted of a clock flanked on either side by a statuette cast in the same metal as the clock case. The statues are now often to be seen either as part of an arrangement or a composition.

If you want to elevate flowers there are many ways you can do so. For a large display take three bowls which may be either the same size or graded. In all but the top bowl stand an empty flower pot and fit a bowl on to it. You can use more than one bowl if you want to make a tower of bloom. My table decoration of tulips shows a tower constructed on much the same principle except that wine glasses were used instead. Plasticine pills can be used under the glass base.

Usually, the main purpose of building an arrangement is to raise the flowers and you will find many objects around you which can be used for this purpose. I have seen a well-turned piece of oak staircase used to hold a wooden bowl.

Mixed chrysanthemums in a candlestick. Both the flowers and the candle are held fast in a candle-cup, a little footed bowl is made to fit in the candle socket. Some candle-cups come ready fitted with stem holders.

A piece of wrought iron fixed to a stand and supporting a bowl makes an elegant holder for a winter arrangement of red cotoneaster berries, ivy trails and leaves and a pretty white ornamental cabbage.

A little silver birch log has been hollowed out so that it will hold a Christmas decoration. The hole is lined with cooking foil and then packed with a cylinder of Oasis into which all stems can be inserted easily.

Open work wicker baskets such as this which holds hellebores can be made quite watertight by lining them with foil or sheet polythene and using one of the foamed plastic stem holders.

Roses and gypsophila are arranged in an antique pewter sugar scoop. Keeping stems moist is no problem nowadays. Foamed urea, such as Florapak will hold water and also keep stems well-anchored. There is no fear of drips damaging furniture surfaces.

A modern wrought iron candelabrum can be made to hold flowers if a block of Oasis is fixed on the centre portion. This foamed plastic, water-absorbent stem holder must be moistened daily because it evaporates more quickly being ex-container.

A tin lid, nailed to a base on which pieces of driftwood have also been fixed, will hold sufficient Oasis to provide water for flowers so long as it is inspected regularly to make sure it has not become dry.

An old-fashioned cutlery box divided into two compartments makes it possible to separate the flowers from the fruit. For the flowers the compartment is foil-lined. The stems are held in moist Florapak.

A tall glass supports a plate of fruit and flowers. There are a few anemones in the water held down by a tiny pinholder. Flowers among the fruit are in a block of Oasis hidden by kale leaves.

A pair of balances, whether real or a copy like these, makes an unusual side table decoration. Modern foamed plastics make arrangement considerably easier.

A conch shell holds the chrysanthemums which flow across the line of driftwood. Other shells and a sand-coloured wooden base completes the composition.

GROUPING OBJECTS FOR EFFECT

When I described the purpose and the pleasures of making pictorial and scenic flower arrangements, I briefly explained the role that accessories can play and I mentioned a few of the most popular of them. We shall see later, when we come to discuss actual arrangement, that these often can play more than one part and that they can have a practical value as well as one which is purely decorative.

Meanwhile, we should not imagine that the accessories, no matter what they are, should be used only within the flower arrangement itself or that they are always arranged inside the container, for this is not so. Sometimes they play a more important and decorative part by being outside an arrangement. Yet because it is obvious that they have a purpose, they are seen as an essential part of a composition of related objects.

You will find, and I hope that my arrangements on this page show, that a grouping is often much more effective than a single vase. Do not imagine that composing a group is a complicated affair . . . but it is highly engaging!

One lesson a flower arranger soon learns is that it is not a bit of good planning a composition unless it can be practically translated. Not only must flowers stay in the required position, but everything else must stay in place also.

There are many tricks of the trade! Much depends on how well things can be camouflaged. Napkin rings, pastry cutters or any other open ring can be used to lift and support many objects either in water or out. You can keep a pineapple in almost any position by using this method. It is also effective if you want to 'float' a flower in water. Flower pots, cream cartons and similar vessels will hold fruit or other objects. Several can stand inside each other.

Modelling clay holds many things in position but only if surfaces are perfectly dry. You can make small pills of the clay and fix these lightly to the base of any object to be held in place. Then press the object on to the place where it is to be anchored. The pills will flatten and hold. Or an alternative method is to roll out a length of clay, form it into a circle or oval and place the object to be held within it.

What could be more economical than this ? Six daffodils, a cutting of chlorophytum, which can be potted up when it roots, and four lemons.

Look around you for inspiration

Once you become interested in composition you will find that ideas come fast, for inspiration is all around you. Take the china that you use every day for example. Study it to give you a theme for colour or design. If it is a good shape, use it, though not necessarily as a container, for you may be able to use it some other way. A plate might make a good base for a low arrangement; a lid with an attractive pattern or perhaps an essential colour can be used as a focal point.

Matching flowers with china is a useful as well as an entertaining exercise which you will find repays you well when you are looking for ways to decorate your table for a special occasion. I have more to say about this in my chapter on table decoration.

You might like to make a composition using some favourite object you own and linking it with flowers. A painting, for example, can be linked beautifully with flowers, fruits and leaves and some other accessory that will 'tie' them to the

Five white irises and a few stems of pussy willow are arranged with dried hosta leaves, gilded to match the rim on the willow pattern china.

Christmas decorations without flowers. (*Above*) a gloriously coloured winter cabbage is the centrepiece of this composition. (*Right*) Tree baubles on false stems play the flowers' role in the tankard and add a little cheer.

painting. If your painting hangs over the fireplace, the mantelpiece will give a useful area for flowers. Otherwise you will need some other surface below the picture.

Among other things, I collect shells and driftwood and I have an alcove in one of my rooms where a few shells are always on display. Here I enjoy making compositions that speak of the sea, or seem to do so to me. It is surprising how many flowers and plants seem apposite, spiky daisies remind one of starfish, so do cryptanthus and some other bromeliads; all rush-like leaves, seaweed-like fronds – even if they are no more than pteris ferns – play a part in setting the scene. Elsewhere I have a modern painting which reminds me both of a leaf and of an entire tree, of the soil and yet of the sky and here I tend to make compositions of treen, wood and wooden things such as hard, brown seed pods, leathery, preserved leaves, and fossil-thick oolite.

Flower arrangement, thank goodness, is no static art! Once you learn the basic 'rules' – how to keep a stem in place, and a flower happy and long-lived – you can set off on a thousand journeys of discovery not only about nature and the world around you but also about yourself!

A base is an integral part of a design

Many people automatically place a mat under a vase of flowers, just as they do under a glass or beaker containing a drink, to prevent the surface of the furniture from being stained if the vessel is wet. Often these protectors are at variance with the arrangement in colour, pattern, shape or in some other way.

A cosy crocheted mat seems a long way from a beautiful stand holding an oriental arrangement, but there is a link. The Japanese place their flowers on a stand or base, in fact, this is often an important and integral part of the design and is known as 'dai'. But this stand also, originally served to protect the polished surface of the little table or platform on which the flowers stood.

Because I am essentially a practical person, I look for practical applications in floral art and it is obvious to me that even with modern furniture that will not mark, or stem holders that will not spill water, and other advantages, many arrangements are improved by being stood on a base. Displayed this way, an arrangement becomes 'lime-lighted'– your attention is drawn to it. From the purely practical point of view, a flower arrangement on a stand is often much more easily moved for dusting than a single vase, and from a further practical point, we return to the old question of economy, less flowers are needed for an arrangement displayed in this way because the base lends importance. It can also add colour, texture, line and mood!

From the point of view of design a base often provides the extra little something which you feel is lacking in an otherwise pleasing arrangement. For example, even something as simple as a thick, dark, circular mat can bring a seemingly too-frail arrangement to earth and give it a more stable quality. If you feel that your few flowers do not bring quite enough colour you can add more by repeating their colour, or alternatively, complementing it or harmonising with it through the base.

From this you will see that not all bases are stands or platforms although if you are lucky enough to possess one or more of these you are certain to find them useful at times. Bases like so much else in flower arrangement are really what you make them – or perhaps it should be from what you make them! I have used plates, upturned ash-trays, a scroll of thick paper, the base of a Victorian glass dome, a plinth of a challenge cup, driftwood, slate, marble, trays and cake tins. But, remember, a base is not essential!

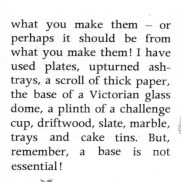

(*Above*) A base for flower arrangement can give importance to the design. It can also add colour, texture, mood and style. The two bamboo mats under this simple yet lovely arrangement of just two chrysanthemums and jasmine leaves emphasise its oriental quality.

(*Left*) In most oriental styles the base is an integral part of a design. These roses are on the traditional 'dai' of the Japanese.

63

Peonies and the rough textured, hollow stems of cholla wood are arranged on a large pinholder. Driftwood and a billbergia plant hide the holder from view.

STEM HOLDERS

If you want to be able to arrange your flowers not only as you want them but also quickly and easily, it is vital that you should be able to assemble any kind of arrangement with confidence. The most important part of any flower arrangement, from the practical point of view, is the stem holder. Sometimes more than one is necessary for it all depends on what kind of arrangement is being planned.

If the stem holder is to be hidden within a container then we are not so concerned with its appearance. The main thing is that it should work. Quite the cheapest and most efficient of all stem holders for this purpose is large mesh wire netting. It is important that the mesh is large, one-and-a-half to two inches, because only the large size is malleable enough to be easily crumpled up and squashed into a container. Another point worth noting is that should a thick woody stem have to be inserted through the wire it passes through easily because if it pushes against the wire it will move it. Small mesh is much more rigid and thick stems either will not pass through the small mesh at all or will be unable to influence it.

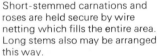

Short-stemmed carnations and roses are held secure by wire netting which fills the entire area. Long stems also may be arranged this way.

Stem holders should not be visible through glass. First arrange and tie the stems in the hand. Leaves or accessories added later can hide the tie.

Mesh used to be obtainable only as galvanised wire but now there is plastic-covered mesh in black, green and white. It has the advantage of not marking the interior of precious china, but I think that it has the disadvantage of being a little slippery. This means that it may move in highly-glazed containers until many stems are locked together. As the trickiest part of assembly comes at the beginning this fault can be off-putting to a beginner. It also takes up a little more room in small containers because it is thicker. For large containers and those which have a ridge at the rim which holds netting well, it is excellent.

If you store your containers you will find it best to keep the netting inside them after you have cleaned them. If you are afraid that it might mark the vase, store it in a plastic bag.

As a general rule the netting is cut to the size of the part of the container which holds the water, cut it twice its depth and match its width with the widest part.

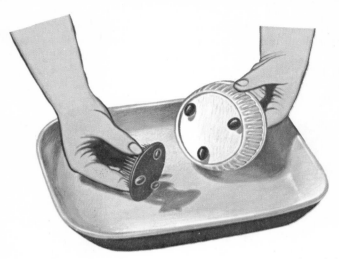

Pills of Plasticine make good washers and can be placed under any container or on a pinholder to secure one surface to another.

Tricks of the Trade

There is no point in doing flower arrangement the hard way! You are sure to discover a few tricks of your own, meanwhile here are a few of mine!

In the first place I have found that the best way to fill a container with wire netting is first to bend it in a 'U' and then push it into the mouth of the vessel so that the cut ends of the netting are just protruding above the rim. These then can be curved over the rim to hold it firm.

Fasten netting high in glass.   Florist wire lengthens short stems

Cut ends will also help to hold very heavy stems in place especially if these are rather branched. I make a rule that the taller or heavier the stem the more netting I use. At times this protrudes above the rim, but it is easily hidden later. The important point is that the netting can be taken round the lower portion of the stem in more than one place until it is as firm as a rock.

The snag ends are also useful in pinning stems in place. For example, you may need a low hanging leaf which will flow prettily over the rim, but it may be that the leaf hasn't really grown the way you want it. In this case a snag end can be passed round the leaf stem at rim level and then the wire – not the stem – can gently be bent so that the leaf reaches the point required. If you press hard on the stem you may snap it, but if the wire is bent, the stem it embraces is protected yet curves with it.

At other times the wire can be used just like a pin, by which I mean that a piece can be pushed through a stem at some point where it is necessary to hold it.

Although stems are held best if the netting fills the container from rim to base this is not a pretty thing to do when glass is used. Here the technique is to fix the netting in the top portion only and to make it shallow enough to be well hidden by the materials arranged lowest down. The plastic-covered netting I referred to earlier can sometimes be left in its original roll and fitted into the mouth of a glass. To arrange flowers on the side of a container, make a ball of netting, fix it on the side and pass the stems through.

Stem anchor

Stems inserted

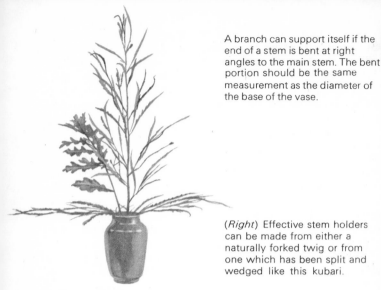

A branch can support itself if the end of a stem is bent at right angles to the main stem. The bent portion should be the same measurement as the diameter of the base of the vase.

(*Right*) Effective stem holders can be made from either a naturally forked twig or from one which has been split and wedged like this kubari.

Other types of stem holders

Often one lovely branch is enough decoration in itself yet it is not always easy to arrange it if you rely on the support of the rim of the container alone. It is possible to wedge it firmly in a narrow-necked vase by pushing short thick pieces of bare stem between the branch and the vase. Another method is to use modelling clay pushed behind the branch. Patterns of other home-made stem holders can be borrowed from the Japanese who use forked and crossed sticks. They should always be cut from living twigs. Forked kubari – this is the Japanese term – can be made from naturally forked twigs by cutting the stems to the required length. Otherwise they can be made by splitting a piece of twig; cupressus is excellent. Split twigs may need an extra piece of twig inserted in the fork so that the two arms remain apart. They may need to be held a distance apart by raffia or fine twine, or by using a rubber band to prevent them from springing open too far. Cross twigs are merely fastened in the centre with raffia or fine twine.

The purpose of these holders is to prevent the branch from moving or to enable one to arrange a group of flowers

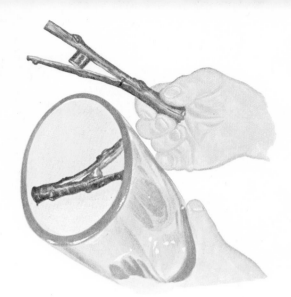

flowing at a required angle.

For very tall vases, an upright forked twig standing a little higher than half the depth of the container can hold a leaning branch, the end of which is also forked. When the branch is arranged the end is fixed into the forked twig holder in such a way that only a small portion is actually in water as it lies across the container in a diagonal line.

Pinholders hold stems which are impaled on their points. Woody stems cut on a slant can be arranged at almost any angle. Very thick stems are best split for an inch and forked.

(*Below*) A small pinholder can be fixed to the side of a container by clay pills. Upright stems can then be pushed against the pin points where they will hold firm. They will also hide the holder from view.

(*Left and below*) A block of Oasis holds the mixed pinks and wild vetch arranged in a shallow container.

(*Above*) Oasis cylinders are joined together — the first stage in making this tall arrangement.

Foamed plastic stem holders

When we look around us for new or unusual containers we see many which have an appealing shape, an interesting texture or perhaps a certain period charm and yet, they seem to be unsuitable mainly because they are much too shallow to hold water satisfactorily or in sufficient quantities to keep stems turgid. At one time these would be passed by; today, thanks to the introduction of foamed, water-absorbent plastics, the range of containers and flower holders of all types has been greatly enlarged.

I visualise the way in which I would like to display the flowers and then select the appropriate stem holder.

The plastics concerned are types of foamed urea. The important thing is their texture, soft, sponge-like and unresistant. You can insert a stem and if the flower is only a short one, you need push in no more than an inch of the base (which obviously, is a great advantage), and it will hold quite firm even if you hold the block of plastic upside down.

Because the plastics absorb and hold water they can be used for arrangements which have to be stood on polished

(*Right*) A block of Oasis holds this carnation tree.

surfaces where spilled water would cause damage.

They are divided into two types. One, Florapak should be used inside containers. It can be used time and time again, but as more and more stems are inserted and taken out the material crumbles. I find that the crumbled mass can be pressed down to compact it and a new piece laid over it. The other, much firmer, Oasis, keeps its form and so can be used ex-container.

Florapak holds water for a long period because it is not exposed. For this reason it is ideal for arrangements which have to be placed out of reach. Even so, materials which are very long-lasting take a lot of moisture and so the plastic should be inspected from time to time and water replenished where necessary.

Oasis, on the other hand, because it is used ex-container loses water quickly and needs soaking afresh each day. The exception is when the Oasis block is held in a vessel into which some water can be poured, as in the urn base shown on the opposite page. The moisture will then be taken up by capillary action as the block dries.

71

Attractive ways to hide stem holders

In many ways it is a good thing that a pinholder in a low dish or other type of container should have to be hidden because the way you decide to camouflage it can add to the interest of the arrangement as a whole. Hiding the stem holder often anchors the flowers in a way that really makes them and the container become one unit. Whatever you use should bear some relation to the flowers. Sometimes all you need is one large flower from the group which forms the arrangement with its stem cut short so that, as it leans out from the holder, either it or the leaves which grow close to it, hide the stem holder completely.

At other times other accessories are needed and it really is worth while building up a collection of stones, shells, small but broad and well-shaped pieces of driftwood, cork, bark and any natural material which appeals to you, so that you can always find something which will suit the flowers you are using. All of these things are so diverse that you are sure to find some to blend with all containers.

Five Dutch irises are firmly fixed on a pinholder which is hidden by abalone shells, chosen to harmonise with the bleached adiantum fern.

Fruits of all kinds are useful for hiding stem holders. Most will have to be kept out of water otherwise they are likely to spoil or rot. There are several ways in which this can be done. Any Oasis blocks, with their bases covered in foil so that they do not draw up the water and become wet, can also be used. These also can be stacked or halved to give different levels if necessary. The fruit can either be pressed into the plastic and thus made to stay in place or, it can be mounted on a false stem which can then be held secure by the Oasis.

Often it is quite simple to lay a piece of bark, wood, or cork mat, or even a piece of small-mesh wire netting, or folded large mesh, across the container from one side to the other at the foot of the flowers, and to arrange the fruit on this. One advantage of netting is that it can be shaped to fit in between stems and the rim of a container. It can also be curved easily so that, should this be necessary, it can follow the shape of a container. It can also be moulded to form a bowl or a trough to take fruits of all shapes and sizes.

Assorted gourds hide the pin-holder on which these hippeastrums are held. Together with the flowers and autumn leaves they match the container's colours.

73

Three formal dahlias with richly coloured ligularia leaves, which supplement the flowers, furnish and colour-match the bowl, and hide the stem holder.

Leaves also may be used

Often one of the quickest, most practical and, at the same time, prettiest ways of hiding any kind of ugly stem holder is by leaves which can also form an important feature of the arrangement.

There are so many lovely kinds of foliage which can be used but even if you have no garden, often you can use the leaves from the flowers you buy. Look over stems before you strip them to see if there are not some extra good samples which will do, if not for one arrangement then maybe for another. Lay them carefully one on the other and stand them in water until you are ready for them. Many leaves, such as those of gladioli, bulbous irises and daffodils seem only to be useful for tall arrangements when their contrast of shape can be exploited, but actually these can also be used at low levels if they are first looped and arranged in 'ribbon' bows.

Some of the leaves which cry out to be used because they are so lovely may not generally be considered to be flower arrangement material, but they will cover a holder very prettily. These include the outside leaves of winter cabbage which often is tinged with lovely hues, the yellow leaves of forced rhubarb, raspberry, strawberry, celery, and many other humble plants.

Town dwellers should keep a look out when walking in the park in autumn for many of the fallen leaves can be pressed, oiled and used again and again. It is wise to collect many kinds and store them flat in plastic bags until they are required. Evergreens are extremely useful.

Leaves should be gathered with stems (petioles), as long as possible so that they can be easily arranged. Those for pin-holders need only to be impaled on the points or laid across them but those which are to flow over the rim of deeper containers may need a little help. It is often quite easy to insert a florist wire up the fleshy petiole either to the margin of the leaf or just far enough to hold firm. The protruding portion can then be inserted down into the wire netting or other stem holder. Alternatively, pipecleaners can be twisted round the base of the petiole to elongate it and to make it easier to arrange.

Tall crown imperials are in a matching vase which is filled with stem-holding large mesh wire netting. Fatsia leaves are artificially elongated by wires inserted in the stem ends.

STYLES OF ARRANGEMENT

Personal tastes play as important a part in the art of flower arrangement as they do in other visual arts. The style of decoration favoured will depend in the first place upon what kind of flowers you like to grow or buy. These will be (or ought to be) influenced by the colours of your home interior decoration. Also, the flowers are likely to influence, not only the choice of the type of container used, but also the setting in which the finished arrangement is placed. And, of course, the flowers must suit their surroundings.

Certain people want to be surrounded by flowers and flowers alone! Take, for example, the man or woman whose hobby is growing chrysanthemums, dahlias, gladioli, roses or some other specialist flower. Such people often have dozens of plants which yield many hundreds of flowers all destined for cutting. Such enthusiasts will not be interested in a few blooms, arranged in oriental styled designs!

But not everyone has masses of flowers nor wants to have so many around him.

An arrangement is often more likely to be an ornament than a true flower piece. Here the line of the complete ensemble was designed to fit a certain scene and to bring to it a touch of colour and a hint of atmosphere.

Shrub roses are arranged in a simple manner in a modern but traditionally styled Wedgwood vase. This free, loose bunch style is especially suitable for old-fashioned garden flowers like these.

Modern flowers look well arranged in the modern manner. As most flowers grown from bulbs and corms last best in shallow water there is a further advantage in choosing a style such as this for gladioli.

There are those who prefer to see just a few flowers aesthetic-ally displayed rather than a great mass. There are others who lead such busy lives that leisurely flower arrangement is either impossible or a seldom indulged luxury. These people tend to look on flower arrangement from a different view-point than those I first mentioned. But there are methods of easy arrangement for them also and later these also will be explained.

The lover of pure flower decoration is often puzzled by the stark simplicity of modern floral art and claims that this has nothing in common with the traditional manner of dis-playing blooms. Inevitably, we find that the term 'flower arrangement' really is too restricting and does not satisfac-torily describe all the forms of floral art we see. Yet there is no other term for it and we must use it whether we are thinking in terms of putting roses in a jug, building a cone of seed heads, arranging a piece of driftwood with a succulent plant or filling an altar vase.

Arrangements of informal flowers like these clustered floribunda roses can be used in many ways according to their size and content. These were to decorate a long table.

Formal or informal

Once, to do the flowers meant little more than arranging a few choice blooms in a vase designed to hold as much water as possible. Modern arrangers find old-fashioned vases very difficult to use which is one reason why containers not originally made to hold flowers are used.

Styles fall roughly into two groups, formal and informal. These groups are also subdivided, as we shall see. The type of flowers often, but not always, dictates the group into which their arrangement falls.

Generally speaking you will find that, since commercially produced blooms have to be as perfect and as uniform as possible, these tend to fall into formal styles when they are arranged even if the arranger was not, in fact, following a well-defined theme.

On the other hand, most flowers which are allowed to grow in a perfectly natural way, by which I mean not disbudded, staked or trained, tend to fall easily and happily into informal styles. A suitable choice of both stem holder and container increases this informality and results in a charming arrangement. Yet it is possible to arrange even the most unsophisticated flowers, the species rather than the man-made hybrids, into an informal design.

After many years I have learned that you can let flowers work for you! Informality is easily achieved when simple flowers grown quite naturally are used. They usually want to go their own way and the wise arranger follows them. So far as shop bought flowers are concerned, you may find, as I do, that their perfect uniformity is often best exploited. They can be arranged in highly formal and sophisticated designs and look quite wonderful, often much more distinctive than if they had been reduced to an artificiality by having been smothered with softening agents like fussy fern.

Formality exploited ! These uniform narcissi are arranged in a long curve by shortening stems to different lengths. Later the cut ends are also arranged.

Let your individuality show through

Except when we are arranging flowers for exhibition and competition there is really no reason at all why we should not arrange flowers exactly as we like. If we have personal tastes why should we subdue them?

At this point I feel that I should stress that I, personally, am not attempting to dictate how *you* should arrange *your* flowers. Instead, I am endeavouring to tell you how I do mine. I also believe that if, on the other

Formal flowers like these daffodils, often strongly individualistic, need to be arranged with both skill and understanding.

80

hand, you conform and accept or adopt the present popular styles of arrangement you can use them also as a means of self-expression. I make the plea that as you learn to arrange flowers efficiently you are not content to copy but strive to develop a style of your own. You will find it a rewarding experience.

My own first journey into making individual flower arrangements was down the daffodil path. For years I had arranged these flowers in a simple pitcher or mixed them with spring blossom in a vase, but one day, confronted with several almost identical bunches of flowers I decided to make some arrangements quite different. I hit on the idea of 'stepping' the stems, cutting each a different length so that every bloom could be displayed, and then standing them on a pinholder in a shallow dish.

Since that time a simple curve of formal flowers has become one of the accepted styles and one is likely to see many adaptations of it at all times of the year.

In this winter decoration, the orange-hued Galaxy chrysanthemums are matched by the undersides of the distinctive leaves of *Rhododendron Falconeri*.

Traditional flower arrangement tends to fall mainly into a few patterns based on certain shapes. This, roughly a half globe, is one of them.

Traditional patterns

Patterns which have been in vogue for many decades, even centuries, have a right to be called traditional. They are based on the simple bunch which was once placed in water, as it was with the stems still bound. One can imagine that a round posied bunch would be stood on a low table where it could be properly admired and that a tall bunch, or a sheaf, would be stood in a taller vessel with its back to the wall.

Then flower arrangement became more sophisticated. Instead of being bunched they were arranged individually yet the old patterns were still followed. In a bowl, flowers were

Even when loosely arranged and informal in character many designs are fundamentally traditional. In this mixture of sweet peas, pinks and roses the pattern once more, can be described as a portion of a globe, as an outline round the outer stems will show.

arranged to represent the round dome of the posy. The sheaf shape, which traditionally was made with some protective green fern fronds at the back, was repeated in side vases.

We have never really broken away from these old styles mainly because there is nothing which quite replaces them. Also flowers tend to fall into these patterns themselves.

I think that it helps the arranger to study natural plant shapes and in the imagination to convert them into styles for flowers using their proportions as a guide.

If you think about it a little you will see that there are just a few shapes which are continually repeated. The pyramid or cone is to be seen all around us and there are many variations played upon this theme from the stylised spruce pyramids to the slim leaf shapes of the cypress or the distinctive triangular outlines of pines. The globe which we have seen in fruits of all kinds is halved along its equator when it forms a bush or an alyssum plant. As these are nature's own shapes what is more natural than that we should have taken them as guides for our own art forms?

An arrangement designed to be placed against a wall needs a flat back. It is, in effect, a bunch or sheaf, with stems hidden by the vase.

A table centre for Christmas based on the posy theme. It has chincherinchees and chrysanthemums on a circular base of green.

Arctotis and pansies are set in a wide-angled triangle which enables one to make a wide band of colour with only a few flowers.

Hybrid tea roses fall beautifully into globular or semicircular designs which repeat the outline of the flowers themselves.

For a winter arrangement, a few pruned stems of eucalyptus contain within their pattern three tulips and three lilies-of-the-valley. The figure three is used here to emphasise the triangle theme.

Pink and blue chicory make a triangle of colour round an inner triangle of kale leaves, framing pompon chrysanthemums and pineapple mint.

In this summer arrangement of peonies, sweet peas, delphiniums, pinks and spiraeas the flowers are arranged in almost an entire globe.

The triangle is a favourite pattern in flower arrangement. Here, the lichen covered twigs are set in a triangular shaped pattern and the one chrysanthemum and gourds are placed within their outline.

Even large flowers like dahlias can be arranged in a posy. Here with pungent yellow fennel, they are arranged in a copper mug to decorate a kitchen dresser.

(*Above*) The first stems to be arranged are the centre one, which defines the height, and the two side stems at roughly right angles to it which define the width of the arrangement. The intermediate stems should never be taller than the centre or the proportions will be unbalanced.

It is important that no stems are seen to cross but that each one appears to flow out from a main centre source at the foot of the centre, vertical stem.

Variations on a theme

In spite of the great variety of flowers and plant materials we use, most of them fall very easily into traditional shapes based on the globe, semi-circle and circle. They are often very elegant.

If an arrangement is to be viewed from all points, the stems should radiate from the centre in all directions, but if it is to be faced one way, like the arrangement illustrated, they need only flow in a semicircular sweep radiating from the centre stem.

I would say that of all the styles or patterns of flower arrangement, those which are based on the globe are the most useful.

This all-round arrangement, as it is often called, is a basis for so many decorations as we shall see when we come to the next chapter.

A true cone, by which I mean a pointed shape on a round base, is also useful, but tends to be more formal than the rounded shapes. Flowers are easily arranged in this pattern and it entails only a simple matter of changing the lengths of the stems. The central stem, which goes into place first should be very much taller than the side stems. The shorter the side

Pyrethrums and sweet peas in a circular pattern are really a section of a globe split down the middle. Their tips almost make a full circle.

stems are and the greater the difference between them and the centre stem, the more pronounced the shape of the cone will be.

If an arrangement has to be spreading, say a low bowl close to the table's surface, then the central stem must be much shorter than the side stems. Again, the way they are cut and arranged will make the arrangement either conical or circular.

One thing is most important and this is that all the stems should appear to be radiating from a common source at the very centre of the arrangement. This they cannot do practically, but if every one of them leans away from the centre stem, the only vertical one, they will give this effect.

FLOWERS
FOR THE TABLE

Down through the ages there have been many occasions when table decorations have been extremely elaborate although their original purpose was simple enough. In Roman times, for instance, certain flowers were thought to be efficacious in warding off drunkenness! For this reason they were generously (and thoughtfully) heaped in front of the guest known to be bent on enjoying himself to the full. Roses were said to be particularly good for this purpose, so much so that these flowers were often made into garlands and given to a guest to hang round his neck as he sat down to wine and dine. Sometimes the wreaths were placed on the table instead.

Other flowers were said to ward off fever and for this reason sweet-smelling kinds were highly valued. These flowers, with sweet smelling leafy herbs were made into posies, sometimes called tussie-mussies, and placed on tables about the house. When a special guest was to be entertained, the posies would be somewhat larger and consequently sweeter than usual. Sometimes there would be many on a table, one for each guest.

Although the necessity for having prophylactic posies has disappeared, the custom of placing a bowl of flowers in the centre of a table has remained. So customary is it that to many of us a table does not look complete unless flowers are set upon it, even if it is otherwise bare.

In the home, flower arrangements on the table should add to the intimacy and friendliness of the occasion, but this has not always been so. There have been times when, after the first gasp of wonder or surprise, they must have been more intimidating than otherwise. This was, as one might expect in Victorian and even on into Edwardian times, when flower arrangements literally reached great heights! I understand that the purpose of such ostentation was to add to the general effect of gorgeousness of the room and that they should be visible over the heads of the guests. Now table decorations need to be low so that they do not form a screen between one person and another. They look best if they harmonise with the table linen and china and if they are not scented the food will taste better!

(*Right*) an example of a Victorian table decoration taken from a contemporary magazine.

A far cry from Victorian opulence! Gleanings from the garden: leek flower heads, lupin, poppy and honesty seed heads and mixed foliage match modern china.

The candle is the main 'stem' in the Christmas decorations above.

Methods of arrangement

As I said earlier, the 'all-round' arrangement is a good basic shape and lies at the root of many designs which can be as varied as a large decoration on a pedestal to grace a great hall or a table decoration for a little Christmas party.

The most important stem is the central one. It is well worth while spending a little time on this to ensure that it is both properly placed and well-anchored so that no stems arranged later be likely to move its position.

If candles are used these should be treated as flowers, or

(*Below*) First define dimensions, make all other stems lean from centre.

(*Above*) imaginary axis. (*Above right*) Flowering stems.

stems. One candle should be set in the very centre and all subsequent stems should radiate from points round its base. If two candles are used you should imagine that the central space between them is the axis of the arrangement. This way lines and proportions will be pleasing.

Candles are easily arranged. Wire netting will hold them quite well although you may have to hold them erect while the first few stems are arranged. These will soon wedge them in place. I use a combination of Florapak or Oasis, and place the netting over and/or around this. The base of the candle then goes through the upper layers of netting and down into the plastic where it is held firm.

If you want to arrange a candle on a pinholder first warm the pinholder by standing it in hot water. The candle will then fit easily on the points, but don't forget to make the pinholder base quite dry again before fixing the clay pills on. Remove the candle in the same way.

If using a basket with a handle, you should take this into consideration. Decide where the centre point lies and if it is not possible to stand an upright stem under it, and this will depend upon both the style of the basket and how high the handle stands from the container, then imagine an axis immediately under the centre of the handle. Arrange the stems so that they radiate from this.

If you want to build an arrangement using two or more bowls one above the other, determine the centre of the top bowl and imagine it extends to the centre of the lower bowl.

To celebrate a Golden Wedding, this little bowl contains some very straight stems but natural golden foliage and ribbon bows bring a soft touch to them.

If the tip of the centre stem is directly over the centre of the base of the container the arrangement will always be well balanced no matter how mixed the components. Side stems at wide angles to the centre stem will flow low and add an informal note.

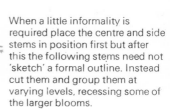

A raised container brings grace to a bowl arrangement especially if the stems of some components are stiff. It also allows the arranger to use short-stemmed materials.

When a little informality is required place the centre and side stems in position first but after this the following stems need not 'sketch' a formal outline. Instead cut them and group them at varying levels, recessing some of the larger blooms.

A pineapple of carnations with croton leaves and Christmas tree baubles is arranged for a party table. In this case the stems are short but the principles of arrangement are the same as for the longer stems seen here.

Formal and traditional, chrysanthemums are arranged in a silver punch bowl. Spray flowers are sometimes so clustered that the stem for the centre needs thinning or it will look top heavy.

An all round arrangement is not necessarily one held in a low bowl. This little shell-shaped container held by a dolphin raises short stemmed pansies and pinks so that they may be easily admired and smelled !

When mixed shapes are used they often look attractive if they are grouped in their kinds or colours. However, if this is done, do not separate the zones too severely but allow them to merge one with another.

An arrangement placed at the end of a table can be tailored to fill the space by extending or shortening the side stems as required.

Ideas for table settings

Obviously, where table settings are concerned, a great deal depends upon the size of the table and the number of guests to be seated round it, but if we realise that we do not have to be restricted to a plain bowl in its centre area we are much more likely to devise original and pleasing decorations.

Take, for example, the small room in which one end of the table is often flush against a wall. If the decoration is placed at this point it will not only look very attractive but you will find that its site is also practical. The rest of the table will be clear for china, glass and linen.

If you choose this position you can place a long arrangement made to measure, or a triangular design almost flat against the wall. Pairs of arrangements look well in this position and you will find that decorations made in candle-cups look appropriate. Tiers of flowers, or fruit and flowers mixed, can flank a central mass of fruit.

One advantage of this style of placement is that the flowers are never likely to impede the guests' view!

But what about free standing tables? Sometimes two or more arrangements running the length but leaving the actual centre clear are more convenient than one main bowl, for then an area is left free for fruit or some other dish. When you do this take care none of the flowers stand high.

Arrangements running across the table diagonally, divide the table prettily. This line need not be dense with flowers but can be determined by foliage, ivy trails for example, superimposed with troughs of flowers according to the size of the table and the importance of the occasion.

On a really large table, flowers at varying heights look very attractive especially if the lower stemmed ones in the taller decorations are brought down prettily to touch, or almost touch, those at a lower level. Sometimes the difference in levels can be effected and accentuated by candles.

Study the pattern and colours on both china and table linen so that you can select plant materials to harmonise.

Often two or more arrangements look prettier than one bowl, especially if they are placed diagonally, leaving room in the centre.

Flowers which carry their blooms at an angle to their stems are known as 'faced' flowers and are ideal for arrangements designed to face into a room.

FLOWERS TO FACE INTO A ROOM

There are many places about the home where flowers will be displayed against a wall and in this case, it will be much more convenient (and as we shall see, economical) if they have flat backs. Yet, even if this is so, the arrangement itself should never appear flat and contourless.

Most formal arrangements could be said to be all-round styles sliced down the middle. Thus we can have a half cone which will appear to be triangular in outline and a half globe which will have a circular or a semicircular shape, and with these we can have all the variations that one would expect to be played on these two important shapes.

The only real difference between these styles and the all-round designs we have been discussing is that all the action, as it were, is on one side of the arrangement only. But if you take the idea of an arrangement sliced down the centre too literally, you are likely to find that the finished design may be too flat-backed to be pleasing. It all depends on where it is to stand in the home but beware, it may look

An arrangement with a flat back is ideal for floral mixtures. Tall graceful stems can be used to provide height while smaller stemmed flower masses can be used low down, centrally, at rim level or even lower than this.

ugly when viewed from the side. So it is important that such arrangements should always look well in profile. Fortunately, this is something which is easily done.

Even though, in a sense we halve the mass of flowers, there is no need to halve the area of container in which their stems are to be placed. So, if when we begin assembling them we take the tallest vertical stem and, as before, place it in the centre of the arrangement but, instead of also placing it in the middle of the container, we take it back as near to the rim as possible, we shall leave almost all the area of the container to be filled. Then we can arrange the following stems in the same way as before, allowing each one to lean away gradually from the central vertical stem which defines the height of the arrangement.

As work proceeds, look occasionally at the profile of the arrangement and view it as it might be seen by, say, someone entering a room.

Often you need no more than a leaf or a short spray flowing over the back rim. Sometimes you will need to take the flowers round more than the 180° of a half circle.

Containers are important

Once again, we realise that an attractive arrangement does not depend solely upon the flowers. As I have stressed before, while it is by no means important that they should be valuable, containers need to be chosen with care. For example, a stemmed or pedestal vase will lift short-stemmed flowers and give them an air of elegance and importance. Many gorgeous short-stemmed blooms are ideal for massing at rim level in mixed designs.

Many of the mass-produced flowers bought from the shop have very straight and stiff stems which often offer problems to the flower arranger. A pedestal vase will help dispel any over-stiff effect. The tulips in the arrangement illustrated on the opposite page have straight stems which are unlikely to curve much in water, but both the container and the twigs behind them have helped to make them look a little less formal. One advantage a pedestal vase has over deep, tall ones is that you do not need many flowers to fill it!

It is important that the flowers and their container should not only belong to

(Below top) Many of the flowers in this arrangement : pansies, scabious, snapdragons, sweet peas and petunias are short stemmed but the pedestal dolphin vase raises them gracefully.

(Below bottom) This little footed vase which so prettily matches the colour of the ivy and tulip foliage brings a dignity to a dozen short-stemmed double tulips.

each other but should be seen to belong. By this I mean that not only is it important to select a container which suits the flowers in size, colour and texture, as we have seen, but that it and the flowers should merge.

This is not at all difficult to achieve. If you study the illustrations on these two pages you will see that in every case, flowers and other materials arranged more or less at rim level and below it, have been made to flow out over, and below the actual rim. This way they eliminate any hard and well-defined line which might otherwise exist.

This effect also serves another purpose for by bringing the flowers out over the rim you make the arrangement greater in depth at its base. This improves its profile.

Again, you will see that all the stems do not flow out over the rims for the same distance. Some, like pansies, ivy clusters and forget-me-nots, are much shorter than the others.

If flowers are allowed to flow out and below the rim of a vase, an arrangement becomes well integrated. But these flowing stems should not be of equal lengths.

Styles unlimited

There is really no limit to the styles you can choose for arrangements to stand against a wall or in some other place where it is not essential that they shall be viewed from all angles. Whether these are formal or informal will really depend as much upon the flowers and other materials as upon the type of container and the nature of the setting in which the arrangement is to be placed.

Generally speaking, mass-produced, uniform flowers tend to fall into formal patterns. They can only be made to look informal by using certain accessories. Actually, a great deal of entertainment and pleasure can be derived from trying to create an informal scene from seemingly unsympathetic materials.

If time is important to you it might be wisest and best to compromise. Have by you a selection of suitable containers which will suit florist flowers. Devise a pattern of arrangement which suits you and which you can carry out quickly and easily. Do not think that the sameness will become monotonous! The seasons bring their own variety.

Remember that the formal styles are symmetrical and are

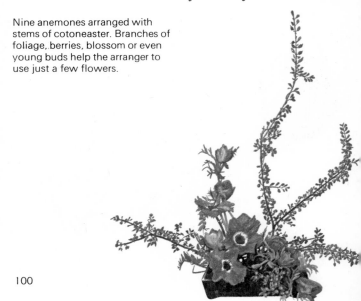

Nine anemones arranged with stems of cotoneaster. Branches of foliage, berries, blossom or even young buds help the arranger to use just a few flowers.

fundamentally based either on the globe or the cone. Take the triangle for example. Nothing is easier than to arrange six uniform flowers into a triangle merely by shortening the stems so that beginning at the tip, you have one, two (one on each side of it at a lower level) then, one again, in the centre and lower than the two side flowers; and then two, as above but leaning just a little further out. If the flowers are well supplied with their own foliage the arrangement might be complete, but it is more likely that it will be improved by some complementary material arranged within the line of the triangle.

If you exercise your imagination you will find many ways of using just a few flowers even for a large arrangement. A flat branch of beech, spruce, pine or maple, for example, can be placed at the back of a container so that it forms a triangle or semicircle defining the size and shape of the finished arrangement. Lower or misplaced side stems should be trimmed away and re-arranged to flow over the rim or set aside to arrange later among the straight-stemmed blooms. The backcloth of foliage will help eliminate their formality and, also, give you a lovely and quickly assembled decoration.

A gorgeous head of variegated kale not only furnishes a large area of an arrangement but by its frilly, informal pattern complements the formal, uniform chrysanthemums. Extra kale and leaves of grevillea turned to show their silver undersides add to the informality.

Containers and colours can be selected to suit the room in which the flower arrangement stands. In this arrangement for the kitchen, a copper saucepan holds everlasting flowers.

Flowers add to the beauty of a home

As I said earlier, if flowers are to be an important part of your interior decoration they should be neither chosen nor displayed too casually. With a little thought you can get them working for you!

You can use your flowers to create illusions. If your rooms are low, try using the flowers to suggest height and place them nearer the floor than the ceiling and choose styles in which there are good vertical lines. If the opposite is true and the ceilings are high, place your flowers on shelves, tall slim tables, or torchères, or hang them in wall vases. If you have dark corners, light them up with floral pillars or cones of white, yellow or pastel tints which will reflect even the smallest amount of light. If you have patterned wallpaper use a monochrome colour scheme.

You can save time and trouble if you place an arrangement where it is unlikely to be disturbed. A good place is the wall between two windows where the sun does not glare and yet it is in good light. If this wall is opposite the door they will speak a welcome!

In winter dark browns of preserved materials give a surprisingly warm impression. In summer lots of cool greens and white give a cool, airy effect which is pleasant and restful. Your fireplace can be made to glow with flowers. A bare wall can be beautifully furnished with a wall vase.

Clever placing of certain colours will help give new proportions to the rooms. Place red flowers at the end of a room rather than in the middle, because red appears to make a room smaller. Conversely, use blue to give an impression of space. A blue arrangement against a far wall in a small room will help to make it appear larger. If the setting is right, a pair of blue arrangements will achieve an even better effect.

A Byzantine cone of single chrysanthemums makes a striking decoration for the corner of a room, especially if the floral colour matches that of the furnishing.

Pairing them off

There are many places in the home where a pair of flower arrangements look more attractive than a single decoration. A mantelpiece, sideboard, a long side table, even a dressing table, can be given new beauty and importance this way. For parties, a buffet table can be made both attractive and entertaining if it is decorated with pairs of arrangements.

You really do not need many more flowers for a pair of arrangements than for one large one. If the theme of two floral ornaments fits in well with your interior decor schemes you might consider making a semi-permanent framework of preserved materials which is attractive enough to stand alone yet capable of being dressed up for parties. Nicely curved branches of willow or broom, for example, terminating in a cluster of preserved leaves and a knot of some lovely dried fruits such as camphor buds or agave seed-pods can be quickly brought to life by a single orchid or a little curve of a few blooms of some other kind. A tube for holding tablets pushed in among the leaves will hold water for them.

Narcissi, tulips, irises and hyacinths, in bud and bloom, and maple and viburnum, look well raised on a pair of old Sheffield plate candlesticks.

It is not wise to make first one arrangement and then the other to match. Somehow the flowers that are left never seem to pair. Instead, assemble both arrangements side by side and if one has a low stem which flows to the right, try to find a similar stem which flows to the left in the other.

Obviously, it will depend upon where you stand the pair what their style should be. You might want them to be quite formal and symmetrical. On the other hand they might look much more attractive and effective if they were asymmetrical. Supposing, for example, you placed a pair on the mantelpiece, one each side of a picture. You could shape each into a crescent so that the picture was 'embraced' within the curve made by each of them.

Alternatively, you could arrange the flowers in a tall triangle, each upright following a parallel line with the frame of the picture and its base running along below it. If you want to 'spread' the width of the shelf or the wall against which it stood, the base of the triangles could run in the other direction.

When you make a pair of arrangements, assemble them both at the same time so that you can make sure that they are equally balanced.

USING ONLY A FEW FLOWERS

It is not necessary to use a great many flowers to create a beautiful arrangement. I have made many in which only one flower was featured and I often use just three blooms – the result of dividing a market bunch of a dozen into four so that I can spread the flowers round the home.

Sometimes a scarcity of flowers inspires you to create a decoration in which the beauty of the individual flower becomes revealed.

Japanese flower arrangement, an ancient art practised for centuries, uses very few flowers or little plant material, but relies instead on stylised line, beautiful containers, and other accompaniments. This and other modern oriental styles derived from it, have influenced the art of flower arrangement all over the world.

Western flower arrangement has in the past been robust in character – after all, in temperate climates, plant materials are plentiful! However, with the increase of population and the growth of commercial flower production, with warmer homes where the atmosphere hastens the maturity of cut flowers so that they become a costly item of expenditure, with less time to spend on doing the flowers and also with a new look at indoor decoration generally, there is now a tendency for arrangers to use fewer flowers *en masse* and to concentrate instead on the beauty of line.

Such arrangements often are exciting and sometimes, even dramatic but, like all floral decorations, they need to suit

their surroundings. Usually, they look their best in a contemporary setting, but they can be made to harmonise by observing one or two points, for instance, choosing a container in character with the rest of the room.

We shall see, in the pages to come, how each line has meaning and in a well-designed arrangement if even one of them were removed, the arrangement would look incomplete.

The eye becomes trained to appreciate line. Often at the beginning, a new flower arranger tends to try to mass line, arranging say, many bare twigs where three or five would have been enough and only later realises that space and voids also have decorative values. You will soon find that a space left between lines accentuates their beauty.

Arrangements using the minimum of materials : (*Left*) a single hyacinth bloom and prunings from a clematis. (*Above*) even a cabbage leaf is beautiful enough to accompany three daffodils. (*Right*) One arum lily with a beautiful leaf and two rushes are enough for a lovely arrangement if stems are skilfully placed.

107

The tallest stem which represents heaven is known as *shin*, its tip should always be over its base. The second stem, *soe*, is two-thirds the height of the main stem. *Hikae* representing man always assumes a lowly position and again is shorter than the stem which proceeds it. This rule applies when flowers are grouped together or when they stand apart as these irises do.

The principles behind oriental design

Rules for Japanese arrangement are strict but helpful. Those who wish to follow them faithfully will need to study hard for a long time – not only floral art but also philosophy! Others who do not wish to be too bound by rules can also benefit by studying them, for they are based on good sense.

The basic shape is an irregular triangle, the main lines of which are described by three stems, known as *shushi*. Some arrangements call for additional stems and these known as *jushi*, should

always be placed within pattern of the *shushi*.

Centuries ago, a teacher reverently taught that these three stems represented heaven, earth and man. They are known as *shin, soe* and *hikae*. *Shin* is of the greatest importance and is always the tallest. This stem should be curved and its tip should always be over its base, a sensible rule because this always leads to good balance and pleasant placement. If the branch or stem is undulating it may move away from the centre on its upward course, but it should return immediately over its base.

The *soe* is next in importance and this is placed to the side of the main stem. As it rises from the surface of the water, *shin* and *soe* should run closely together but after a little space the *soe* should move away to follow its own path reaching two-thirds the height of the main stem. *Hikae*, the short, third stem, assumes a lowly position. This should always be kept low in an arrangement and should flow forward, giving the arrangement a third dimension, although it should not be allowed to assume a drooping position. The *jushi* are added last, usually three or five are sufficient.

Picture or scenic arrangements

Today, many people are interested in Ikebana, which although it means 'keeping cut flowers alive in water', is really Japanese flower arrangement as interpreted by various schools and teachers. Now, there seem to be as many styles of Ikebana as there are of Western arrangements!

Generally though, it represents a way of using a few flowers which can be effectively arranged by following definite rules. Its popularity is due to the fact that it can be enjoyed by anyone with or without a garden, rich or poor. It is really not so very different from a simple and free-style way of arranging flowers which many of us have practised and enjoyed for years.

As a flower arranger who has gone her own way from the beginning, I have often been delighted to find that concepts I discovered for myself, have in fact, been expounded by those who have gone before. Take Ikebana, for example, one rule is that the water in the container is important and represents the soil from which the plants spring.

In Ikebana also, the stem ends at the bases – which are

Pine and nerines describe a little scene of trees and flowers growing from rocks, which in fact, hide the pinholder securing the stems.

always visible – should be close together so that they give the illusion of combined springing up from the soil which bore them. I have always felt that the components of an arrangement, no matter what its style, should appear to spring from a common source, and this is something I have stressed in former chapters in this book.

Actually, as well as being visually pleasing, this is good sense! It is so much easier to arrange stems in a line arrangement this way just as it is so much easier to hide the mechanics of the actual arrangement when stems are close together than if they are widely distributed.

One way that this natural effect can be featured – even exploited – is when we use a few flowers and accessories in an arrangement which tells a story or describes a scene, really, an adaptation of more subtle Japanese arrangements. For these you will need firm, solid containers that suggest the earth. They should be wide enough to show an expanse of water or, alternatively, for you to spread 'grass'. They should be deep enough to sustain a good branch as well as frail flowers, if these are used.

Pussy willow, daffodils and hellebores paint a picture of spring. The Iceland-moss keeps the flowers fresh and hides their holders.

(*Top left*) Variegated dogwood parrot tulips, and wild arums are arranged to make a crescent of colour in a slim, black vase of modern design.

(*Top right*) In this unusual arrangement brass bowl and leaves of my own design give importance to a bunch of violets and join them in complementary harmony.

(*Bottom left*) A long-lasting winter arrangement of London pride and ferns in a brass bowl. Burned gorse gives additional height as well as providing interest.

(*Bottom right*) Three English iris are arranged in a triangle. Two hosta leaves accentuate the flowing line of the flowers and lotus seed heads provide an attractive contrast of texture.

(*Top left*) Two separate groups of snowdrops standing on pin-holders arranged with sprays of wild ivy tell a story of spring gardens. The piece of wood provides a decorative base.

(*Top right*) Only three chrysanthemum blooms are used, but swirled aspidistra leaves and thin-cat-tails give them height and add interest to the arrangement.

(*Bottom left*) Seven short-stemmed tulips sit in an arc of grevillea leaves. This is, in fact, two triangular arrangements linked together by one centre flower.

(*Bottom right*) A handful of flowers are placed in a modern Scandinavian mug. The daffodils are first tied together in the hand and later, wedged in place with the bunch of primroses and ivy.

Accessories are both helpful and important

If you want to paint an attractive picture you need materials as well as inspiration, but the difference between the flower arranger and the painter is that to the flower arranger materials are often the source of inspiration!

A wise decorator builds up a good store of accessories. These are likely to be extremely varied and there is no limit to what you can use, except for competition, when the schedule will define what or what is not allowed. Today's 'pop' floral artists even go so far as to use bed springs and feathers among other things! My own tastes lead me to search for materials from the same basic sources as the flowers, although I also like to use shells and other marine objects.

If you decide to stock a store cupboard for your arranging you will find that you are never at a loss for something to place with any type of flower as it comes into season. There are a few materials which, to me at any rate, seem classic. Shells, for example, seem to suit all flowers equally well.

Obviously, as these vary so considerably, some shells will be more suitable for certain blooms or plant materials than others. However, there is something akin to flowers in the satin texture and rainbow colours of some, or to the bark of trees in the rough grainy surfaces of others.

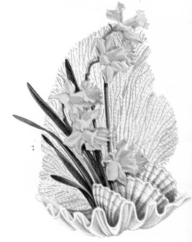

A crescent of five yellow daffodils within the leaf-shape of a sea-fan. The curve is repeated in the scallop shells at the base of the flowers.

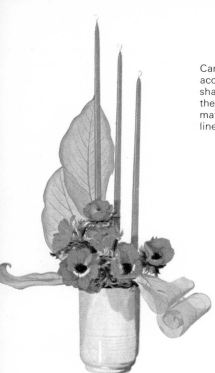

Candles and leaves are classic accessories for flowers. Here shadow leaves, dyed red to match the anemones, hold three matching candles in their curving line.

I have a selection which ranges from some tiny yellow periwinkles to scatter in a glass bowl holding daffodils, to great clams in which flowers and plants are arranged.

Leaves of all kinds may be pressed and preserved and set aside to use some other time. Some can be skeletonised and can be bought under the name of 'shadow' leaves. These are usually magnolia although often ficus are included. You can preserve your own foliage. I describe how this is done in the chapter on Dried Flowers.

A complete contrast to such natural objects are candles which help the flower arranger in providing colour, either when this is scarce or lacking altogether, or in setting the scene. If you have a stately coloured candle as the centre pivot in an arrangement you will need only few flowers to accompany it!

Good companions

Driftwood is another classic accessory that shares the beauty of a composition as much with an orchid as a daisy. However, I feel that it must be true driftwood, worn smooth and silky by the action of sea and sand. Sometimes a simulated driftwood is prepared by stripping the bark from a branch, but it does not please me.

Lichen-covered branches are also very beautiful and well

An accessory to flowers can play more than one role. Here, five parrot tulips are supported as well as supplemented by the driftwood shells and rocks.

(*Above*) A towering branch of hazel catkins, which will open prettily in the warmth of a room, and a spray of ivy has transformed a low bunch of violets into a decoration suitable for the corner of a room.

(*Left*) Cat-tails or reed mace and the true rushes may be dried and kept to use time and time again. Cones and preserved leaves suit autumnal flowers.

worth using. Actually, if you handle them carefully and spray the lichen itself occasionally, they can be used many times. Sometimes you can find lichen festooned larch branches which are also thick with cones.

Fresh, edible mushrooms can be used, especially in table and buffet decorations. If you have no young children in the house you can also use the more brightly coloured toadstools. Best of all are the tree-oysters, a bracket fungi, which you see attached to tree trunks. These dry naturally, with no special treatment. I like to use clusters of this fungus among green leaves at the foot of a branch of early spring blossom.

Branches of early blossom seem a natural choice but some, catkins and pussy willow, for instance, can be dried and kept in use for many weeks.

However, for a scenic arrangement, look for a prettily-shaped living branch and let it play the part of a tree in the arrangement.

There are many grasses which can be stored successfully. Do not think of them only as accompaniments for dried flowers; some look pretty with fresh flowers too.

(*Left*) Thick stems are not always easily impaled on a pinholder but if the stem is split upwards for about the same length as the depth of the water the two parts can then be easily impaled.

(*Middle left*) Sometimes, driftwood can be arranged like any other stem. Here, some of the snag ends of the wire netting stem holder in the vase have been wrapped round the lower two or three inches of the driftwood.

Techniques for arrangement

If you are going to employ all kinds of accessories you must be able to arrange and position them with confidence! There is no virtue in doing flower arrangement the hard way! If an easy way does not appear to exist, look for it or devise one for yourself. Often what appears to be an important visual part of an arrangement or composition is also of practical use. For example, stones and shells can be used to hold down pinholders which are suporting heavy stems or used to wedge leaning branches and

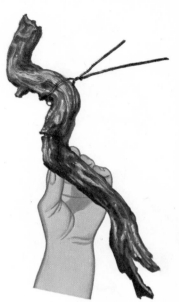

(*Below left*) Some of the weight of this piece is supported by the edge of the container but extra security is given by passing florist wire around the driftwood and passing the ends through the points of the pinholder.

(*Right*) If a piece of driftwood is to flow over the rim of a container, it should be mounted on florist wire. The ends of the wire can then be inserted into the stem holder easily.

to hide other ways and means employed to keep materials well anchored.

As long as it does not show, do not hesitate to use a wire if you will ensure that a stem is firmly held. I find that an 18 gauge florist wire, or two or more if a thicker gauge is needed, bent like a hairpin, is one of the best means of holding a crooked piece of driftwood in position over the rim of a container. Pass the wire over the wood and the legs down firmly into the stem holder. This is sometimes effective in holding down a branch when you want it to flow downwards in a low line. Use long wires for deep vases.

Pieces of driftwood can be mounted on wires or they can be screwed on to a wooden base. But usually, you find that it is possible to stand one piece upright and then straddle it with another. The pinholders and rocks do the rest. However, various gadgets have been invented by some flower arrangers and are sold through the National Association of Flower Arrangement Societies.

Fungi can usually be mounted by inserting 18 gauge wire in the soft base. Cocktail sticks may also be used.

119

Daffodils, cryptanthus, scindapsus and hedera (ivy) — house plants are so varied and colourful that it is possible to harmonise them with most flowers.

LONG-LASTING ARRANGEMENTS

Among the many accessories for flower arrangement we ought to consider the most natural of all — entire plants! Often, you can arrange a plant with a root as a focal point, a rosette of London pride, a soft, silvery grey verbascum, or a gloriously coloured ornamental cabbage, for example. You can also arrange cut flowers and pot plants together in a *pot-et-fleur* arrangement and in this way devise ways and means of making long-lasting arrangements.

It is also possible to make the ensemble in such a way that the flowers are easily removed and replaced after they have faded as some plants will go on for months even though they may be tilted or raised to suit the arrangement.

If you like *pot-et-fleur*, which offers a form of flower arrangement as well as of indoor gardening, you will find that the accessories referred to in the previous chapter are essential. You will want plenty of material both to hide, wedge and support pots.

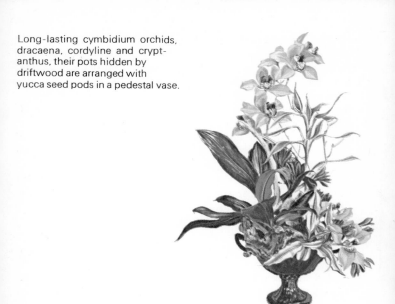

Long-lasting cymbidium orchids, dracaena, cordyline and crypt-anthus, their pots hidden by driftwood are arranged with yucca seed pods in a pedestal vase.

If you are also a greenhouse gardener you will be able to create a great variety of *pot-et-fleur* arrangements, for you will have the facilities to look after and revive faded pot plants until they are once again lovely enough to accompany flowers. You could also propagate a selection of plants with *pot-et-fleur* arrangements in mind.

Plant and flower arrangements can be designed to fit in with your colour schemes just as arrangements of flowers alone. You will find also that they can be just as dramatic in appearance and as exciting as outline. It all depends on what kind of plants you choose.

Many of us have containers which are really too large to be filled with flowers yet these look lovely filled with plants and coloured with fresh-cut blooms. You will find also that *pot-et-fleur* can be as elegant as a flower arrangement, especially when it is displayed in a pedestal vase. Keep this in mind when you are selecting plants. Choose some which will scramble prettily over the rim, others that will tower above them and some that can be tilted.

How the containers are filled

It is best to arrange the pot plants and the vessels to hold water for the flowers at the same time so that one can wedge, hold and hide the other. In most containers you can use Florapak or Oasis into which either the whole pot or just its base (according to the depth of the container) can be pushed. You will find also that plants can be easily and firmly tilted this way. Another advantage in using Florapak or Oasis is that when dampened the evaporation creates a micro-climate round the plants which is beneficial to them.

The containers for the flower themselves will have to suit the size of the arrangement as well as the thickness of the flowers' stems, although if you have used Florapak or Oasis you can also arrange the flower stems in this.

I have several metal cones, painted green so that they are inconspicuous, of various sizes and lengths. I also have some mounted on thin canes. Other vessels I use are individual cigar tubes, tablet bottles, cream cartons, plastic funnels and metal florist cones. The latter just hold a cylinder of Oasis and are useful for strong-stemmed flowers. Party balloons filled with water and tied to a flower stem will make a creeper 'bloom'. Mounted containers enable you to arrange flowers at different levels.

Wide-mouthed containers, such as the cream cartons, need stem holders in them. I find too that it often helps to put a small screw of netting in the mouth of a cone, otherwise all the stems drop in vertically.

You can also use soil, sand, bulb fibre or peat as a 'plunge' or as packing for the pot plants. Not only does a covered surface look more attractive but it slows down evaporation. Mosses look attractive, bun mosses especially so. Iceland moss or lichen needs to be pushed in firmly so that it stands well. Watch that they do not siphon the water out.

(*Top*) Vessels to hold water for the flowers can be pushed down among the plants and hidden by them. (*Centre*) Plants need to be selected for their practical value as well as for their beauty. Wide spread plants like this chlorophytum, furnish the centre of the arrangement and conceal the vessel for the flowers plunged behind it. (*Bottom*) *Pot-et-fleur* arrangements can be simple like this trug holding a syngonium and a holly ivy.

Flowers which suit pot plants

Some flowers seem to have a natural affinity with greenhouse-grown pot plants and you can feel this even if you have no botanical knowledge. Generally speaking, those which have very leafy or very downy or hairy stems look ill at ease and often unattractive. Where the pot plants themselves have a lot of leaves, flowers with other foliage is distracting. An exception to this rule is the rose, which seems to fit in with everything else, but even here it might be necessary to remove a few leaves. Save them to arrange low in the container and use them to wedge the stems in place and to hide the rim.

Arums look well – but then many of the house plants are aroids, which probably accounts for it. Smooth-stemmed bulb flowers are ideal. In fact a *pot-et-fleur* offers one a way to use just three blooms from a divided bunch which I described in a former chapter.

It is not always the upper surface of a leaf which is the most vivid. Look below and there, often, you will find the most gorgeous hues! Match white and creamy tints with

Arranged in a large dried fungus, *Dracaena sanderiana* flanks the driftwood, *Cordyline terminalis* spreads between the tulips, *Cryptanthus tricolour* nestles below.

chlorophytum, ivy, *Cryptanthus tricolour*, *Dracaena sanderiana* and *Scindapsus aureus*.

Many plants carry somewhere on them, perhaps on stems, stipules or bracts, that lovely glowing plant purple – nearer to magenta than violet. Many pink flowers are really a tint of this colour. Place them together and you will see! Try *Cordyline terminalis* with double pink tulips.

Study a few plants and you will find the lavender blue of Dutch iris, the rosy red of nerines, all the subtle tints and tones – and the greens – of orchids, the soft hues of modern lilies and the gay tulip colours. And even if you have no great collection and must rely only on the old and well-tried favourites such as ivy, rhoicissus or even aspidistra, you will find the strong greens offer fine foil for all floral colours.

Shells, dried seed heads and even fresh fruits can be mixed in a *pot-et-fleur* to add colour and will look delightful.

Another pleasant thing is that many of the house plants have foliage which bears some resemblance to the leaves of the flowers. As so many of these flowers are marketed without their own foliage the plants fill a need!

Smooth-stemmed flowers such as arums (really zantedeschias) and bulbous iris look well with sansevieria, cyperus, scindapsus, tradescantia and ivy.

DRIED FLOWERS

At the beginning of this book I said that if you want your flowers to live for many days, you must see that they are young and in perfect condition when you pick or buy them. And this is so, but under certain conditions no flowers can live for long. Central heating, for example, can kill frail flowers very quickly. The *pot-et-fleur* arrangements described in the previous chapter are better for such conditions than cut flowers alone because a growing plant raised in a greenhouse and later supplied with humidity will go on growing. But even plants succumb eventually!

Fortunately, there are many flowers, leaves and other plant materials which will stand up to the hottest and driest atmospheres! These are the everlastings, immortelles and all the fascinating perpetuelles. With these you need never be without flower arrangements. Do not imagine for one minute that they are dull. They can be as bright or alternatively, as subtly coloured as you wish.

I have many of these dried flower arrangements myself. In fact, they are not reserved for winter decoration only but tend to become part of the fixtures! There is such a wide range of materials that it is possible to select dainty, summery, feminine flowers such as soft pink daisies, roses or blue hydrangeas for bedrooms or other places where pastel tints are best and more robust colours and textures for hall or living rooms.

Blue echinops or globe thistle, with white statice and lavender in a Chinese bowl with matching colours make a charming and long-lasting table decoration.

126

Mostly from my garden — pressed vine leaves, achillea, strawdaisies, golden rod, tulip and plantain seed heads, barley and wild rushes.

Surprising as it may sound, you can wash some of these everlastings. They can then be dried out and rearranged!

I grow most of my own materials. The rest I collect from the country or seaside. These are supplemented by others bought from the florist sundries' man who imports from all over the world and this range grows yearly.

Many of the perpetuelles can be used to complement and supplement arrangements of fresh flowers and I have referred to them from time to time in previous chapters. For this reason it is wise to collect more than you anticipate using for dried decorations alone.

From varied helichrysums you can make many colour schemes. With these are achillea, orange seed pods of *Iris foetidissima*, clematis seed heads and burdock.

Some flowers are everlasting

As you know, most flowers will, when cut and left out of water, just shrivel and die, but there are some which produce blooms with tough, papery or straw-like petals which remain stiff and firm. If these are gathered at the correct time, before they are pollinated and begin to make seed, they will keep their shape, form and colour.

Most of these plants are from the daisy or *Compositae* family. These are the everlastings and immortelles. There are both annual and perennial kinds. There are some lovely varieties and strains of these, particularly helichrysums. The annual form of this comes in white, yellow, gold, orange, pale pink, rose, red, crimson and deep bronze which is almost black.

True everlastings can be distinguished by the papery or straw-like texture of the flower parts. But there are other flowers which, although they are not 'straw flowers' can in fact be dried quite naturally. These are the perpetuelles. When dried, they do not retain their beauty quite so well as the true everlastings. Even so, they are useful and decorative. Some unexpectedly fresh looking flowers come into this category, larkspurs and delphiniums for example, golden rod, hydrangeas, some roses, pompon chrysanthemums and others.

Ornamental grasses to go in winter bouquets have been cultivated for centuries. The great quaking grass, *Briza maxima*; Job's tears, *Coix Lacryma Jobi*; squirrel's tail, *Hordeum jubatum* and hare's tail, *Lagurus ovatus* are favourites.

There are also wild grasses well worth gathering. Also highly decorative are the farm cereals, oats, wheat, barley, maize (including some attractive garden hybrids) and, if you live in the right place, rice and millet.

The important thing about all of these is that they must really be cut when the flower or grass is at the correct point of maturity, success depends on this! Young flowers' colours are clearer, their stems stronger.

Helipterum daisies have clear yellow centres. White and yellow statice, and *Briza maxima*, the quaking grasses, surround them.

Flowers to grow

If you would like to grow some of these flowers for yourself you will find them listed in all good seedsman's catalogues. Usually available are *Ammobium alatum* or sand flower; *Gomphrena globosa* or Globe Amaranth; *Helichrysum bracteatum*, the straw daisy of which there are many varieties and strains; *Helipterum manglesii*, sometimes listed as *Rhodanthe manglesii* and *H. roseum*, often called *Acroclinium roseum*; *Limonium bonduelli, sinuatum, suworowii*; *limoniums* are also listed as *statice*; *Lonas inodora*; *Xeranthemum annuum, X. a. ligulosum* and *X. a. perligulosum*. There are also perennials, *Anaphalis margaritacea* or pearly everlasting, many helichrysums including some with attractive downy or 'silver' foliage, and *Limonium latifolium* and *incanum*.

Among the non-everlastings are *Amaranthus caudatus* or love-lies-bleeding, and its near relatives the showy cock's combs or celosia, didiscus, the lace flower; salvias – those

showy bedding plants which are now in other colours than scarlet; tagetes among which are the African and French marigolds and zinnias – but not the red ones. All of these are annuals.

There are many perennials and, before I list them, I would like to urge you to experiment with drying others. A great deal seems to depend upon the season. In hot dry summers I have found flowers like rambler roses, pelargoniums, helianthemums, cornflowers, even aquilegia, dry well.

Perennials which I dry often are: many of the achilleas including the filipendulina varieties and the white ptarmica; echinops or globe thistle and the eryngium or sea holly (the wild sea-shore holly will also dry but it is very prickly, so beware!); gypsophila – the double is better, *Salvia farinacea*, the lovely blue salvia, stachys and verbascum. Among shrubs I dry buddleia, erica or heathers, hydrangea, lavender and catkins of all kinds.

(*Left*) Seedheads such as teasels, grasses, bulrushes and everlastings like helichrysums and statice have long lives. (*Right*) Not true everlastings but hydrangeas, larkspur and mimosa may also dry.

(*Top left*) Poppy heads are often imported but any of the garden poppies can also be used. Green pods retain much of their colour.

(*Middle left*) Yucca seed pods are almost wooden — a texture they share with other seed vessels of the same lily tribe. Large clusters can be divided.

(*Below left*) Sweet corn husks can be opened to make a giant 'flower.' Some of the Indian or squaw corn with brightly multi-coloured kernels looks attractive displayed this way.

(*Below*) Okra pods, the seed cases of the succulent lady fingers' vegetable can be mounted individually.

(*Right*) Artichokes and cardoons are handsome perpetuelles and ideal for large arrangements. Cut them while still young.

(*Middle right*) Many trees have fruits which are well worth harvesting. Maple keys should be cut while young and brightly coloured. They dry to a biscuit tint.

(*Below right*) The star thistle, and all others are highly decorative, but need handling carefully.

(*Below*) The gorgeous magnolia blossoms are followed by seed pods of interesting form and texture. False stems have to be attached when these are used in tall decorations.

Pressed ferns mixed with teasels, seedheads, and larch cones are used as a permanent background for a few scarlet anemones arranged separately in water.

Preserving other perpetuelles

As you can see by the illustrations on the previous page, there are other parts of plants included in the ever-growing list of perpetuelles which can be dried. These are not only leaves but even roots. Seed stems of all kinds abound.

Most of these dry on the plant and must be gathered before they become deteriorated by rain or frost.

Most of the true everlastings and the other flowers I have already described should be made into small bunches and hung head downwards in a cool but very dry place. It should also be dark, for then the colours will be brightest. Sunshine and bright light will make grasses hay-like.

Always gather all materials on dry days only and before frosts occur. Remember that materials gathered in wet seasons when growth is lush take longer to dry and for this reason you should make the bunches quite small. Hang them well apart so that the air can circulate round them.

Flowers such as roses, and indeed all but the true everlastings which would become too brittle if treated this way, are often best dried quickly in a warm place such as an airing cupboard. A rack or 'table' of wire netting will enable you to support round flat flowers such as zinnias and even helichrysums. Insert the stem through the mesh and let the flower rest on it.

Helichrysums sometimes sever easily from their stems. To avoid this gather the flower with a small portion of stem, insert a florist wire up the stem until the flower's centre is reached, but do not let the wire penetrate it, and either hang up head downwards or support through wire mesh until the flower is dry (when stem has shrivelled).

To preserve branches, feathery seed heads such as *Clematis vitalba* or old man's beard, immature seed heads or downy flower spikes such as verbascum, among many other things, make a solution of one-third glycerine and two parts water. Mix and boil this and pour into a deep narrow vessel so that the stem ends can be stood in about two or three inches of the hot solution, according to their own length. If a tin or glass jar is used, stand this inside a bucket to prevent it tipping over.

To skeletonise leaves let them soak for a few weeks in rain water until you can remove the outer tissues by slipping a leaf between the fingers. Then wash under running water, soak in a solution of household bleach and water. Dry in newspaper. Press flat ferns between newspaper or books under a weight until they are dry

Drying flowers in a desiccant

You may have heard of flowers being dried by being buried in sand and this is possible but it is not really to be recommended because the sand is so heavy that it cannot be safely used to any great depth or it will damage the flower. But it is cheap! Much lighter in weight are borax and silica gel but these are more costly. However, the crystals can be used again and again. Some people mix borax and sand together. I prefer to use silica gel.

Unless you are going to have great quantities of the desiccant, enough to fill deep boxes to take the entire flower stem, the stems have to be shortened and this, in turn, means that false wire stems have to be applied later. It may also be necessary to tape them with florist tape or crepe paper tapes so that they look as natural as possible.

Airtight boxes should be used and if there is any doubt that their lids do not fit tightly these should also be sealed with tape.

The procedure is first to pour a layer of the desiccant on

Flowers may be dried by burying them in a desiccant such as silica gel, which should surround the flowers and be sifted between the petals.

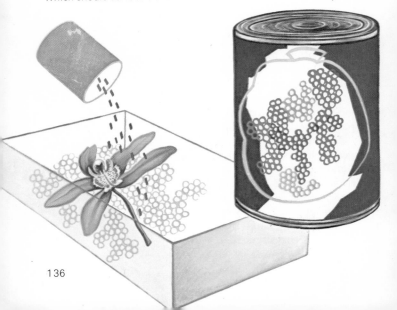

the floor of the box. Place the flowers in position on this layer according to the type of flower, e.g. whether it has a face like a pansy and will lie flat, or whether it is like a rose and will need desiccant sifted carefully in between its petals or whether it is like a flat daisy, which should be laid face down.

You will find that the upward facing ones will have to be supported while you pour the desiccant over, under and around them so that it can flow in every crevice, for flowers must be buried. The actual time taken for a flower to dry will depend very much on the type of flower. As a general rule, flowers take from one to five days. Some kinds will dry in an airing cupboard, cornflowers and large individual florets of delphiniums, for example, and these will dry quicker than a fleshy flower. But this is very much a matter of trial and error. If you find that some flowers shatter when they have dried, try fixing the petals by painting the bases with gum arabic before burying. Test by gently brushing or pouring away the desiccant until a flower is exposed and can be felt.

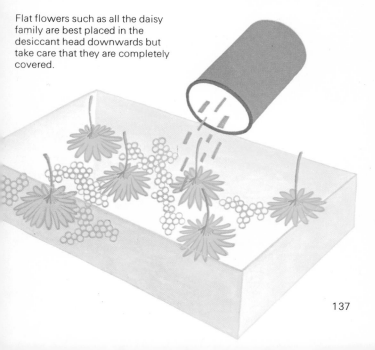

Flat flowers such as all the daisy family are best placed in the desiccant head downwards but take care that they are completely covered.

Pine cones and many other stem-less scaly or rough-textured subjects can be mounted as shown. Use a long florist wire to do so and place it between the scales.
Put pressure on it so that the wire is hidden in the bases of the scales.

Twist one wire round the other and bring the two legs down to roughly the same point as one would expect the stem to be. The wire portion can be used as a stem. It can also be made longer and joined to another wire or a slim cane. Several canes can be bunched together by binding their mount wires together.

Pull the florist wire round the cone so that it fits snugly in the crevices between the scales and is hidden by them.
It is possible to keep the wire quite flat against the cone's surface as the legs are brought down and under before being twisted together.

If the short stem below a subject like this lotus seed head, is soft or hollow, take a short wire and insert it up the stem as far as possible. Then push the protruding portion into the centre of a hollow stem or straw. Push the ends of stem and straw together.

False stems of wire are usually strong enough for all but very large leaves. Mount as directed for leaf loops, below.

Smaller leaves can be slightly reinforced if the loop is laid on the back surface to reach about two thirds the length of the leaf before the wire is passed round the stem.

Mount leaf loops by looping one end of wire to lie against the back of the leaf. Pass the long end round the leaf or leaves binding them together. Bring it down to make the 'stem'.

Soft leaves may need to be stitched with fine wire. Do this before pressing or drying but after preserving.

Posies of field daisies, each with its own collar of ivy leaves, are simply placed in a ring round a candle in a shallow dish.

PARTY FLOWERS

Flower arrangements for parties need to look lovely but they can also be quite simple and their assembly takes no more than a matter of minutes.

If they are expendable, one of the prettiest ways to decorate a table is merely to place a posy or a corsage by each place. Ivy trails and other graceful foliage can help you here, for with them you can outline shapes, say a long lazy 'S' on a table surface, or festoons on a buffet table apron, and stud this foliage with neat posies at suitable intervals. My illustration of a very simple decoration made from posied daisies can be used for other kinds of flowers and there are many variations you can play on this theme. You can, for example, stack up bowls and make posy pyramids.

To save time you can mix your fruit and flowers on the table. Camellias, arums, chincherinchees, gladioli and orchids are just a few which can be arranged out of water so that there will be no need to worry about water spilling.

Gladioli and laurel leaves are arranged on a pinholder in a shallow vase at the back of the tray on which the fruit is arranged.

If you use cylinders or sections of dry Oasis you can use them to stand fruit at varying levels. Even the roundest apple will stay in place if it is lightly pressed into the plastic. At the same time these will serve to hold the flowers' stems in position.

The spicate shape of gladioli contrasts attractively with the rounded forms of most fruits. Colour harmonises easily, for in the reds, oranges, apricots and yellows of the flowers you are certain to find some of the fruit colour.

So little water is needed for these flowers when they are to last for a few days that you can choose a really shallow container to hold the heavy pinholder on which they should be impaled. Being shallow this is easily hidden. Indeed, if you can lay a tough leaf, such as laurel, over it you will be able to arrange the fruit quite close to the flower's stems. Gladioli and daffodils and iris can be quickly arranged for all you need to do is to bunch them with their heads at different levels, cut the stem ends level and merely press the bunch on the pinholder.

Your flowers can break the ice!

Novel flower decorations can provide a talking point at any party but they should be attractive as well as original. Often originality springs from looking for a quick and easy way of displaying flowers or of creating a mass of colour. Have by you a few party accessories; cake boards on which fruit and flowers can be arranged; doilys to act as stemholders, as well as mats; heavy but low candle holders which can be hidden among flowers and fruit spread out on the table.

In the past chapters we have often seen how a flower container can be built up by using a combination of various vessels and ornaments. For a dinner party pieces of table china matching that on which the food is being served, can be used for the flowers.

On page 54 there is an illustration showing small dishes piled one on the other. Spare lids of vegetable dishes can be used in much the same way. If they are upturned they will usually fit quite securely into a glass, sometimes even into an egg-cup; it really depends on what you you have available.

Pineapple candle-holders sit easily in wine glasses. The doilys give each a party frill. Pompon chrysanthemum stems are threaded through the 'lace'.

A plate stood on end in a block of Oasis can hide the base of the stems of the flowers arranged behind it while other, shorter flowers can be arranged to appear to flow out from it thus hiding its support.

I see no reason why plant materials should not be dressed up for certain occasions. Cycas leaves, for example, when raised on strong false stems, make distinctive backgrounds in large arrangements. But the deep green of preserved fronds is often too heavy for the colour scheme of, say, a wedding reception buffet decoration. However, if they are first lightly sprayed with clear varnish and then dusted with glitter, a transformation scene takes place. Silver, gold, blue, ruby and even green glitter can be used with effect on pressed or preserved ferns. Christmas tree baubles also bring a little sparkle to party arrangements. Small samples can be bought ready mounted on chenille stems. Others can be mounted on pipe cleaners. They can be distributed or grouped according to the type of arrangement. Purple and green baubles look splendid arranged like bunches of grapes.

(*Left*) Tall or raised decorations suit buffet tables. Cones like this one, enable you to use snippets of green and short-stemmed flowers. Baubles add a party note and are mounted on pipe cleaners

(*Right*) For special occasions, plant materials can be given a party dress of paint and glitter. Christmas tree baubles look well among flowers. They need to be mounted on false stems.

143

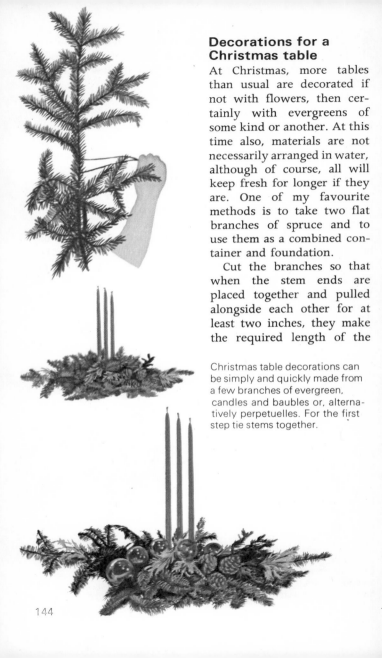

Decorations for a Christmas table

At Christmas, more tables than usual are decorated if not with flowers, then certainly with evergreens of some kind or another. At this time also, materials are not necessarily arranged in water, although of course, all will keep fresh for longer if they are. One of my favourite methods is to take two flat branches of spruce and to use them as a combined container and foundation.

Cut the branches so that when the stem ends are placed together and pulled alongside each other for at least two inches, they make the required length of the

Christmas table decorations can be simply and quickly made from a few branches of evergreen, candles and baubles or, alternatively perpetuelles. For the first step tie stems together.

table decoration. Lash the large stem ends firmly together. Test that the tied branches lie flat on the table.

Take a roll of wire netting, place it in the centre of the decoration over the tied stems and tie it to them by threading wire or twine through the netting and round the stems. Arrange the candles pushing their bases down through the netting. Do not worry if they lean a little because they can be wedged upright as the other snippets of green are inserted in the wire around them.

This is the basic shape! The 'all-round' arrangement in another guise. Use pieces of netting and single candles for small decorations.

The foliage should be varied so that you have plenty of contrast to the green. Variegated and silver downy sprigs look good, so do berries and other fruits, baubles, everlasting lichen and even artificial toadstools!

If you prefer to make a decoration on a base, the method is rather similar. I find that cake boards are useful as foundations. Make a slight depression in the centre to anchor the candle after it has passed through the wire netting.

Remember the taller and/or the heavier the candle the more netting you will need.

In this Christmas decoration, a cakeboard is used as a base. Wire netting holds all the foliage and the colourful baubles contrast with the green of the plant material.

Anemones, golden cupressus and holly. To make the most of their vivid colour, holly sprigs may need to have some leaves removed.

Other Christmas decorations

The flat shape of the spruce and some other evergreens used at Christmas is both useful and attractive and is well worth exploiting for its seasonal effect. If you cut a side branch you will see that it is pyramidal in outline.

I like to use a branch as the background of an arrangement against which just a few blooms can be displayed.

If the flowers have short stems they can be arranged effectively quite low leaving the branch to show its shape. I have often glittered branches and hung them with stars and baubles, or with dainty glittered cones.

To add a little height and variety of shape, colour and atmosphere you can arrange baubles rising above the low placed rounded flowers. Long, bare florist wires to support the baubles are inconspicuous against the branch. Grade the baubles so that the smallest are at the top.

Evergreens usually need grooming. Leaves should be wiped over with tepid water and if you want them to be really glossy use a little olive oil on them after washing. Heavily berried sprigs of holly provide more colour if some of the leaves are carefully snipped away with scissors. Although some berries can be sprayed with clear varnish to keep them plump, this may turn holly berries black, so test first. To keep the berries plump and the evergreens fresh, arrange them in water to which a little plant food has been added.

Blue spruce seldom drops its needles; instead it is more inclined to dry like other perpetuelles. Thuja, cypress and others will also dry but become brittle and then tend to drop if touched. All these can be held faster if sprayed with clear varnish or painted with Polycell.

A branch of flat-growing spruce or some other evergreen makes an aptly shaped background for a few flowers in a Christmas decoration. With these forced daffodils are variegated elaeagnus and holly berries.

147

FLOWERS FOR EXHIBITIONS

One of the delightful things which has been promoted by flower clubs everywhere is that more flowers than ever are on exhibition and can be enjoyed by the general public who usually are overwhelmed at both the beauty of the flowers and the skill of those who arranged them.

Suddenly, it seems, our churches regain their medieval glory as a band of flower arrangers move in to celebrate a festival of flowers. Glorious country houses become young again as great vases and pedestals are set against the wall or blooms flank the great staircase. The local village hall becomes transformed as club members move in with drape backgrounds, tables and a multitude of flowers.

This is only one of the good things for which flower clubs are responsible. Another is that often beautiful arrangements are just exhibited and not judged. This does not mean that the quality of the arrangements is any lower for, always, the highest standard is demanded from anyone who has been given the honour of being allowed to exhibit.

Creamy daffodils and tulips with lighter gladioli and lily-like hippeastrums frame tall pure white candles in an arrangement for Easter.

Flower show arrangements are not necessarily large or ornate. This one was designed for a class calling for an arrangement using only three flowers.

However, there are also times when competitions are held and flower arrangements are judged. These have to be assembled and staged and later, judged, according to the schedule drawn up by the club.

It is not always flower clubs alone who hold competitions, but when they do, all exhibits are judged by accredited judges strictly according to the rules laid down by the flower club. At other flower shows, usually held by a horticultural society, a judge may not be called upon to observe the same rules.

Inevitably, the schedule must be the guide. This also varies considerably according to the size and nature of the flower show. A little village show's schedule may also be very simple and give the competitor little guidance, while a larger show's schedule is not only likely to have many more classes but also to define much more clearly what is expected. If the arrangement is 'not according to schedule' it is likely to be disqualified and passed over when judging takes place.

149

Before using grasses, berries or any plant material other than flowers, check that this is according to the schedule.

Attention to detail is important

As a judge, I have so often been disappointed when my co-judges and I have regretfully had to pass over a really lovely arrangement because one little thing was against the schedule rules. For example, in an arrangement which calls for foliage only, someone may use a flower bud or an immature seed head or a cone, because these are green.

There is sometimes misunderstanding over the use of a term which to the botanist may mean one thing and to the layman another. For instance, to me, 'fruits' could include anything which follows a flower whether it be a gourd, a seed pod or a banana. But the schedule makers might mean edible fruit only! It is as important for those who draw up schedules to make them concise and perfectly understood as it is for the arranger to interpret them correctly.

The size of an arrangement is also important. Because space is often at a premium, flower arrangers are given a precise place for each exhibit. A good schedule should inform you just what the dimensions are.

I find that exhibitors tend to misunderstand the importance of these dimensions. Usually those who stage the show so arrange it that each exhibitor has his or her own alcove. Often I have stood before an arrangement which was so large that it crowded its space and lost its beauty in doing so and, on the other hand, I have often admired an arrangement and regretted that because it was so small and seemed swamped by its surroundings, that it could not be given a prize.

Among the qualities that judges look for in an arrangement are balance and proportion. If the arrangement is not scaled to its surroundings its own good balance and proportions will not be evident. Many arrangers find that it helps them to make a practise arrangement at home.

Many a beautiful arrangement has failed to win the top prize because one stem, leaf or flower has wilted before the judges got to it. Materials for show must be well prepared and hardened. The earliest pages in this book deal with care and transport of flowers.

When accessories and figures are used, a composition, not an arrangement, is made as it is here where arums surround a candle, and 'Ming' tree.

The colour and condition of materials can do much to accentuate the beauty and quality of an arrangement. Accessories used must also be immaculate.

Advice on staging

It often surprises me at an exhibition to see an arrangement into which, obviously, so much time and thought has gone, displayed on a piece of fabric which is creased and sometimes even soiled. Judges like to see attention paid to the slightest detail. Foliage should be groomed, vases cleaned, drapes pressed.

Spend a little time when all is done looking hard and critically for faults. In one class I once judged, what should have been the first prize had to be down-pointed because the tallest and most noticeable stem, a foxglove, had its top two or three inches crawling with aphis! Often a spray of lovely foliage will have holes cut in its leaves by various insects.

Make sure also that none of the materials is causing a siphon. The old Japanese rule about the lower stem not resting on the container may be based on common sense! Sometimes when a leaf, especially a downy one, is resting on the rim it conveys or siphons the water from the vase on to the table.

Another thing which sometimes gets overlooked is the

A well-groomed appearance is important and particularly so where the arrangement depends upon the contrasts of textures and shapes rather than on vivid colours. Echeveria, *Begonia Rex* foliage, zebrina and the immature flowers of eryngium harmonise with the pure metal sheen of the pewter stand and plate.

(*Below*) Stem holders can be hidden by all kinds of accessories. Here, the strata of the stones repeat both the line and colours of the stems of the yellow arums, really zantedeschias. The greys in them repeat shades.

stem holder. No part of this should ever show, even from the side where no judge is likely to look.

It is my experience that stem holders are often much larger than they need to be. So long as anchorage is secure, pinholders can be quite small and, consequently, easily hidden. And, as I commented in an earlier chapter, the means employed to hide a stem holder can often add to the character and general effectiveness of the arrangement. But make sure that whatever accessories you employ suit the mood and style of the arrangement.

Interpretive arrangements

In many flower shows there are classes in which you are asked to interpret a subject. Sometimes the show itself has a theme, in which case the classes will have relation to the overall title. At other times, just one or two classes may be included to give the exhibitor an opportunity of creating something out of the ordinary. Usually, these classes are of great interest to the visitors to a show.

Practised flower arrangers can take them in their stride, but during the year I seem to receive many letters from puzzled readers, new to exhibition work, who ask me to explain how they can possibly make a flower arrangement which also depicts a song title or some similar theme. This is hard for me because I know that when the arrangements are being judged some points are given for originality. The theme should be the exhibitor's own idea. Therefore, I use a simple example *The Last Rose of Summer* in which one rose is used with materials suggesting the onset of autumn.

Perhaps I should say that often what might seem a novel

idea to an exhibitor may be hackneyed to a judge who visits many shows in places round the country or even the world. Therefore originality really needs to be just that if you hope to be a prize winner!

To be given a theme is often a great deal easier than to think of one for yourself. But where the first applies you are much more likely to find another exhibitor working along the same lines as yourself. In such a situation, don't be dismayed or put out. Carry on but remember that judging is likely now to be highly competitive, so see that you attend meticulously to details and take care not to lose points on arrangement.

One last point. It may not have occurred to you that there really are both very modern and old-fashioned flowers, distinctive enough to be recognised as such. Most of those you buy from the florist are modern introductions, so if you seek to interpret something from bygone days remember that you are much more likely to strike the right atmosphere if you search for flowers that were known then.

(*Far left*) In the Dresden manner. Spring blossom, pieris, currant, apple and deutzia, with hyacinths, narcissi, primroses and forget-me-nots in a lovely container which repeats their colours.

'Heaven and Earth,' was the title I gave to my little arrangement of three hydrangea blooms, ligularia leaves and clematis seed heads.

155

BOOKS TO READ

Amateur Gardening Picture Book of Flower Arrangement by Violet Stevenson. Collingridge, London and Sydney.

Better Homes and Gardens Flower Arranging. Meredith, U.S.A.

Conway's Encyclopaedia of Flower Arrangement by J. Gregory. Conway, Routledge and Kegan Paul, Knopf, U.S.A.

Conway's Treasury of Flower Arrangements by J. Gregory Conway, Routledge and Kegan Paul, Knopf, U.S.A.

Decorating with Flowers and Plants by Violet Stevenson. Transatlantic, U.S.A.

Enjoy Flower Arranging by Sally Ades. Faber, London.

Flower Arrangement by Betty Stockwell. Pitman, London.

Flower Arrangement in Colour by Violet Stevenson. Studio Viking, U.S.A.

Flower Arranging by Joyce Rogers. Hamlyn, London and Sydney.

Flower Arranging in Colour by Betty Massingham. Hamlyn, London and Sydney.

Flower Decoration by Constance Spry. Dent, London.

Flower Decoration in Churches by Sheila Macqueen. Faber, London.

Handbook for Flower Arrangers by Phyllis Page. Blandford Press, London; International Publications Series, U.S.A.

Party Pieces by Julia Clements. Newnes, London and Sydney.

Sheila Macqueen's Encyclopedia of Flower Arranging. Faber, London.

Simple Flowers by Constance Spry. Aldine Paperback, London.

The Eye of the Flower Arranger by Lim Bian Yam. Collingridge, London and Sydney.

Woman's Own Book of Flower Arrangements, Pearson, London and Sydney.

INDEX

158

TITLES IN THIS SERIES

Arts
Art Nouveau for Collectors/Collecting and Looking After Antiques/
Collecting Inexpensive Antiques/Silver for Collectors/Toys & Dolls for
Collectors

Domestic Animals and Pets
Cats/Dog Care/Dogs/Horses and Ponies/Tropical Freshwater Aquaria/
Tropical Marine Aquaria

Gardening
Flower Arranging/Garden Flowers/Garden Shrubs/House Plants

General Information
Aircraft/Beachcombing and Beachcraft/Espionage/Freshwater Fishing/
Modern Combat Aircraft/Modern First Aid/Photography/Sailing/Sea
Fishing/Trains/Wargames

History and Mythology
Witchcraft and Black Magic

Natural History
Bird Behaviour/Birds of Prey/Birdwatching/Butterflies/Fishes of the
World/Fossils and Fossil Collecting/A Guide to the Seashore/Prehistoric
Animals/Seabirds/Seashells/Trees of the World

Popular Science
Astronomy/Biology/Computers at Work/Ecology/Economics/Electricity/
Electronics/Exploring the Planets/Geology/The Human Body/
Microscopes and Microscopic Life/Psychology/Rocks, Minerals and
Crystals/The Weather Guide

Enid Blyton™

THE
WISHING-CHAIR
AGAIN

EGMONT

EGMONT

We bring stories to life

First published in Great Britain 1950 by Newnes
Mammoth edition first published 1992
This edition published 2008
by Egmont UK Limited
239 Kensington High Street
London W8 6SA

ISBN 978 1 4052 3959 2

7 9 10 8 6

www.egmont.co.uk

A CIP catalogue record for this title is available from the British Library

Printed and bound in Great Britain by the CPI Group

Also by Enid Blyton

The Enchanted Wood
The Magic Faraway Tree
The Folk of the Faraway Tree

Naughty Amelia Jane!
Amelia Jane is Naughty Again!
Amelia Jane gets into Trouble!
Amelia Jane Again!
Good Idea, Amelia Jane!

The Adventures of the Wishing-Chair
More Wishing-Chair Stories

The Mystery of the Burnt Cottage
The Mystery of the Disappearing Cat
The Mystery of the Secret Room
The Mystery of the Spiteful Letters
The Mystery of the Missing Necklace
The Mystery of the Hidden House
The Mystery of the Pantomime Cat
The Mystery of the Invisible Thief
The Mystery of the Vanished Prince
The Mystery of the Strange Bundle
The Mystery of Holly Lane
The Mystery of Tally-Ho Cottage
The Mystery of the Missing Man
The Mystery of the Strange Messages
The Mystery of Banshee Towers

CONTENTS

I

HOME FOR THE HOLIDAYS

Mollie and Peter had just arrived home for the holidays. Their schools had broken up the same day, which was very lucky, and Mother had met them at the station.

They hugged her hard. 'Mother! It's grand to see you again. How's everyone?'

'Fine,' said Mother. 'The garden's looking lovely, your bedrooms are all ready for you, and your playroom at the bottom of the garden is longing for you to go there and play as usual.'

The two children looked at one another. They had a big Secret. One they couldn't possibly mention even in their letters to one another at school. How they were longing to talk about it now!

'Can we just pop down to our playroom first of all?' asked Peter when they got home.

'Oh, no, dear!' said Mother. 'You must come upstairs and wash – and help me to unpack your things. You will have plenty of time to spend in your playroom these holidays.'

The children's Secret was in their playroom – and they so badly wanted to see it again. They went upstairs and washed and then went down to tea.

'Can we go to our playroom after we've helped you to unpack?' asked Peter.

Mother laughed. 'Very well – leave me to unpack, and go along. I expect you want to see if I've given away any of your things. Well, I haven't. I never do that without asking you.'

After tea Peter spoke to Mollie in a low voice.

'Mollie! Do you think Chinky will be down in our playroom waiting for us – with the Wishing-Chair?'

'I do hope so,' said Mollie. 'Oh, Peter, it was dreadful trying to keep our Secret all the term long and never saying anything to anyone.'

'Well, it's such a marvellous Secret it's worth keeping well,' said Peter. 'Do you remember when we first got the Wishing-Chair, Mollie?'

'Yes,' said Mollie. 'We went to a funny little shop that sold old, old things to get something for Mother's birthday, and we saw heaps of strange enchanted things there. And we were frightened and huddled together in an old chair . . .'

'And we wished we were safe back at home,' said Peter, 'and, hey presto! the chair grew little red wings on its legs, and flew out of a window with us, and took us back to our playroom!'

'Yes. And it wouldn't go back to the shop even when we commanded it to,' said Mollie. 'So we had to keep it – our very own Wishing-Chair.'

'And do you remember how we went off in it again, and came to a castle where there was a giant who kept a little servant called Chinky?' said Peter. 'And we rescued him and took him home in the Wishing-Chair with us.'

'That was lovely,' said Mollie. 'And after that Chinky lived down in our playroom and looked after the chair for us . . .'

'And told us when it grew its wings so that we could all fly off in it again and have wonderful adventures,' said Peter. 'Then we had to go to school and leave it.'

'But it didn't matter really, because Chinky took the chair home to his mother's cottage and lived with her and took care of it for us,' said Mollie.

'And he said he'd come back as soon as we came home for the holidays, and bring the chair with him so that we could go adventuring again,' finished Peter. 'If Mother only knew that's the reason we want to get down to the playroom – to see if Chinky is there, and to see the dear old Wishing-Chair again.'

Peter found the key. 'Come on, Mollie – let's go and see all our toys again.'

'And the Wishing-Chair,' said Mollie in a whisper. '*And* Chinky.'

They rushed downstairs and out into the garden. It was the end of July and the garden was full of flowers; it was lovely to be home! No more lessons for eight weeks, no more preps.

They raced down to the playroom, which was really a big, airy shed at the bottom of the garden. Peter slid the key into the lock. 'Chinky!' he called. 'Are you here?'

He unlocked the door. The children went into the playroom and looked round. It was a nice room, with a big rug on the floor, shelves for their books and toys, a cot with Mollie's old dolls in it, and a large dolls' house in the corner.

3

But there was no Wishing-Chair and no Chinky the pixie! The children stared round in dismay.

'He's not here,' said Peter. 'He said he would come to-day with the chair. I gave him the date and he wrote it down in his note-book.'

'I hope he's not ill,' said Mollie. They looked all round the playroom, set the musical box going and opened the windows.

They felt disappointed. They had so looked forward to seeing Chinky, and to sitting once more in the Wishing-Chair. Suddenly a little face looked in at the door.

Mollie gave a shout. 'Chinky! It's you! We were so worried about you! We hoped you'd be here.'

Both children gave the little pixie a hug. Chinky grinned. 'Well, how could I be here waiting for you if the door was locked and the windows fastened, silly? I may be a pixie, but I can't fly through locked doors. I *have* missed you. Were you very bored away at school?'

'Oh, *no*,' said Peter. 'Boarding school is simply lovely. We both loved it – but we're jolly glad to be home again.'

'Chinky, where's the Wishing-Chair?' asked Mollie anxiously. 'Nothing's happened to it, has it? Have you got it with you?'

'Well, I brought it here this morning,' said Chinky, 'but when I found the door of the playroom was locked and couldn't get in I hid it under the hedge at the bottom of the garden. But you'd be surprised how many people nearly found it!'

'But nobody goes to the bottom of the garden!' said Peter.

'Oh, don't they!' said Chinky. 'Well, first of all your gardener thought he'd cut the hedge there to-day, and I had an awful job dragging the chair from one hiding place to another. Then an old gipsy woman came by, and she almost saw it, but I barked like a dog and she ran away.'

The children laughed. 'Poor old Chinky! You must have been glad when we got here at last.'

'Let's go and get it,' said Peter. 'I'm hoping to sit in it again. Has it grown its wings much since we left it with you, Chinky?'

'Not once,' said Chinky. 'Funny, isn't it? It's just stood in my mother's kitchen like any ordinary chair,

5

and never grown even one red wing! I think it was waiting for you to come back.'

'I hope it was – because then it may grow its wings heaps of times,' said Peter, 'and we'll go off on lots of adventures.'

They went to the hedge. 'There it is!' said Mollie in excitement. 'I can see one of its legs sticking out.'

They dragged out the old chair. 'Just the same!' said Peter in delight. 'And how well you've kept it, Chinky. It's polished so brightly.'

'Ah, that was my mother did that,' said Chinky. 'She said such a wonderful chair should have a wonderful polish, and she was at it every day, rub, rub, rub till the chair groaned!'

Peter carried the chair back to the playroom. Chinky went in front to make sure there was nobody looking. They didn't want any questions asked about why chairs should be hidden in hedges. They set it down in its old place in the playroom. Then they all climbed into it.

'It's just the same,' said Peter. 'We feel a bit more squashed than usual because Mollie and I seem to have grown at school. But you haven't grown, Chinky.'

'No. I shan't grow any more,' said Chinky. 'Don't you wish the chair would grow its wings and go flapping off somewhere with us now?'

'Oh, yes,' said Mollie. 'Chair, do grow your wings – just to please us! Even if it's only to take us a little way up into the air and back.'

But the chair didn't. The children looked anxiously down at its legs to see if the red buds were forming that sprouted into wings, but there was nothing there.

6

'It's no good,' said Chinky. 'It won't grow its wings just because it's asked. It can be very obstinate, you know. All I hope is that it hasn't forgotten *how* to grow wings after being still so long. I shouldn't like the magic to fade away.'

This was a dreadful thought. The children patted the arms of the chair. 'Dear Wishing-Chair! You haven't forgotten how to grow wings, have you?'

The chair gave a remarkable creak, a very long one. Everyone laughed. 'It's all right!' said Chinky. 'That's its way of telling us it hasn't forgotten. A creak is the only voice it's got!'

Mother came down the garden. 'Children! Daddy's home. He wants to see you!'

'Right!' called back Peter. He turned to Chinky. 'See you to-morrow, Chinky. You can cuddle up on the old sofa as usual, with the rug and the cushion, for the night. You'll live in our playroom, won't you, as you did before, and tell us when the chair grows its wings?'

'Yes. I shall like to live here once more,' said Chinky.

The children ran back to the house. They had a very nice evening indeed telling their parents everything that had happened in the term. Then off they went to bed, glad to be in their own dear little rooms again.

But they hadn't been asleep very long before Peter began to dream that he was a rat being shaken by a dog. It was a very unpleasant dream, and he woke up with a jump.

It was Chinky shaking him by the arm. 'Wake up!' whispered the pixie. 'The chair's grown its wings

7

already. They're big, strong ones, and they're flapping like anything. If you want an adventure hurry up!'

Well! What a thrill! Peter woke Mollie and they pulled on their clothes very quickly and ran down the garden. They heard a loud flapping noise as they reached the playroom shed. 'It's the chair's wings,' panted Chinky. 'Come on – we'll just sit in it before it goes flying off!'

II

OFF ON AN ADVENTURE

The children raced in at the playroom door and made
for the Wishing-Chair. They could see it easily in the
bright moonlight. It was just about to fly off when they
flung themselves in it. Chinky squeezed between them,
sitting on the top of the back of the chair.

'Good old Wishing-Chair!' said Peter. 'You didn't
take long to grow your wings! Where are we going?'

'Where would you like to go?' said Chinky. 'Wish,
and we'll go wherever you wish.'

'Well – let me see – oh dear, I simply can't think of
anywhere,' said Mollie. 'Peter, you wish – quickly.'

'Er – Wishing-Chair, take us to – to – oh, goodness
knows where I want it to go!' cried Peter. 'I simply
don't . . .'

But dear me, the Wishing-Chair was off! It flapped
its wings very strongly indeed, rose up into the air, flew
towards the door and out of it – then up into the air it
went, flapping its red wings in the moonlight.

Chinky giggled. 'Oh, Peter – you said "Take us to
Goodness Knows Where",' said the pixie. 'And that's
just about where we're going!'

'Gracious! – is there *really* a land called Goodness
Knows Where?' said Peter, in surprise.

'Yes. Don't you remember when we went to the Land of Scallywags once, the Prince of Goodness Knows Where came to see me,' said Chinky. 'I was pretending to be a King. Well, I suppose it's *his* Land we're going to.'

'Where is it?' said Mollie.

'Goodness knows!' said Chinky. 'I don't. I've never met anyone who did, either.'

'The Wishing-Chair seems to know,' said Peter, as it flew higher and higher in the air.

But it didn't know, really. It dropped downwards after a time and came to a tiny village. Peter leaned out of the chair and gazed with great interest at it. 'Look at that bridge,' he said. 'Hey, Chair, whatever are you doing now?'

The chair hadn't landed in the village. It had flown a few feet above the strange little houses and had then shot upwards again.

The chair flew on again, and then came to a heaving mass of water. Was it the sea? Or a lake? The children didn't know. 'Look at that lovely silver moon-path on the sea,' said Mollie, leaning out of the chair. 'I'm sure it leads to the moon!'

The chair seemed to think so, too. It flew down to the water, got on the moon-path and followed it steadily, up and up and up.

'Hey! This isn't the way to Goodness Knows Where!' said Chinky, in alarm. 'It's the way to the moon. Don't be silly, Chair!'

The chair stopped and hovered in mid-air as if it had heard Chinky and was changing its mind. To the

10

children's great relief it left the moon-path and flew on till it came to a little island. This was perfectly round and flat, and had one big tree standing up in the middle of it. Under the tree was a boat and someone was fast asleep in it.

'Oh, that's my cousin, Sleep-Alone,' said Chinky, in surprise. 'He's a funny fellow, you know – can't bear to sleep if anyone else is within miles of him. So he has a boat and an aeroplane, and each night he takes one or the other and goes off to some lonely place to sleep. Hey there, Sleep-Alone!'

Chinky's shout made the children jump. The chair jumped, too, and Mollie was almost jerked off. She clutched at the arm.

The little man in the boat awoke. He was more like a brownie than a pixie and had a very long beard, which he had wound neatly round his neck like a scarf. He was most surprised to see the Wishing-Chair landing on the island just near him. He scowled at Chinky.

'What's all this? Coming and shouting at me in the middle of the night! Can't I ever sleep alone?'

'You always do!' said Chinky. 'Don't be so cross. Aren't you surprised to see us?'

'Not a bit,' said Sleep-Alone. 'You're always turning up when I don't want to have company. Go away. I've a cold coming on and I feel gloomy.'

'Is that why you've got your beard wound round your neck – to keep it warm?' asked Mollie. 'How long is it when it unwinds?'

'I've no idea,' said Sleep-Alone, who seemed a

11

disagreeable fellow. 'Where are you going in the middle of the night? Are you quite mad?'

'We're going to Goodness Knows Where,' said Chinky. 'But the chair doesn't seem to know the way. Do *you* know it?'

'Goodness knows where it is,' said Sleep-Alone, pulling his beard tighter round his neck. 'Better ask her.'

The children and Chinky stared. 'Ask who?' said Chinky.

'Goodness, of course,' said Sleep-Alone, settling down in his boat again.

'Oh – is Goodness the name of a person then?' said Mollie, suddenly seeing light.

'You are a very stupid little girl, I think,' said Sleep-Alone. 'Am I to go on and on saying the same thing over and over again? Now good night, and go and find Goodness if you want to disturb someone else.'

'Where does she live?' bellowed Chinky in Sleep-Alone's ear, afraid that he would go to sleep before he told them anything else.

That was too much for Sleep-Alone. He shot up and reached for an oar. Before Chinky could get out of the way he had given him such a slap with the oar blade that Chinky yelled at the top of his voice. Then Sleep-Alone turned on the two children, waving the oar in a most alarming manner.

Peter pulled Mollie to the chair. He put out a hand and dragged Chinky to it too, shouting, 'Go to Goodness, Chair, go to Goodness, wherever she is!' Up rose the chair so very suddenly that Chinky fell off and had to be dragged up again.

Sleep-Alone roared after them. 'Now I'm thoroughly awake and I shan't go to sleep to-night. You wait until I see you again, Chinky, I'll fly you off in my aeroplane to the Land of Rubbish and drop you in the biggest dustbin there!'

'He's not a very nice cousin to have, is he?' said Mollie, when they had left Sleep-Alone well behind. 'I hope we don't see him again.'

'Who is this Goodness, I wonder?' said Peter.

'Never heard of her,' said Chinky. 'But the chair really seems to know where it's going this time, so I suppose it knows Goodness all right!'

The Wishing-Chair was flying steadily to the east now. It had left the water behind and was now over some land that lay shining in the moonlight. The children could see towers and pinnacles, but they were too high up to see anything clearly.

The chair suddenly flew downwards. It came to a small cottage. All three of its chimneys were smoking. The smoke was green, and the children knew that was a sign that a witch lived there.

'I say – that's witch-smoke,' said Peter, nervously. He had met witches before on his adventures, and he knew quite a bit about them.

'I hope the chair has come to the right place,' said Mollie, as it landed gently on the path just outside the door of the little cottage.

They jumped off the chair, dragged it under a tree and went to knock at the door. A little old woman opened it. She looked so ordinary that the children felt sure she wasn't a witch.

13

'Please, is this where Goodness lives?' asked Chinky, politely.

'Not exactly. But I keep a Book of Goodness,' said the old woman. 'Have you come to seek advice from it?'

'Well – we rather wanted to know where the Land of Goodness Knows Where is,' said Chinky. 'And we were told that only Goodness knew where it was!'

'Ah, well – you will have to consult my Goodness Book then,' said the old woman. 'Wait till I get on my things.'

She left them in a tiny kitchen and disappeared. When she came back, what a difference in her! She had on a tall, pointed hat, the kind witches and wizards wear, and a great cloak that kept blowing out round her as if she kept a wind under its folds. She no longer looked an ordinary little old woman – she was a proper witch, but her eyes were kind and smiling.

She took down from a shelf a very big book indeed. It seemed to be full of names and very tiny writing. 'What are your names?' she asked. 'I must look you up in my Goodness Book before you can be told what you want to know.'

They told her, and she ran her finger down column after column. 'Ah – Peter – helped a boy with his homework for a whole week last term – remembered his mother's birthday – owned up when he did something wrong – my word, there's a whole list of goodness here. And Mollie, too – gave up her half-holiday to stay in with a friend who was ill – told the truth when she knew she would get into trouble for doing so – quite a long list of goodness for her, too.'

14

'Now me,' said Chinky. 'I've been living with my mother. I do try to be good to her.' The old woman ran her finger down the list again and nodded her head. 'Yes – did his mother's shopping and never grumbled – took her breakfast in bed each day – never forgot to feed the dog – yes, you're all right, Chinky.'

'What happens next?' said Peter. The witch took her Book of Goodness to a curious hole in the middle of the kitchen floor. It suddenly glowed as if it were full of shining water. The witch held the book over it, and out of it slid little gleaming streaks of colour. 'That's your Goodness going into the magic pool,' she said. 'Now, ask what you want to know.'

Chinky asked, in rather a trembling voice, 'We want to know where the Land of Goodness Knows Where is.'

And dear me, a very extraordinary thing happened! On the top of the shining water appeared a shimmering map. In the middle of it was marked 'Land of Goodness Knows Where.' The children and Chinky leaned over it eagerly, trying to see how to get there.

'Look – we fly due east to the rising sun,' began Chinky; then he stopped. They had all heard a very peculiar noise outside. A loud creaking noise.

'The chair's calling to us!' cried Chinky and he rushed to the door. 'Oh, look – it's flying away – and somebody else is in it. Somebody's stolen the Wishing-Chair! Whatever shall we do?'

III

WHERE CAN THE
WISHING-CHAIR BE?

'Who's taken our chair?' cried Peter, in despair. 'We can't get back home now. Come back, Chair!'

But the chair was under somebody else's command now, and it took no notice. It rose higher and higher and was soon no more than a speck in the moonlight. The three stared at one another, very upset indeed.

'Our very first adventure – and the chair's gone,' said Mollie, in a shaky voice. 'It's too bad. Right at the very beginning of the holidays, too.'

'Who was that taking our chair – do you know?' Chinky asked the witch, who was busy smoothing the surface of the water in the hole in the floor with what looked like a fine brush. The map that had shone there was now gone, and the water was empty of reflection or picture. The children wondered what would appear there next.

The witch shook her head. 'No – I don't know,' she said. 'I didn't hear anyone out there because I was so busy in here with you. All kinds of people come to ask me questions, you know, just as you did, and watch to see what appears in my magic pool. Some of the people are very odd. I expect it was one of them – and he saw your chair, knew what it was and flew off in it at once.

16

It would be very valuable to him.'

'I do think it's bad luck,' said Mollie, tears coming into her eyes. 'Our very first night. And how are we to get back home again?'

'You can catch the Dawn Bus if you like,' said the witch. 'It will be along here in a few minutes' time. As soon as the sky turns silver in the east it comes rumbling along. Now, listen, I can hear the bus.'

Wondering whatever kind of people caught the Dawn Bus, Mollie and the others went out to catch it. It came rumbling along, looking more like a toy bus than a real one. It was crammed with little folk of all kinds! Brownies with long beards leaned against one another, fast asleep. Two tiny fairies slept with their arms round each other. A wizard nodded off to sleep, his pointed hat getting more and more crooked each moment – and three goblins yawned so widely that their mischievous little faces seemed all mouth!

'The bus is full,' said Mollie, in dismay.

'Sit in front with the driver, then,' said the witch. 'Go on, or you'll miss it!'

So Mollie, Peter and Chinky squashed themselves in front with the driver. He was a brownie, and wore his beard tied round his waist and made into a bow behind. It looked very odd.

'Plenty of room,' he said, and moved up so far that he couldn't reach the wheel to drive the bus. 'You drive it,' he said to Chinky, and, very pleased indeed, Chinky took the wheel.

But, goodness gracious me, Chinky was no good at all at driving buses! He nearly hit a tree, swerved violently and went into an enormous puddle that splashed everyone from head to foot, and then went into a ditch and out of it at top speed.

By this time all the passengers were wide awake and shouting in alarm. 'Stop him! He's mad! Fetch a policeman!'

The bus-driver was upset to hear all the shouting. He moved back to his wheel so quickly that Chinky was flung out into the road. He got up and ran after the bus, shouting.

But the bus-driver wouldn't stop. He drove on at top speed, though Mollie and Peter begged him to go back for Chinky.

'I don't know how to back this bus,' said the brownie driver, solemnly. 'I keep meaning to learn but I never seem to have time. Most annoying. Still, I hardly ever want to back.'

'Well, *stop* if you don't know how to back,' cried Peter, but the brownie looked really horrified.

'What – stop before I come to a stopping-place? You must be mad. No, no – full speed ahead is my motto. I've got to get all these tired passengers back home as soon as possible.'

'Why are they so tired?' said Mollie, seeing the wizard beginning to nod again.

'Well, they've all been to a moonlight dance,' said the driver. 'Very nice dance, too. I went to it. Last time I went to one I was so tired when I drove my bus home that I fell asleep when I was driving it. Found myself in the Land of Dreamland in no time, and used up every drop of my petrol.'

This all sounded rather extraordinary. Mollie and Peter looked at him nervously, hoping that he wouldn't fall asleep this time. Mollie could hardly keep her eyes open. She worried about Chinky. Would he find his way back to the playroom all right? And, oh dear, what were they going to do about the Wishing-Chair?

Just as she was thinking that she fell sound asleep. Peter was already asleep. The driver looked at them, gave a grunt, and fell asleep himself.

So, of course, the bus went straight on to Dreamland again, and when Peter and Mollie awoke, they were not in the bus at all but in their own beds! Mollie tried to remember all that had happened. Was it real or was it a dream? She thought she had better go and ask Peter.

She went to his room. He was sitting up in bed and rubbing his eyes. 'I know what you've come to ask me,' he said. 'The same question I was coming to ask *you*. Did we dream it or didn't we? And how did we get back here?'

'That bus must have gone to the Land of Dreamland again,' said Mollie. 'But how we got here I don't know. I'm still in my day-clothes – look!'

'So am I,' said Peter, astonished. 'Well, that shows it was real then. Oh, dear – do you suppose Chinky is back yet?'

'Shall we go and see now?' said Mollie.

But the breakfast bell rang just then. They cleaned their teeth, did their hair, washed and tidied their crumpled clothes – then down they went.

After breakfast they ran down to the playroom at the bottom of the garden.

Chinky was there! He was lying on the sofa fast asleep.

'Chinky, wake up!' shouted Mollie.

He didn't stir. Mollie shook him.

'Don't wake me, Mother,' murmured Chinky, trying to turn over. 'Let me sleep.'

'Chinky – you're not at home, you're here,' said Peter, shaking him again.

Chinky rolled over on his other side – and fell right off the sofa!

That woke him up with a jerk. He gave a shout of alarm, opened his eyes and sat up.

'I say, did you tip me off the sofa?' he said. 'You needn't have done that.'

'We didn't. You rolled off yourself,' said Mollie with a laugh. 'How did you get back last night, Chinky?'

'I walked all the way – so no wonder I'm tired this morning,' said Chinky, his eyes beginning to close again. 'I did think you might have stopped the bus and picked me up.'

'The driver wouldn't stop,' explained Peter. 'He was awfully silly, really. We were very upset at leaving you behind.'

'The thing is, Chinky – how are we going to find out where the Wishing-Chair has gone?' said Peter, seriously. 'It's only the beginning of the holidays, you know, and if we don't get it back the holidays will be very dull indeed.'

'I'm too sleepy to think,' said Chinky, and fell asleep again. Mollie shook him impatiently.

'Chinky, do wake up. We really are very worried about the Wishing-Chair.'

But there was no waking Chinky this time! He was so sound asleep that he didn't even stir when Mollie tickled him under the arms.

The two children were disappointed. They stayed in the playroom till dinner-time, but Chinky didn't wake up. They went indoors to have their dinner and then came down to see if Chinky was awake yet. He wasn't!

Just then there came a soft tapping at the door and a little voice said: 'Chinky! Are you there?'

Peter opened the door. Outside stood a small elf, looking rather alarmed. He held a leaflet in his hand.

'Oh, I'm very sorry,' he said. 'I didn't know you were here. I wanted Chinky.'

'He's so fast asleep we can't wake him,' said Peter. 'Can we give him a message?'

'Yes. Tell him I saw this notice of his,' said the little elf, and showed it to the children. It was a little card, printed in Chinky's writing:

'Lost or stolen. Genuine Wishing-Chair.
Please give any information about it to
CHINKY.
(I shall be in the playroom.)'

'Anything else?' asked Peter.

'Well – you might tell him I think I know where the chair is,' said the little elf, shyly.

'*Do* you?' cried both children. 'Well, tell us, then – it's our chair!'

'There's to be a sale of furniture at a brownie's shop not far away,' said the elf, 'and there are six old chairs to be sold. Now, I know he only had five – so where did the sixth come from? Look, here's a picture of them.'

The children looked at the picture. Peter gave a cry. 'Why, they're *exactly* like our chair. Are they *all* wishing-chairs, then?'

'Oh, no. Your chair is very unusual. I expect what happened is that the thief who flew off on your chair wondered how to hide it. He remembered somebody who had five chairs just like it and offered it to him to make the set complete.'

'I don't see why he should do that,' said Mollie, puzzled.

'Wait,' said the elf. 'Nobody would suspect that one of the six chairs was a wishing-chair – and I've no doubt that the thief will send someone to bid a price for all six; and when he gets them he will suddenly say that he has discovered one of them is a wishing-chair, and sell it to a wizard for a sack of gold!'

'I think that's a horrid trick,' said Mollie, in disgust. 'Well, it looks as if we'll have to go along to this furniture shop and have a look at the chairs, to see if we can find out which one is ours. Oh, dear, I do wish Chinky would wake up.'

'You'd better go as soon as you can,' said the elf. 'The thief won't lose much time in buying it back, with the other chairs thrown in!'

So they tried to wake Chinky again – but he just wouldn't wake up! 'We'll have to go by ourselves,' said Peter at last. 'Elf, will you show us the way? You will? Right, then off we go! Leave your message on the table for Chinky to see, then he'll guess where we've gone!'

IV

HUNTING FOR THE CHAIR!

The elf took them a very surprising way. He guided them to the bottom of the garden and through a gap in the hedge. Then he took them to the end of the field and showed them a dark ring of grass.

'We call that a fairy ring,' said Mollie. 'Sometimes it has little toadstools all the way round it.'

'Yes,' said the elf. 'Well, I'll show you a use for fairy rings. Sit down on the dark grass, please.'

Mollie and Peter sat down. They had to squeeze very close together indeed, because the ring of grass was not large. The elf felt about in it as if he was looking for something. He found it – and pressed hard!

And down shot the ring of grass as if it were a lift! The children, taken by surprise, gasped and held on to one another. They stopped with such a bump that they were shaken off the circle of grass and rolled away from it, over and over.

'So sorry,' said the elf. 'I'm afraid I pressed the button rather hard! Are you hurt?'

'No – not really,' said Mollie. As she spoke she saw the circle of grass shoot up again and fit itself neatly back into the field.

'Well – we do learn surprising things,' she said. 'What next, elf?'

'Along this passage,' said the elf, and trotted in front of them. It was quite light underground, though neither of the children could see where the lighting came from. They passed little, brightly-painted doors on their way, and Peter longed to rat-tat at the knockers and see who answered.

They came to some steps and went up them, round and round in a spiral stairway. Wherever were they coming to? At the top was a door. The elf opened it – and there they were, in a small round room, very cosy indeed.

'What a strange, round room,' said Peter, surprised. 'Oh – I know why it's round. It's inside the trunk of a tree! I've been in a tree-house before!'

'Guessed right first time!' said the elf. 'This is where I live. I'd ask you to stop and have a cup of tea with me, but I think we'd better get on and see those chairs before anything happens to them.'

'Yes. So do I,' said Peter. 'Where's the door out of the tree?'

It was fitted in so cunningly that it was impossible to see it unless you knew where it was. The elf went to it at once, of course, and opened it. They all stepped out into a wood. The elf shut the door. The children looked back at it. No – they couldn't possibly, possibly tell where it was now – it was so much part of the tree!

'Come along,' said the elf and they followed him through the wood. They came to a lane and then to a very neat village, all the houses set in tiny rows, with a little square green in the middle, and four white ducks looking very clean on a round pond in the centre of the green.

'How very proper!' said Peter. 'Not a blade of grass out of place.'

'This is Pin Village,' said the elf. 'You've heard the saying, "As neat as a pin," I suppose? Well, this is Pin – always very neat and tidy and the people of the village, the Pins, never have a button missing or a hair blowing loose.'

The children saw that it was just as the elf said – the people were so tidy and neat that the children felt dirty and untidy at once. 'They all look a bit like pins dressed up and walking about,' said Mollie with a giggle. 'Well,

I'm glad I know what "neat as a pin" really means. Do they ever run, or make a noise, or laugh?'

'Sh! Don't laugh at them,' said the elf. 'Now look – do you see that shop at the corner? It isn't kept by a Pin; it's kept by Mr. Polish. He sells furniture.'

'And he's called Polish because he's always polishing it, I suppose,' said Mollie with a laugh.

'Don't be too clever!' said the elf. 'He doesn't do any polishing at all – his daughter Polly does that.'

'Here's the shop,' said Mollie, and they stood and looked at it. She nudged Peter. 'Look,' she whispered, 'six chairs – all exactly alike. How are we to tell which is ours?'

'Come and have a look,' said Peter, and they went inside with the elf. A brownie girl was busy polishing away at the chairs, making them shine and gleam.

'There's Polly Polish,' said Mollie to Peter. She must have heard what they said and looked up. She smiled. She was a nice little thing, with pointed ears like Chinky, and very green eyes.

'Hallo,' she said.

Mollie smiled back. 'These are nice chairs, aren't they?' she said. 'You've got a whole set of them!'

'Yes – my father, Mr. Polish, was very pleased,' said Polly. 'He's only had five for a long time, and people want to buy chairs in sixes, you know.'

'How did he manage to get the sixth one?' asked Peter.

'It was a great bit of luck,' said Polly. 'There's a goblin called Tricky who came along and said he wanted to sell an old chair that had once belonged to his grandmother – and when he showed it to us, lo and behold, it was the missing sixth chair of our set! So we bought it from him, and there it is. I expect now we shall be able to sell the whole set. Someone is sure to come along and buy it.'

'Which chair did the goblin bring you?' asked Peter, looking hard at them all.

'I don't know now,' said Polly, putting more polish on her duster and rubbing very hard at a chair. 'I've been cleaning them and moving them about, you know – and they're all mixed up.'

The children stared at them in despair. They all looked exactly alike to them! Oh, dear – how could they possibly tell which was their chair?

Then Polly said something very helpful, though she didn't know it! 'You know,' she said, 'there's something strange about one of these chairs. I've polished and polished the back of it, but it seems to have a little hole there, or something. Anyway, I can' t make that little bit come bright and shining.'

The children pricked up their ears at once. 'Which chair?' said Peter. Polly showed them the one. It certainly seemed as if it had a hole in the back of it. Peter put his finger there – but the hole wasn't a hole! He could feel quite solid wood there!

And then he knew it was their own chair. He whispered to Mollie.

'Do you remember last year, when somebody made our Wishing-Chair invisible? And we had to get some paint to make it visible again?'

'Oh, yes!' whispered back Mollie. 'I do remember –

27

and we hadn't enough paint to make one little bit at the back of the chair become visible again, so it always looked as if there was a hole there, though there wasn't really!'

'Yes – and that's the place that poor Polly has been polishing and polishing,' said Peter. 'Well – now we know that this is our chair all right! If only it would grow its wings we could sit on it straight away and wish ourselves home again!' He ran his fingers down the legs of the chair to see if by any chance there were some bumps growing, that would mean wings were coming once more. But there weren't.

'Perhaps the wings will grow again this evening,' said Mollie. 'Let's go and have tea with the elf in his tree-house and then come back here again and see if the chair has grown its wings.'

The elf was very pleased to think they would come back to tea with him. Before they went Peter looked hard at the chairs. 'You know,' he said to Mollie, 'I think we'd better just tie a ribbon round our own chair, so that if by any chance we decided to take it and go home with it quickly before anyone could stop us, we'd know immediately which it was.'

'That's a good idea,' said Mollie. She had no hair-ribbon, so she took her little blue handkerchief and knotted it round the right arm of the chair.

'What are you doing that for?' asked Polly Polish in surprise.

'We'll tell you some other time, Polly,' said Mollie. 'Don't untie it, will you? It's to remind us of something. We'll come back again after tea.'

They went off with the elf. He asked them to see if they could find his door-handle and turn it to get into his tree-house – but, however much they looked and felt about, neither of them could make out where the closely-fitting door was! It's no wonder nobody ever knows which the tree-houses are!

The elf had to open the door for them himself, and in they went. He got them a lovely tea, with pink jellies that shone like a sunset, and blancmange that he had made in the shape of a little castle.

'I do wonder if Chinky's woken up yet,' said Mollie, at last. 'No, thank you, elf, I can't possibly eat any more. It was a really lovely tea.'

'Now what about going back to the shop and seeing if we can't take our chair away?' said Peter. 'We'll send Chinky to explain about it later – the thing is, we really must take it quickly, or that goblin called Tricky will send someone to buy all the set – and our chair with it!'

So off they went to the shop – and will you believe it, there were no chairs there! They were all gone from the window! The children stared in dismay.

They went into the shop. 'What's happened to the chairs?' they asked Polly.

'Oh, we had such a bit of luck just after you had gone,' said Polly. 'Somebody came by, noticed the chairs, said that the goblin Tricky had advised him to buy them – and paid us for them straight away!'

'Who was he?' asked Peter, his heart sinking.

'Let me see – his name was Mr. Spells,' said Polly, looking in a book. 'And his address is Wizard Cottage. He seemed very nice indeed.'

29

'Oh dear,' said Peter, leading Mollie out of the shop. 'Now we've *really* lost our dear old chair.'

'Don't give up!' said Mollie. 'We'll go back to Chinky and tell him the whole story – and maybe he will know something about this Mr. Spells and be able to get our chair back for us. Chinky's very clever.'

'Yes – but before we can get it back from Mr. Spells, that wretched goblin Tricky will be after it again,' said Peter. 'He's sure to go and take it from Mr. Spells.'

The elf took them home again. They went into the playroom. Chinky wasn't there! There was a note on the table.

It said: 'Fancy you going off without me! I've gone to look for you – Chinky.'

'Bother!' said Mollie. 'How annoying! Here we've come back to look for him and he's gone to look for us. Now we'll have to wait till to-morrow!'

V

OFF TO MR. SPELLS OF
WIZARD COTTAGE

Mollie and Peter certainly could do no more that day, because their mother was already wondering why they hadn't been in to tea. They heard her calling as they read Chinky's note saying he had gone to look for them.

'It's a pity Chinky didn't wait for us,' said Peter. 'We could have sent him to Mr. Spells to keep guard on the chair. Come on, Mollie – we'll have to go in. We've hardly seen Mother all day!'

Their mother didn't know anything about the Wishing-Chair at all, of course, because the children kept it a strict secret.

'If we tell anyone, the grown-ups will come and take our precious chair and put it in a museum or something,' said Peter. 'I couldn't bear to think of the Wishing-Chair growing its wings in a museum and not being able to get out of a glass case.'

So they hadn't said a word to anyone. Now they ran indoors, and offered to help their mother shell peas. They sat and wondered where Chinky was. They felt very sleepy, and Mollie suddenly gave an enormous yawn.

'You look very tired, Mollie,' said Mother, looking at her pale face. 'Didn't you sleep well last night?'

'Well – I didn't sleep a *lot*,' said Mollie truthfully, remembering her long flight in the Wishing-Chair and the strange bus ride afterwards.

'I think you had both better get off early to bed,' said Mother. 'I'll bring your suppers up to you in bed for a treat – raspberries and cream, and bread and butter – would you like that?'

In the ordinary way the children would have said no thank you to any idea of going to bed early – but they really were so sleepy that they both yawned together and said yes, that sounded nice, thank you, Mother!

So upstairs they went and fell asleep immediately after the raspberries and cream. Mother was really very surprised when she peeped in to see them.

'Poor children – I expect all the excitement of coming home from school has tired them out,' she said. 'I'll make them up sandwiches to-morrow and send them out on a picnic.'

They woke up early the next morning and their first thought was about the Wishing-Chair.

'Let's go down and see Chinky,' said Mollie. 'We've got time before breakfast.'

So they dressed quickly and ran down to their playroom. But no Chinky was there – and no note either. He hadn't been back, then. Wherever could he be?

'Oh dear, first the Wishing-Chair goes, and now Chinky,' said Mollie. 'What's happened to him? I think we'd better go and ask that elf if he's seen him, Peter.'

'We shan't have time before breakfast,' said Peter.

'We'll come down as soon as we've done any jobs Mother wants us to do.'

They were both delighted when Mother suggested that they should take their lunch with them and go out for a day's picnicking. Why – that would be just right! They could go and hunt out the elf – and find Chinky – and perhaps go to Mr. Spells with him. Splendid!

So they eagerly took the packets of sandwiches, cake and chocolate that Mother made up for them, and Peter put them into a little satchel to carry. Off they went. They peeped into their playroom just to make sure that Chinky still hadn't come back.

No, he hadn't. 'Better leave a note for him, then,' said Peter.

'What have you said?' asked Mollie, glancing over her shoulder.

'I've said: "Why didn't you wait for us, silly? Now we've got to go and look for you whilst you're still looking for us!"'

Mollie laughed. 'Oh dear – this really is getting ridiculous. Come on – let's go to the tree-house and see if the elf is in.'

So off they went, down the garden, through the hedge, and across the field to where the dark patch of grass was – the 'fairy-ring.' They sat down in the middle of it and Mollie felt about for the button to press. She found something that felt like a little knob of earth and pressed it. Yes – it was the right button!

Down they went, not nearly as fast as the day before, because Mollie didn't press the button so hard. Then along the passage, past the strange bright little doors, and up the spiral stairway. They knocked on the door.

'It's us – Mollie and Peter. Can we come in?'

The door flew open and there stood the elf. He looked very pleased. 'Well, this is really friendly of you. Come in.'

'We've come to ask you something,' said Mollie. 'Have you seen Chinky?'

'Oh, yes – he came to me yesterday, after I'd said good-bye to you, and I told him all you'd told me – and off he went to find Polly Polish and get the latest news,' said the elf.

'Well, he hasn't come back yet,' said Mollie. 'Where do you suppose he is!'

'Gone to see his mother, perhaps?' suggested the elf. 'I really don't know. It's not much good looking for him, really, you know – he might be anywhere.'

'Yes – that's true,' said Peter. 'Well, what shall we do, Mollie? Try and find Mr. Spells of Wizard Cottage by ourselves?'

'Oh, I know where *he* lives,' said the elf. 'He's quite a nice fellow. I'll tell you the way. You want to take the bus through the Tall Hill, and then take the boat to the Mill. Not far off on the top of a hill you'll see a large cottage in the shape of a castle – only you can't call it a castle because it's not big enough. Mr. Spells lives there.'

'Oh, thank you,' said Peter, and off they went to catch the bus. It was one like they had caught the other night, but it had a different driver, and was not nearly so crowded. In fact there would have been plenty of

34

room inside for Peter and Mollie if they hadn't noticed that one of the passengers happened to be Mr. Sleep-Alone, Chinky's strange and bad-tempered cousin.

'We'd better travel with the driver on the outside seat again,' said Peter. 'Sleep-Alone might recognize us and lose his temper again.'

The bus travelled fast down the lane, going round corners in a hair-raising style. 'Do you like going round corners on two wheels?' asked Peter, clutching at Mollie to prevent her from falling off.

'Well, it saves wear and tear on the others,' said the driver.

The bus suddenly ran straight at a very steep hill and disappeared into a black hole, which proved to be a long and bumpy tunnel. It came out again and stopped dead beside a little blue river, its front wheels almost touching the water.

'I always do that to give the passengers a fright,' said the driver. 'Must give them something for their money's worth!'

The children were really very glad to get out. They looked for a boat and saw plenty cruising about on the water, all by themselves. 'Look at that!' said Peter. 'They must go by magic or something.'

One little yellow boat sailed over to them and rocked gently beside them. They got into it. The boat didn't move.

'Tell it where to go, silly!' called the bus-driver, who was watching them with great interest.

'To the Mill,' said Peter, and immediately the boat shot off down-stream, doing little zigzags now and again in a very light-hearted manner. It wasn't long before they came to an old Mill. Its big water-wheel was working and made a loud noise. Behind it was a hill, and on the top was what looked like a small castle.

'That's where Mr. Spells lives,' said Peter. 'Come on – out we get, and up the hill we go.'

So up the hill they went and came at last to the curious castle-like house.

But when they got near they heard loud shouts and thumps and yells, and they stopped in alarm.

'Whatever's going on?' said Mollie. 'Is somebody quarrelling?'

The children tiptoed to the house and peeped in at one of the windows, the one where the noise seemed to be coming from. They saw a peculiar sight!

Chinky and a nasty-looking little goblin seemed to be playing musical chairs! The children saw the six chairs there that they had seen the day before in Mr. Polish's shop, and first Chinky would dart at one and look at it carefully and try to pull it away, and then the goblin would. Then Mr. Spells, who looked a very grand kind of enchanter, would pull the chairs away from each and then smack both the goblin and Chinky with his stick.

Roars and bellows came from the goblin and howls from Chinky. Oh, dear. Whatever was happening?

'Chinky must have found out that the chairs had gone to Mr. Spells, and gone to get our own chair,' said Peter. 'And the goblin must have gone to get it at the same time. Can you see the blue handkerchief we tied on our own chair, Mollie?'

'No. It's gone. Somebody took it off,' said Mollie. 'I

believe I can see it sticking out of Chinky's pocket – I expect he guessed we marked the chair that way and took the hanky off in case the goblin or Mr. Spells guessed there was something unusual about that particular chair.'

'Sir!' cried Chinky suddenly, turning to Mr. Spells, 'I tell you once more that I am only here to fetch back one of these chairs, a wishing-chair, which belongs to me and my friends. This goblin stole it from us – and now he's come to get it back again from you. He'll sell it again, and steal it – he's a bad fellow.'

Smack! The goblin thumped Chinky hard and he yelled. Mr. Spells roared like a lion. 'I don't believe either of you. You're a couple of rogues. These chairs are MY CHAIRS, all of them, and I don't believe any of them is a wishing-chair. Wishing-chairs have wings, and not one of these has.'

'But I tell you . . .' began Chinky, and then stopped as the enchanter struck him lightly with his wand, and then struck the goblin, too.

Chinky sank down into a deep sleep and so did the goblin. 'Now I shall have a little peace at last,' said Mr. Spells. 'And I'll find out which chair is a wishing-chair – if these fellows are speaking the truth!'

He went out of the room, and the children heard him stirring something somewhere. He was probably making a 'Find-out' spell!

'Come on – let's get into the room and drag Chinky out whilst he's gone,' said Peter. 'We simply must rescue him!'

So they crept in through the window and bent over

37

Chinky. And just at that very moment they felt a strong draught blowing round them!

They looked at each of the chairs – yes, one of them had grown wings, and was flapping them, making quite a wind! Hurray – now they could fly off in the Wishing-Chair, and cram Chinky in with them, fast asleep.

'Quick, oh, quick – Mr. Spells is coming back!' said Peter. 'Help me with Chinky – quick, Mollie, QUICK!'

VI

MR. SPELLS IS VERY MAGIC

The Wishing-Chair stood with the other five chairs, its red wings flapping strongly. The children caught hold of the sleeping pixie and dragged him to the chair. He felt as heavy as lead! If only he would wake up.

'He's in a terribly magic sleep,' said Mollie in despair. 'Now – lift him, Peter – that's right – and put him safely on the seat of the chair. Oh dear, he's rolling off again. Do, do be quick!'

They could hear Mr. Spells muttering in the next room, stirring something in a pot. In a few moments he would have made his find-out spell to see which was the Wishing-Chair, and would come back into the room. They *must* get away first!

The chair's wings were now fully grown, and it was doing little hops on the ground as if it were impatient to be off. The children sat down in it, holding Chinky tightly. Tricky the goblin was still lying on the floor, fast asleep. Good!

'Fly home, chair, fly home!' commanded Peter. Just in time, too, because as he spoke the children could hear the wizard's steps coming towards them from the next room. He appeared at the door, carrying something in a shining bottle.

The chair had now risen in the air, flapping its wings, and was trying to get out of the window. It was an awkward shape for the chair to get through, and it turned itself sideways so that the children and Chinky almost fell out! They clung to the arms in fright, trying to stop Chinky from rolling off.

'Hey!' cried the wizard in the greatest astonishment. 'What are you doing? Why, the chair's grown wings! Who are you, children – and what are you doing with my chair? Come back.'

But by this time the chair was out of the window and was the right way up again, much to the children's relief. It flew up into the air.

'Good! We've escaped – and we've got both the chair *and* Chinky,' said Peter, pleased. 'Even if he is asleep, we've got him. We'll have to ask the elf if he knows how to wake him up.'

But Peter spoke too soon. Mr. Spells was too clever to let the chair escape quite so easily. He came running out into the little garden in front of his castle-like cottage, carrying something over his arm.

'What's he going to do' said Mollie. 'What's he got, Peter?'

They soon knew! It was a very, very long rope, with a loop at the end to lasso them with! Mr. Spells swung the loops of rope round for a second or two, then flung the rope up into the air. The loops unwound and the last loop of all almost touched them. But not quite! The chair gave a jump of fright and rose a little higher.

'Oh, do go quickly, chair!' begged Mollie. 'The wizard is gathering up the rope to throw it again. Look

out – here it comes! Oh, Peter, it's going to catch us –
it's longer than ever!'

The rope sped up to them like a long, thin snake.
The last loop of all fell neatly round the chair, but,
before it could tighten, Peter caught hold of it and
threw it off. He really did it very cleverly indeed.

'Oh, Peter – you *are* marvellous!' cried Mollie. 'I
really thought we were caught that time. Surely we are
out of reach now – the wizard looks very small and far
away.'

Once more the rope came flying towards the
Wishing-Chair, and it tried to dodge it, almost
upsetting the children altogether. The rope darted after
the chair, fell firmly round it – and before Peter could

throw it off it had tightened itself round the chair and the children too!

Peter struggled hard to get a knife to cut the rope – but his arms were pinned tightly to his sides and he couldn't put his hands into his pockets. Mollie tried to help him, but it was no use. Mr. Spells was hauling on the rope and the chair was going gradually down and down and down.

'Oh dear – we're caught!' said Mollie in despair. 'Just when we had so nearly escaped, too! Peter, do think of something.'

But Peter couldn't. Chinky might have been able to think of some spell to get rid of the rope but he was still fast asleep. Mollie had to use both hands to hold him on the chair in case he fell off.

Down went the chair, pulling against the rope and making things as difficult as possible for the wizard, who was in a fine old temper when at last he had the chair on the ground.

'What do you mean by this?' he said sternly. 'What kind of behaviour is this – coming to my house, stealing one of the chairs I bought – the Wishing-Chair, too, the best of the lot? I didn't even know one of the chairs was a magic chair when I bought the set.'

Mollie was almost crying. Peter looked sulky as he tried to free his arms from the tight rope.

'You'll keep that rope round you for the rest of the day,' said Mr. Spells. 'Just to teach you that you can't steal from a wizard.'

'Let me free,' said Peter. 'I'm not a thief, and I haven't stolen this chair – unless you call taking something that really belongs to us *stealing*. I don't!'

'What do you mean?' said Mr. Spells. 'I'm tired of hearing people say this chair is theirs. Tricky said it – Chinky said it – and now you say it! It can't belong to all of you – and, anyway, I bought it with my money.'

'Mr. Spells, this Wishing-Chair is ours,' said Peter patiently. 'It lives in our playroom, and Chinky the pixie shares it with us and looks after it. Tricky stole it and sold it to Mr. Polish, who had five other chairs like it.'

'And then Tricky told you about the six old chairs and you went and bought them,' said Mollie. 'And Tricky came to-night to get back the Wishing-Chair because it's valuable and he can sell it to somebody else!'

'And then Chinky came to try and tell you about it before Tricky stole it,' went on Peter. 'And I suppose they came at the same time and quarrelled about it.'

'Well, well!' said Mr. Spells, who had been listening in surprise. 'This is a queer story, I must say. It's true that I came in from the garden to find the goblin and the pixie behaving most peculiarly. They kept sitting down first on one chair and then on another – trying to find out which was the Wishing-Chair, I suppose – and shouting at one another all the time.'

'I'd tied my blue hanky on the right arm of the Wishing-Chair,' said Mollie.

'Yes – I saw it there and wondered why,' said Mr. Spells. 'I can see it in Chinky's pocket now – he must have recognized it as yours and taken it off. Well, I suppose you came in just at the moment when I was

43

angry with them both, and put them into a magic sleep.'

'Yes,' said Peter. 'Then you went out and we thought we'd escape if we could, taking Chinky with us. The chair suddenly grew its wings, you see.'

'Mr. Spells, can we have back our chair, please, now that you've heard our story?' begged Mollie. 'I know you've paid some money to Mr. Polish for it – but couldn't you get it back from Tricky the goblin? After all, he's the rogue in all this, isn't he – not us or Chinky?'

'You're quite right,' said Mr. Spells. 'And I think it was very brave of you to come to rescue Chinky. I'm sorry I put him into a magic sleep now – but I'll wake him up again. And now I'll take the rope off and set you free!'

He took the rope off Peter and then lifted Chinky from the Wishing-Chair and laid him down on the floor. He drew a white ring of chalk round him and then a ring of blue inside the white circle. Then he called loudly.

'Cinders! Where are you? Dear me, that cat is never about when he's wanted!'

There was a loud miaow outside the window. In jumped a big black cat with green eyes that shone like traffic signals! He ran to Mr. Spells.

'Cinders, I'm going to do a wake-up spell,' said the wizard. 'Go and sit in the magic ring and sing with me whilst I chant the spell.'

Cinders leapt lightly over the chalk rings and sat down close to the sleeping Chinky. Mr. Spells began to walk round and round, just outside the ring, chanting a curious song. It sounded like: –

> 'Birriloola-kummi-pool,
> Rimminy, romminy, rye,
> Tibbynooka-falli-lool,
> Open your sleepy eye!'

All the time the wizard chanted this strange song the cat kept up a loud miaowing as if he were joining in too.

The spell was a very good one, because at the end of the chant, Chinky opened first one eye and then the other. He sat up, looking extremely surprised.

'I say,' he began, 'what's happened? Where am I? Oh, hallo, Peter and Mollie! I've been looking for you everywhere!'

'And *we've* been looking for you!' said Mollie. 'You've been in a magic sleep. Get up and come home with us. The Wishing-Chair has grown its wings again.'

Then Chinky saw Mr. Spells standing nearby, tall and commanding, and he went rather pale. 'But, I say – what does Mr. Spells think about all this?' he said, nervously.

'I have heard the children's story and it is quite plain that the chair really does belong to you,' he said. 'I'll get the money back from Tricky.'

'Well, he's *very* tricky, so be careful of him,' said Chinky, sitting down in the Wishing-Chair with the children.

'He'll get a shock when he wakes up,' said Mr. Spells, and he suddenly touched the sleeping goblin with the toe of his foot. 'Dimini, dimini, dimini, diminish!' he cried suddenly, and lo and behold the goblin shrank swiftly to a very tiny creature indeed, diminishing rapidly before the astonished eyes of the watching children.

Mr. Spells picked up the tiny goblin, took a matchbox off the mantelpiece, popped him into it, shut the box and put it back on the mantelpiece.

'He won't cause me any trouble when he wakes up!' he said. 'No, not a bit! Well, good-bye. I'm glad this has all ended well – but I do wish that chair was mine.'

The children waved good-bye and the chair rose into the air. 'Shall we go home?' said Peter.

'No,' said Mollie, suddenly remembering the satchel of sandwiches and cake that Peter still carried. 'We'll take Chinky off for the day, picnicking! We deserve a nice peaceful day after such a thrilling adventure.'

'Right!' said Peter, and Chinky nodded happily. 'Wishing-Chair, take us to the nicest picnic spot you know!' And off they flew at once, to have a very happy day together.

VII

OFF ON ANOTHER ADVENTURE!

For a whole week the children watched and waited for the Wishing-Chair to grow its wings again. It didn't sprout them at all! The wings had vanished as soon as it had arrived safely back in the playroom.

'I hope its magic isn't getting less,' said Mollie, one day, as they sat in the playroom, playing ludo together. It was their very favourite game, and they always laughed at Chinky because he made such a fuss when he didn't get 'home' before they did.

As they sat playing together they felt a welcome draught. 'Oh, lovely! A breeze at last!' said Mollie thankfully. 'I do really think this is just about the hottest day we've had these holidays!'

'The wind must have got up a bit at last,' said Peter. 'Blow, wind, blow – you are making us lovely and cool.'

'Funny that the leaves on the trees aren't moving, isn't it?' said Chinky.

Mollie looked out of the open door at the trees in the garden. They were perfectly still! 'But there *isn't* a breeze,' she said, and then a sudden thought struck her. She looked round at the Wishing-Chair, which was standing just behind them.

'Look!' she cried. 'How silly we are! It isn't the

wind – it's the Wishing-Chair that has grown its wings again. They are flapping like anything!'

So they were. The children and Chinky sprang up in delight. 'Good! We could just do with a lovely cool ride up in the air to-day,' said Peter. 'Wishing-Chair, we are very pleased with you!'

The Wishing-Chair flapped its wings very strongly again and gave a creak. Then Chinky noticed something.

'I say, look – it's only grown *three* wings instead of four. What's happened? It's never done that before.'

They all stared at the chair. One of its front legs hadn't grown a wing. It looked rather odd without it.

Chinky looked at the chair rather doubtfully. 'Do you think it can fly with only three wings?' he said. 'This is rather a peculiar thing to happen, really. I wonder if we ought to fly off in the chair if it's only got three wings instead of four.'

'I don't see why not,' said Mollie. 'After all, an aeroplane can fly with three engines, if the fourth one stops.'

The chair gave a little hop up in the air as if to say it could fly perfectly well. 'Oh, come along!' said Chinky. 'We'll try. I'm sure it will be all right. But I wish I knew what to do to get the fourth wing to grow. Something has gone wrong, it's plain.'

They got into the chair, Chinky as usual sitting on the back, holding on to their shoulders. The chair flew to the door.

'Where shall we go?' said Chinky.

'Well – we never did get to the Land of Goodness

Knows Where after all,' said Mollie. 'Shall we try to get there again? We know it's a good way away, so it should be a nice long flight, very cool and windy high up in the air.'

'We may as well,' said Chinky. 'Fly to the Land of Goodness Knows Where, Chair. We saw it on the map – it's due east from here, straight towards where the sun rises – you go over the Tiptop Mountains, past the Crazy Valley and then down by the Zigzag Coast.'

'It sounds exciting,' said Mollie. 'Oh, isn't it lovely to be cool again? It's so very hot to-day.'

They were now high up in the air, and a lovely breeze blew past them as they flew. Little clouds, like puffs of cotton wool, floated below them. Mollie leaned out to get hold of one as they passed.

'This is fun,' she said. 'Chinky, is there a land of ice-creams? If so, I'd like to go there sometime!'

'I don't know. I've never heard of one,' said Chinky. 'There's a Land of Goodies though, I know that. It once came to the top of the Faraway Tree, and I went there. It was lovely – biscuits growing on trees, and chocolates sprouting on bushes.'

'Oh – did you see Moon-Face and Silky and the old Saucepan Man?' asked Mollie, in excitement. 'I've read the books about the Faraway Tree, and I've always wished I could climb it.'

'Yes, I saw them all,' said Chinky. 'Silky is sweet, you'd love her. But Moon-Face was cross because somebody had taken all his slippery-slip cushions – you know, the cushions he keeps in his room at the top of the tree for people to sit on when they slide down from the top to the bottom.'

'I wouldn't mind going to the Land of Goodies at all,' said Peter. 'It sounds really fine. I almost wish we'd told the chair to go there instead of the Land of Goodness Knows Where.'

'Well, don't change its mind for it,' said Chinky. 'It doesn't like that. Look, there are the Tip-Top Mountains.'

They all leaned out to look. They were very extraordinary mountains, running up into high, jagged peaks as if somebody had drawn them higgledy-piggledy with a pencil, up and down, up and down.

On they went, through a batch of tiny little clouds; but Mollie didn't try to catch any of these because, just in time, she saw that baby elves were fast asleep on them, one to each cloud.

'They make good cradles for a hot day like this,' explained Chinky.

After a while, Mollie noticed that Chinky was leaning rather hard on her shoulder, and that Peter seemed to be leaning against her, too. She pushed them back.

'Don't lean so heavily on me,' she said.

'We don't mean to,' said Peter. 'But I seem to be leaning that way all the time! I do try not to.'

'Why are we, I wonder?' said Chinky. Then he gave a cry. 'Why, the chair's all on one side. No wonder Peter and I keep going over on to you, Mollie. Look – it's tipped sideways!'

'What's the matter with it' said Mollie. She tried to shake the chair upright by swinging herself about in it, but it always over-balanced to the left side as soon as she had stopped swinging it to and fro.

They all looked in alarm at one another as the chair began to tip more and more to one side. It was very difficult to sit in it when it tipped like that.

'It's because it's only got three wings!' said Chinky, suddenly. 'Of course that's it! The one wing on this side is tired out, and so the chair is flying with only two wings really, and it's tipping over. It will soon be on its side in the air!'

'Gracious! Then for goodness' sake let's go down to the ground at once,' said Mollie, in alarm. 'We shall fall out if we don't.'

'Go down to the ground, Chair,' commanded Peter, feeling the chair going over to one side even more. He looked over the side. The one wing there had already stopped flapping. The chair was using only two wings – they would soon be tired out, too!

The chair flew heavily down to the ground and landed with rather a bump. Its wings stopped flapping and hung limp. It creaked dolefully. It was quite exhausted, that was plain!

'We shouldn't have flown off on it when it only had three wings,' said Chinky. 'It was wrong of us. After all, Peter and Mollie, you have grown bigger since last holidays, and must be heavier. The chair can't possibly take us all unless it has *four* wings to fly with.'

They stood and looked at the poor, tired Wishing-Chair. 'What are we going to do about it?' said Peter.

'Well – we must try to find out where we are first,' said Chinky, looking round. 'And then we must ask if

51

there is a witch or wizard or magician anywhere about that can give us something to make the chair grow another wing. Then we'd better take it straight home for a rest.'

'Look,' said Mollie, pointing to a nearby sign-post. 'It says, "To the Village of Slipperies." Do you know that village, Chinky?'

'No. But I've heard of it,' said Chinky. 'The people there aren't very nice – slippery as eels – can't trust them or believe a word they say. I don't think we'll go that way.'

He went to look at the other arm of the signpost and came back looking very pleased.

'It says "Dame Quick-Fingers",' he said. 'She's my great-aunt. She'll help us all right. She'll be sure to know a spell for growing wings. She keeps a pack of flying dogs, you know, because of the Slipperies – they simply fly after them when they come to steal her chickens and ducks.'

'Goodness – I'd love to see some flying dogs,' said Mollie. 'Where does this aunt of yours live?'

'Just down the road, round a corner, and by a big rowan tree,' said Chinky. 'She's really nice. I dare say she'd ask us to tea if we are as polite as possible. She loves good manners.'

'Well – you go and ask her if she knows how to grow an extra wing on our chair,' said Mollie. 'We'd better stay here with the chair, I think, in case anyone thinks of stealing it again. We can easily bring it along to your aunt's cottage, if she's in. We won't carry it all the way there in case she's not.'

52

'Right. I'll go,' said Chinky. 'I won't be long. You just sit in the chair till I come back – and don't you let anyone steal it.'

He ran off down the road and disappeared round a corner. Mollie and Peter sat down in the chair to wait. The chair creaked. It sounded very tired indeed. Mollie patted its arms. 'You'll soon be all right once you have got a fourth wing,' she said. 'Cheer up.'

Chinky hadn't been gone very long before the sound of footsteps made the children look round. Five little people were coming along the road from the Village of Slipperies. They looked most peculiar.

'They must be Slipperies,' said Peter, sitting up. 'Now we must be careful they don't play a trick on us and get the chair away. Aren't they odd-looking?'

The five little creatures came up and bowed low. 'Good-day,' they said. 'We come to greet you and to ask you to visit our village.'

VIII

THE SLIPPERIES PLAY A TRICK!

Peter and Mollie looked hard at the five Slipperies. Each Slippery had one blue eye and one green, and not one of them looked straight at the children! Their hair was slick and smooth, their mouths smiled without stopping, and they rubbed their bony hands together all the time.

'I'm sorry,' said Peter, 'but we don't want to leave our chair. We're waiting here with it till our friend Chinky comes back from seeing his Great-Aunt Quick-Fingers.'

'Oh, she's gone to market,' said one of the Slipperies. 'She always goes on Thursdays.'

'Oh dear,' said Peter. 'How tiresome! Now we shan't be able to get a fourth wing for our Wishing-Chair.'

'Dear me – is this a Wishing-Chair?' said the Slipperies, in great interest. 'It's the first time we've seen one. Do let us sit in it.'

'Certainly not,' said Peter, feeling certain that if he let them sit in the chair they would try to fly off in it.

'I hear that Great-Aunt Quick-Fingers has some flying dogs,' said Mollie, hoping that the Slipperies would look frightened at the mention of them. But they didn't.

They rubbed their slippery hands together again and

went on smiling. 'Ah, yes – wonderful dogs they are. If you stand up on your chair, and look over the field yonder, you may see some of them flying around,' said one Slippery.

The children stood on the seat of the chair. The Slipperies clustered round them. 'Now look right down over that field,' began one of them. 'Do you see a tall tree?'

'Yes,' said Mollie.

'Well, look to the right of it and you'll see the roof of a house. And then to the right of that and you'll see another tree,' said the Slippery.

'Can't you tell me *exactly* where to look?' said Mollie, getting impatient. 'I can't see a single flying dog. Only a rook or two.'

'Well, now look to the left and . . .' began another Slippery, when Peter jumped down from the chair.

'You're just making it all up,' he said. 'Go on, be off with you! I don't like any of you.'

The Slipperies lost their smiles, and looked nasty. They laid hands on the Wishing-Chair.

'I shall whistle for the flying dogs,' said Peter suddenly. 'Now let me see – what is the whistle, ah, yes . . .' And he suddenly whistled a very shrill whistle indeed.

The Slipperies shot off at once as if a hundred of the flying dogs were after them! Mollie laughed.

'Peter! That's not really a whistle for flying dogs, is it?'

'No, of course not. But I had to get rid of them somehow,' said Peter. 'I had a feeling they were going to trick us with their silly smiles and rubbing hands and

55

odd eyes – so I had to think of some way of tricking *them* instead.'

'I wish Chinky would come,' said Mollie, sitting down in the chair again. 'He's been ages. And it's all a waste of time, his going to find his Great-Aunt, if she's at the market. We shall have to go there, I expect, and carry the chair all the way.'

'Why, there *is* Chinky!' said Peter, waving. 'Oh, good, he's dancing and smiling. He's got the spell to make another wing grow.'

'Then his Great-Aunt couldn't have gone to market!' said Mollie. 'Hey, Chinky! Have you got the spell? Was your Great-Aunt Quick-Fingers in?'

'Yes – and awfully pleased to see me,' said Chinky, running up. 'And she gave me just enough magic to make another wing grow, so we shan't be long now.'

56

'Five Slipperies came up, and they said your Great-Aunt always goes to market on Thursdays,' said Mollie.

'You can't believe a word they say,' said Chinky. 'I told you that. My word, I'm glad they didn't trick you in any way. They usually trick everyone, no matter how clever they may be.'

'Well, they didn't trick *us*,' said Peter. 'We were much too smart for them – weren't we, Mollie?'

'Yes. They wanted to sit in the chair when they knew it was a Wishing-Chair,' said Mollie. 'But we wouldn't let them.'

'I should think not,' said Chinky. He showed the children a little blue box. 'Look – I've got a smear of ointment here that is just enough to grow a red wing to match the other wings. Then the chair will be quite all right.'

'Well, let's rub it on,' said Peter. Chinky knelt down by the chair – and then he gave a cry of horror.

'What's the matter?' said the children.

'Look – somebody has cut off the other three wings of the chair!' groaned Chinky. 'Cut them right off short. There's only a stump left of each.'

Mollie and Peter stared in horror. Sure enough the other three wings had been cut right off. But how? And when? Who could have done it? The children had been with the chair the whole time.

'I do think you might have kept a better guard on the chair,' said Chinky crossly. 'I really do. Didn't I warn you about the ways of the Slipperies? Didn't I say you couldn't trust them? Didn't I . . .'

'Oh, Chinky – but when could it have been done?'

cried Mollie. 'I tell you, we were here the whole of the time.'

'Standing by the chair?' asked Chinky.

'Yes – or *on* it,' said Peter.

'*On* it! Whatever did you stand *on* it, for?' said Chinky, puzzled. 'To stop the Slipperies sitting down?'

'No – to see your Great-Aunt's flying-dogs,' said Peter. 'The Slipperies said they were over there, and if we would stand up on the chair seat we could just see them flying around. But we couldn't.'

'Of course you couldn't,' said Chinky. 'And for a very good reason, too – they're all at the cottage with my Great-Aunt. I saw them!'

'Oh – the dreadful story-tellers!' cried Mollie. 'Peter – it was a trick! Whilst we were standing up there trying to see the dogs, one of the Slipperies must have quietly snipped off the three wings and put them in his pocket.'

'Of course!' said Chinky. 'Very simple – and you're a pair of simpletons to get taken in by such a silly trick.'

Mollie and Peter went very red. 'What shall we do?' asked Peter. 'I'm very sorry about it. Poor old chair – one wing not grown and the other three snipped away. It's a shame.'

'Thank goodness Chinky has the Growing Ointment for wings,' said Mollie.

'Yes – but I've only got just enough for *one* wing,' said Chinky. 'One wing isn't going to take us very far, is it?'

'No,' said Mollie. 'Whatever are we going to do?'

'I shall have to ask Great-Aunt Quick-Fingers for some more Growing Ointment, that's all,' said Chinky, gloomily. 'And this time you can come with me, *and* bring the chair too. If I leave you here alone with it, you'll get tricked again, and I shall come back and find the *legs* are gone next time, and I can't even grow wings on them!'

'It's not nice of you to keep on and on about it, Chinky,' said Mollie, lifting up the chair with Peter. 'We're very sorry. We didn't know quite how clever the Slipperies were. Oooh – horrid creatures, with their odd eyes and deceitful smiles.'

They followed Chinky down the road and along a lane. Soon he came to his Great-Aunt's cottage. It was very snug and small. To Mollie's enormous delight, five or six little brown dogs, rather like spaniels were flying about the garden on small white wings. They barked loudly and flew to the three of them.

'Now, now – these are friends of mine,' said Chinky, and patted the nearest dog, which was flying round his head.

It was strange to have the little dogs sailing about the air like gulls! One flew up to Mollie and rested its front paws on her shoulder. She laughed, and the dog licked her face. Then off it flew again, and chased after a sparrow, barking madly.

Great-Aunt Quick-Fingers came to the door, looking surprised. 'Why, Chinky – back again so soon!' she said. 'What's happened?'

Chinky told her. 'So you see, Great-Aunt, now that the poor chair has lost *all* its wings, I'm afraid that the Growing Ointment you gave me won't be enough,' said Chinky. 'I'm so sorry.'

'Well, well – it takes a very clever person to see through the Slippery ways,' said his Great-Aunt. 'You'd better come in and have tea now you're all here!'

The children put down the Wishing-Chair and Great-Aunt Quick-Fingers got the little treacle tarts out of the oven. 'There you are,' she said. 'Get your fingers nice and sticky with those! I'll go and make some more Growing Ointment for you. It won't take long.'

She disappeared, and the children sat and munched the lovely treacle tarts.

Just at that moment she came back, with a fairly large jar. She handed it to Chinky. 'There you are. Use that and see what happens. But remember, you can only use it once on anything. The spell doesn't act twice. It's no good trying to use the ointment another time on the chair, to make it grow wings, because it won't be any use.'

Chinky dipped his finger into the jar of ointment. It was curious stuff, bright yellow with green streaks in it.

He rubbed some on to a chair leg and immediately a most wonderful wing sprouted out, big and strong!

'I say – it isn't red, as it always is!' cried Mollie. 'It's green and yellow – and a much bigger wing than before. I say, Chair, you *will* look grand. Make another wing come, Chinky.'

Soon the Wishing-Chair had four grand green and yellow wings, much bigger than its old red ones. It waved them about proudly.

'You'd better get in the chair and go before it tries its new wings out by itself,' said Great-Aunt Quick-

Fingers. So in they all got, Chinky on the back, as usual – and off they went!

'Home, Chair, home!' cried everyone, and it rose high in the air, and flew off to the west. 'Good-bye and thank you very much,' cried Chinky and the children, and Great-Aunt waved till they were out of sight.

'Well, that was quite a nice little adventure,' said Peter. 'And the chair's got some wonderful new wings. I do hope they'll always grow like this in future – big and strong, and all green and yellow!'

IX

MOLLIE AND THE
GROWING OINTMENT

The children were very pleased with the chair's beautiful new green and yellow wings. 'They're much better than the little red ones it used to grow,' said Peter. 'Your Great-Aunt's Growing Ointment is marvellous stuff, Chinky. I only hope the chair will grow its wings more often now.'

The green and yellow wings disappeared, of course, as soon as they were all safely at home again. The chair stood still in its place, looking quite ordinary. The children patted it.

'Good old Wishing-Chair. Grow your wings again soon. You haven't taken us to the Land of Goodness Knows Where yet, you know!'

The chair didn't grow its wings again that week. Friday came, Saturday, Sunday, Monday. The children grew tired of asking Chinky if the chair was growing its wings yet.

On Tuesday a spell of rainy weather began. It really was too wet to play any games out of doors at all. The children went down to their playroom day after day to play with Chinky, and that was fun. But on Friday Chinky said he really must go and see how his dear old mother was.

'I haven't seen her since I came back to you with the chair,' he said. 'I must go to-day.'

'Oh, bother! We shall have to do without you,' said Mollie. 'Just suppose the chair grows its wings, Chinky, and you're not here.'

'Well, that's easy,' said Chinky, with a grin. 'Simply sit in it and wish it to go to my mother's. She will be very pleased to see you, and then we can all three of us go adventuring somewhere.'

'Oh, yes – we'll do that, if only the chair grows wings,' said Peter. 'Well, good-bye, Chinky. Will you be back to-night?'

'Yes,' said Chinky. 'I'll be sleeping on the old sofa as usual, don't worry. I'm not taking my wand with me, by the way, so keep an eye on it, will you?'

Chinky had just bought a new wand, a very useful one that had quite a bit of magic in it. He was very proud of it, and kept it in the cupboard with the toys and games.

'Yes – we'll look after it for you,' said Peter. 'And we won't use it, we promise.'

'I know you won't,' said Chinky. 'Well, see you to-night.'

Off he went to catch the bus to his mother's cottage, dressed in his mackintosh and sou'wester. The children felt decidedly dull when he had gone.

'Game of ludo, Mollie?' said Peter.

'No. I'm bored with ludo to-day,' said Mollie.

'Well, you're not going to be very good company, then,' said Peter, taking down a book. 'I'll read. You can tell me when you've finished being bored and we'll think up an exciting game.'

Mollie lay down on the rug and shut her eyes. What a pity it had rained and rained so long. Even if the Wishing-Chair grew its wings, it wouldn't be much fun going out in the rain. They would have to take an umbrella with them.

Mollie opened her eyes and looked out of the window. Why, the sun was shining – and yet it was still raining.

'I say, Peter, look at this rainbow,' said Mollie. 'It's glorious. Oh – wouldn't it be lovely to fly off to a rainbow in the Wishing-Chair! If it looks as beautiful as this far away, whatever would it look like very near to us? Oh, I do wish the Wishing-Chair would grow its wings this very afternoon.'

Peter took no notice. He was deep in his book. Mollie felt cross. She wandered round the room and opened a little cupboard where Chinky kept some of his things. There on the shelf was the jar of Growing Ointment that Great-Aunt Quick-Fingers had given him to make the wings of the Wishing-Chair sprout again.

Mollie took down the jar and opened the lid. There was plenty of ointment left – yellow with streaks of green in it. She wondered if perhaps it *would* make the chair's wings grow again, although Chinky's Great-Aunt had said it only acted once on anything.

'I'll try it,' thought Mollie. 'And I won't tell Peter! If the wings grow, I'll fly off in the Wishing-Chair without him, and go to Chinky's alone. That will serve him right for not answering when I speak to him!'

She went over to the Wishing-Chair and rubbed a

little of the ointment on one of the front legs. Nothing happened at all. She couldn't feel even a tiny bud of a wing beginning to grow; the Growing Ointment certainly didn't act twice. Great-Aunt Quick-Fingers was right.

Then a wonderful thought came to Mollie. Why shouldn't she try a little of the magic ointment on something else? She looked round. Her dolls, for instance! Oh, if only she could make wings grow on Rosebud, her prettiest doll. That would be really wonderful.

Feeling very excited, Mollie took her doll Rosebud from her cot. She rubbed a little of the green and yellow ointment on to her back – and, hey presto, wing-buds began to form – and little green and yellow wings sprouted out on the doll's back.

And she suddenly left Mollie's knee and flew – yes, *flew* – round the playroom. She flew near Peter and he felt the wind of her little wings. He looked up – and his eyes almost dropped out of his head as he saw Rosebud flying gaily round the room!

Mollie laughed in delight and tried to catch the doll as she flew past. 'I've put some of the Growing Ointment on her back,' she said. 'You know – what Chinky's Great-Aunt gave him for growing wings on the Wishing-Chair. And Rosebud grew wings!'

'Well, I never!' said Peter in amazement. 'I say – do you think my engine would grow wings, too?' said Peter suddenly. He had a wonderful clockwork engine, a perfect model that he was very proud of.

'Oh, *yes* – let's try and see,' said Mollie. So they got

the engine and Peter smeared a little of the ointment on to it. It sprouted out small wings at once!

It flew from Peter's hand and joined the doll. The children laughed till their sides ached to see the two toys behaving like this. They really did look extraordinary.

And then Mollie and Peter went quite mad with the ointment. They smeared it on to a top and that flew round the room, spinning as it went! They smeared the skittles and they all shot round and round, some of them bumping into one another in the air.

They made some of the little toy soldiers fly, and they even gave the bricks in their brick box wings to fly with. All these things flapped their way round the room, and Mollie and Peter screamed with laughter as they tried to dodge the flying toys.

Mollie went to the toy cupboard to see if any toy was there that could be made to fly as well. She picked up Chinky's new wand and put it on one side – but, dear me, her fingers were smeared with the Growing Ointment and the wand at once grew tiny, graceful green and yellow wings, too! It flew out of the cupboard and joined the flying toys.

'Oh dear – there goes the wand,' said Mollie. 'I do hope Chinky won't mind. I just touched it by accident with the ointment smeared on my fingers, and it grew wings.'

'Look – I've made the teapot fly,' said Peter, and roared with laughter to see it flapping its way round the room. 'Look at the skittles colliding again.'

The wind suddenly blew the door wide open. Then a dreadful thing happened. Rosebud the doll, the railway engine, the skittles, the bricks, the top, the teapot, the wand; in fact everything that had grown wings shot straight out of the open door, flew down to the bottom of the garden and vanished!

'Ooooh!' said Mollie in fright.

'They've gone,' said Peter, and rushed to the open door. But he could see nothing. No Rosebud was there, no engine, nothing. They had all vanished into the blue.

'Oh dear – shall we get them back?' said Mollie. 'Why did I ever begin to smear the Growing Ointment on anything? It was a very silly idea. Now I've lost Rosebud.'

'And what about my lovely model engine?' said Peter. 'And I *say* – Chinky's magic wand has gone, too!'

They stared at one another in dismay. Chinky's new wand, that he had saved up for and was so proud of! It had grown wings and now it had flown out of the door and vanished, too. This was dreadful.

'We shall have to tell Chinky when he gets back tonight, and ask him if we can possibly get the things back,' said Mollie. 'If we knew where they had gone we could go and fetch them. Do you suppose they've gone to Great-Aunt Quick-Fingers?'

They said no more to one another, but sat solemnly side by side, hoping and hoping that the things would fly back as unexpectedly as they had flown away. But they didn't.

Chinky came back at half-past six, looking very merry and bright, and bringing a big chocolate cake from his mother. He stopped when he saw their doleful faces.

'What's up?' he said. 'Anything happened?'

They told him, and Chinky listened in astonishment. He leapt to his feet when they spoke about his wand.

'WHAT! You don't mean to tell me you were silly enough to meddle with my wand – surely you didn't make my *wand* grow wings, too!'

'It was an accident,' said poor Mollie. 'I must have had some of the ointment on my fingers when I moved it – and so it grew wings, too. I'm so sorry, Chinky.'

'Where have the things gone, Chinky?' asked Peter.

'I don't know,' said Chinky. 'I haven't the least idea. All I can say is – the next time the Wishing-Chair grows its wings, we'll have to tell it to go wherever the toys have gone – but goodness knows where it will take us to!'

X

OFF TO FIND THE TOYS

Chinky was gloomy and cross that evening. The children were sad, and felt ashamed that they had gone quite so mad with the Growing Ointment. They felt very guilty indeed about Chinky's wand.

'Will you come and tell us if the Wishing-Chair grows its wings again to-night, Chinky?' asked Mollie when it was time for them to go back to the house.

'I might,' said Chinky gruffly. 'And I might not. I might go off by myself in it.'

'Oh, no, don't do that,' begged Mollie. 'That would be horrid of you. Dear Chinky, please be nice and forgive us for losing your wand.'

'All right,' said Chinky, cheering up a little.

'I really do feel very upset about losing my doll Rosebud, you know,' went on poor Mollie. 'I feel just as upset about her as you feel about your wand.'

'And I'm miserable about my engine,' said Peter. 'It was the finest I ever had.'

'Well – we'll hope the Wishing-Chair grows its wings again to-night, then, and we can go and fetch everything,' said Chinky. 'I'll come and tap on your windows if it grows its wings.'

But Chinky didn't tap on their windows at all. The chair didn't grow any wings in the night. Mollie sighed.

'Just when we so badly want it to fly, it won't grow wings! Now to-day we've got to behave nicely and be on our best behaviour, because Mother's got visitors. Perhaps we shan't be able to go down to the playroom at all.'

At eleven o'clock, when the visitors had arrived and Mother was giving them coffee and the children were handing round plates of biscuits and buns, Chinky appeared at the window.

He was horrified when he saw so many people there and disappeared at once. The children caught sight of him.

They looked at one another in despair. Now what were they to do? There was only one thing. They must do something to make Mother send them out of the room.

So Mollie suddenly spilt the plate of biscuits all over the floor, and Peter spilt a cup of coffee.

Mother looked vexed. 'Oh, dear – how clumsy of you!' she said. 'Go and ask Jane if she will please bring a cloth, Mollie. And I think you and Peter had better go now. I don't want anything else spilt.'

'Sorry, Mother,' said Peter.

They shot out of the room. Mollie called to Jane to take a cloth to wipe up the coffee, and then both children raced down to the playroom.

'I hope Chinky hasn't gone off in the chair by himself,' panted Peter. 'If he saw us with all those visitors he might think we couldn't possibly come – and then he'd fly off alone.'

70

They got to the playroom door just as Chinky was flying out in the Wishing-Chair. They bumped into one another, and Peter caught hold of one of the chair's legs.

'Just in time!' he cried. 'Help us up, Chinky!'

Chinky pulled them up with him. Then the chair flapped its green and yellow wings and flew strongly up into the air.

'I was afraid you wouldn't be able to come,' said Chinky. 'I was just setting off by myself. The chair had only grown its wings a few minutes before I peeped in at the window.'

'What fine, big, strong wings it's got now,' said Peter. 'They make quite a draught round my legs. It will be able to fly faster now.'

'Where are we going?' asked Mollie.

'I don't know,' said Chinky. 'I just said to the chair, "Go and find my wand, and Rosebud, and the rest of the toys," and it seemed to know the place I meant, because it rose up at once. I've no idea where we shall land. I only hope it's somewhere nice. It would be awful to go to the Village of Slipperies, or to the Land of Rubbish, or somewhere like that.'

'Oh dear – I hope it's somewhere nice, too,' said Mollie. 'The chair is flying very high, isn't it?'

'Do you think it may be going to Toyland?' asked Peter. 'I wouldn't mind that at all. After all, most of the things were toys. I think it's very likely they may have gone there.'

'It certainly seems to be taking the way to Toyland as far as I remember,' said Chinky, peering down. 'I know we pass over the Village of Teddy Bears before we reach Toyland, and we're very near that now. There's Toyland, far over there. That must be where we're going.'

But it wasn't. The chair suddenly began to fly down and down at a great rate, and it was plain that it was going to land.

'Well! This isn't Toyland!' said Chinky in surprise. 'Good gracious! I do believe it's the school run by Mister Grim, for Bad Brownies. Surely the toys haven't gone there!'

The chair landed in the grounds of a big house, just near a wall. Chinky and the children got off. They pushed the chair under a bush to hide it. Then they looked cautiously round.

From the big building in the distance came a chanting noise. The children and Chinky listened.

'I mustn't scream or whistle or shout
Because Mister Grim is always about,
I mustn't stamp or slam any door
Or jump or slide on the schoolroom floor,
I mustn't be greedy, untidy or lazy
Because Mister Grim would be driven quite
    crazy,
I mustn't be slow, and I MUST be quick,
Because Mister Grim has a very BIG STICK!'

'Ooooh!' said Mollie. 'I don't like the sound of that. That must be the poor Bad Brownie learning verses for Mr. Grim.'

'Yes,' said Chinky. 'I do wish we hadn't come here. I've half a mind to get in the Wishing-Chair and go off again. I've always been told that Mister Grim is a very hard master. We don't want to be caught by him.'

'*Caught!*' said Peter. 'But we're two children and a pixie – we're not brownies – and this is a school for brownies.'

'I know,' said Chinky. 'I just don't like the feel of this place, that's all. If you think it's all right, we'll stay and see if we can possibly find where our toys are.'

'I think we'd better,' said Peter. 'Well – what's the first thing to do?'

'Listen – is that the brownies coming out to play?' said Mollie as a perfect babel of noise reached them. Then came the sound of feet running and in a trice about fifty small brownies surrounded them. They all looked merry, mischievous little fellows, too young to have grown their brownie beards yet.

'Who are you? Are you new pupils for this awful school?' asked a small brownie, pushing himself forward. 'My name's Winks. What's yours?'

All the little brownies crowded round, listening eagerly. Chinky pushed them back.

'Don't crowd so. No, we haven't come to your school. We came because we're looking for things we've lost, and we think they may be somewhere here. My name's Chinky. These are real children, Peter and Mollie.'

'Well, be careful Mister Grim doesn't see you,' said Winks. 'He's in a very bad temper these days – worse than he's ever been.'

73

'Why?' asked Peter.

'Because we found the cupboard where he kept his canes and we broke the whole lot!' chuckled the brownie. 'Every one of them.'

'Can't he slap you or smack you, though?' said Peter.

'Oh, yes – but we dodge,' said Winks. 'Can't dodge a cane very well, though. I say – do be careful he doesn't catch you.'

'What are you looking for?' asked another brownie. 'I'm Hoho; you can trust me.'

'Well,' said Chinky, 'we came here to look for a lot of flying toys – and my new wand. It had wings, too.'

'Flying toys!' said Winks. 'And a flying wand. Well! Have we seen anything like that, boys?'

'Yes!' shouted Hoho at once. 'Don't you remember? Yesterday evening we saw something very peculiar – we thought they were curious birds flying about in the air. They must have been your toys.'

'What happened to them?' asked Peter.

'Well, old Grim was out in the garden smoking his evening pipe,' said Hoho. 'And he suddenly looked up and saw them, too. He was very excited, and called out some words we couldn't hear . . .'

'And what we thought were the peculiar birds came right down to him,' said Winks. 'But they must have been your toys on the way to Toyland! He caught sight of them and made them come to him!'

'Well, whatever can *he* do with them?' said Hoho. 'We are never allowed any toys at all. I suppose he will sell them to his friend the Magician Sly-Boots.'

'Oh dear,' said Mollie. 'Well, we must try and get

them before he does. Will you show us where you think Mister Grim might have hidden our toys?'

'Yes, we'll show you!' shouted the brownies. 'But do be careful you aren't caught!'

They took Chinky and the children to the big building, all walking on tiptoe and shushing each other.

Hoho led them inside. He pointed to a winding stair. 'Go up there,' he whispered. 'You'll come to a little landing. On the left side is a door. That's the storeroom, where I expect Mister Grim has put the toys.'

'Creep in – and see if you can find them,' whispered Winks.

'Come on,' said Chinky to the others. 'It's now or never! If we find our things we'll take them and rush down and out into the garden, and be off in the Wishing-Chair before Mister Grim even knows we're here!'

'Sh!' said Mollie, and they all began to go up the stairs on tiptoe. 'Shhhhhhh!'

XI

MISTER GRIM'S SCHOOL FOR BAD BROWNIES

Up the stairs went the three, treading very quietly indeed, hoping that not one of the stairs would creak or crack.

The brownies crowded round the door at the bottom of the stairs, holding their breath and watching. Up and up and up – and there was the landing at last! Now for the door on the left.

They saw the door. They tiptoed to it and Peter turned the handle. Would it be locked? No, it wasn't!

They peeped inside. Yes, it was the storeroom, and stacks of books, pencils, rulers, ink-bottles, old desks, and all kinds of things were there.

'Can't see our toys,' whispered Chinky. 'Or my wand. Let's look in all the drawers and all the cupboards.'

So they began opening the drawers and hunting in them, and pulling open the cupboard doors and peering in at the shelves. But they could find nothing more exciting than books and pens and rubbers.

And then Chinky gave a soft cry. 'Look here,' he said. 'Here they are!'

The others ran quickly over to him. He had opened a big chest – and there, lying quietly in the top of it, their wings vanished, lay all the toys they had lost – yes,

Rosebud was there, and Peter's engine, and the top and the soldiers – everything.

But wait – no, not quite everything. 'I can't see my wand anywhere,' said Chinky, hunting desperately. 'Oh, where is it?'

They hunted all through the chest, but there didn't seem to be any wand there. They looked in despair at one another. They simply *must* find Chinky's wand.

'I'm glad we've found the toys,' whispered Chinky, 'but it's dreadful that I can't find my wand. It's got a lot of magic in it, you know. I wouldn't want Mister Grim to use that.'

Then the children heard a noise that froze them to the floor. Footsteps – footsteps coming slowly and heavily up the stairs. Not light, quick, brownie steps, but slow, ponderous ones. Would the footsteps come to the storeroom?

In panic the children and Chinky squeezed themselves into a cupboard, not having time to put away the toys they had pulled out of the chest. The door opened – and somebody walked in!

The children hardly dared to breathe and Chinky almost choked. Then a voice spoke.

'SOMEONE has been here. SOMEONE has tried to steal toys. And that SOMEONE is here still. Come out!'

The children didn't move. They were much too scared to do a thing. And then poor Chinky choked! He choked again, then coughed loudly.

Footsteps marched to the cupboard and the door was flung wide open.

There stood Mister Grim – exactly like his name! He was a big, burly brownie, with a tremendous beard falling to the floor. He had pointed ears and shaggy eyebrows that almost hid his eyes.

'HO!' he said in a booming voice. 'So the SOMEONE is not one person, but three!'

Peter, Mollie and Chinky came out, poor Chinky still coughing. Mister Grim took them each firmly by the back of the neck and sat them down on the window-seat.

'And now will you kindly tell me why you came to steal my toys?' he said. 'How did you know they were there, and who told you about them?'

'They're not your toys, sir,' Peter said at last in rather a trembling voice. 'They're ours. We let them grow wings yesterday by using Growing Ointment on them – and they flew away. We came to fetch them.'

'A very likely story indeed,' said Mister Grim scornfully. 'And how did you come here?'

'Up the stairs,' said Mollie.

Mister Grim frowned a fierce frown. 'Don't be foolish, girl,' he said. 'I mean, how did you arrive here – by bus or train – and how did you get into the grounds?'

Chinky gave the others a sharp nudge. Mollie had just been going to say that they had come in their Wishing-Chair, but she shut her mouth again tightly. Of course she mustn't give that away! Why, Mister Grim would search the grounds and find it!

'Well?' said Mister Grim. 'I am asking you a question – and when I ask questions I expect them to be answered.'

Still no reply from any of the three. Mister Grim leaned forward. 'Shall I tell you how you came? You must have friends here among the brownies – and they helped you to climb the wall, and told you to take the toys! Aha! Don't try to say you didn't do that.'

They didn't say a word. Mister Grim got up and put the toys back in the chest. 'You,' he said to Chinky, '*you* are a pixie, and I don't usually take pixies into my school. But you are a very bad pixie, I can see, and I shall keep you here. And I shall keep these two as well. I'm not sure what they are – but even if they are real, proper children, which I very much doubt, they deserve to be punished by being my pupils here for a term.'

'Oh, no!' said Mollie in horror. 'What will our mother say? You can't do that.'

'You will see,' said Mister Grim. 'Now go downstairs, find the brownie called Winks, and tell him you are to come into class when the bell rings. He will give you books and pencils and tell you where to sit.'

The three of them had to go downstairs in a row, Mister Grim behind them. They were frightened! Unless they could manage somehow to get to their Wishing-Chair, they would simply *have* to stay at Mister Grim's school!

They found Winks and told him quickly what had happened. He was very sorry. 'Bad luck!' he said. 'Very bad luck. Come on – I'll get you your books and things. Sit by me in class and I'll try and help you all I can.'

He took them into a big room and gave them books and pencils. Almost at once a bell rang loudly and all the brownies trooped in quickly. Not one of them spoke a word. They took their places quietly and waited.

'Why were you sent here, Winks?' whispered Chinky as they all waited for Mister Grim to appear.

'Because I used my grandmother's Blue Spell and turned all her pigs blue,' whispered back Winks.

'And I was sent here because I put a spell into my father's shoe-tongues and they were rude to him all the way down our street and back,' whispered Hoho.

'And I was sent because . . .' began another brownie, when slow and heavy footsteps were heard. In came Mister Grim and stood at his big desk.

'Sit!' he said, as if the brownies were all little dogs. They sat.

'We have three new pupils,' said Mister Grim. 'I regret to say that I caught them stealing – STEALING – from my storeroom. If I find out who helped them into this school and told them about the toys they came to steal, I shall take my stick to him. Brrrrrr!'

This was very frightening. Mollie didn't even dare to cry. She comforted herself by thinking of the Wishing-Chair hidden under the bush in the garden. They would run to it as soon as ever they could!

'Now we will have mental numbers,' said Mister Grim, and a little groan ran round the class. 'You, boy, what number is left when you take eighty-two and sixty-four from one hundred and three?'

He was pointing at poor Peter. Peter went red. What a silly question! You couldn't take eighty-two and sixty-four from one hundred and three.

'Say six hundred and fifty,' whispered Winks. 'He doesn't know the answer himself!'

'Six hundred and fifty,' said Peter boldly. Everyone clapped as if he were right.

'Er – very good,' said Mister Grim. Then he pointed to Mollie. 'How many pips are there in seven pounds of raspberry jam?'

'Seven pounds of raspberry jam?' repeated Mollie, wondering if she had heard aright. 'Er – well . . .'

'Say none at all, because your mother only makes raspberry jelly and strains the pips out,' whispered Winks.

'Er – none at all,' said Mollie.

'How do you make that out?' thundered Mister Grim in a very frightening voice.

'Because my mother makes raspberry jelly and strains all the pips out,' said Mollie. Everyone clapped again.

'Silence!' said Mister Grim. 'Now you, pixie – and see you are very, very careful in your answer. If I take fifty-two hairs from my beard, how many will there be left?'

Chinky stared desperately at the long beard that swept down to the floor. 'Well,' he began . . . and then Winks whispered to him.

'Say "the rest"!' he hissed.

'Er – well, the rest of the hair will be left,' he said.

Mister Grim suddenly pounded on the desk with his hand. 'You, Winks!' he shouted. 'I heard you whispering then – you told him the answer – and I believe you told the others the answers, too. Come here!

I'll give you the stick. Aha, you think because all my canes were broken that I haven't got one – but I have! You just wait.'

'Please, sir, I'm sorry,' said Winks. 'I just thought I'd help them as they were new. I was trying to be good, sir, and helpful, I really was. You're always telling us to be that, sir.'

'No excuses,' said Mister Grim, and he turned to a cupboard behind him. He unlocked it and took out a long, thin stick.

'Come up here, Winks,' he said, and poor Winks went up. He got two strokes on his hands. Mollie was very upset, but Hoho whispered, 'Don't worry – Winks always puts a little spell in his hands and he doesn't mind a bit if he's whacked. He doesn't feel it!'

Mollie felt comforted. Winks winked at her as he went back to his seat. Mister Grim went to take a book from a shelf – and as he turned his back Chinky clutched Peter by the elbow.

'Peter,' he hissed, 'do you see what his stick is? It's my WAND!'

Peter stared. Yes – the stick on the desk was Chinky's little wand. Oh, if only it had wings now and could fly to Chinky!

But it hadn't. Chinky never took his eyes off it as the class went on and on. 'I must get it,' he kept saying to himself. 'I MUST get it! But how can I? Oh, for a really good idea!'

82

XII

CHINKY IS NAUGHTY

Morning school came to an end at last. Mister Grim rapped on his desk with his stick – Chinky's wand!

'Attention, all of you!' he said. 'Dinner will be in ten minutes' time. Anyone who is late or who has dirty hands or untidy hair will go without.'

Winks groaned. 'It's awful,' he said to Peter when Mister Grim had gone out. 'There's never enough dinner for everyone, so Mister Grim just says, "Here, you, your hair is untidy," or "Here, you, your nails aren't clean," and about a dozen of us have to go without our dinner.'

'What a dreadful school!' said Peter. 'Why don't you run away?'

'How can we?' said Winks. 'You've seen the high wall round the grounds, and all the gates are locked. I wish I could get out of here; it's a horrid place, and I really would be good if I could escape.'

'Would there be room for him in the Wishing-Chair, do you think?' whispered Mollie to Chinky. 'He's so nice. I'd like to help him, Chinky.'

'So would I,' whispered back Chinky. 'Well, we'll see.'

Poor Chinky was one of those who had to go without

his dinner. Mister Grim stood at the door of the dining-hall as each brownie walked in. Every so often he pounced on one and roared at him.

'Here, you, you haven't washed behind your ears! No dinner! Here, you, why aren't your nails scrubbed? No dinner!' And when Chinky tried to slip past him he hit him hard on the shoulder with his hand and roared: 'Here, you, why haven't you brushed your hair? No dinner!'

'I did brush it,' said Chinky indignantly, 'but it's the kind of hair that won't lie down.'

'No dinner to-day for untidy hair, and no dinner to-morrow for answering back,' said Mister Grim.

'Oh, I say, that's not fair,' said Chinky.

'And no dinner for the third day for being rude,' said Mister Grim. 'Another word from you and I'll cane you with this new stick of mine!'

He slapped the wand down so hard on a nearby table that Chinky was afraid it would break in half. But fortunately it didn't.

Chinky went out of the room, looking angry and sulky. Horrid Mister Grim! He joined all the brownies who were also to go without their dinner.

Peter and Mollie were very sorry for Chinky. When the pudding came they tried to stuff two tarts into their pockets to take to him. But the pastry fell to pieces and their pockets were all jammy and horrid. Mister Grim saw the crumbs of pastry around their pockets as they marched past him after dinner. He tapped them with the wand.

'Aha! Trying to stuff food into your pockets. Greedy children! No dinner for you to-morrow!'

Peter tried to snatch the wand away from Mister Grim, hoping to run and give it to Chinky, but Mister Grim was too quick for him. Up in the air it went, and poor Peter got a stinging slash on his arm. Fortunately his sleeve was nice and thick, so he didn't feel it much.

'Bad boy!' roared Mister Grim. 'Stay in after school this afternoon and write out one thousand times "I must not snatch".'

There was a little time before afternoon school. Peter, Chinky, Mollie and Winks had a meeting in a far corner of the grounds.

'Winks, that's my wand Mister Grim has got and is using for a stick,' said Chinky.

Winks whistled. 'I *say*! That's a fine bit of news. We ought to be able to do something about that.'

'But what?' asked Chinky. 'I'm so afraid he will break my wand, and then it will be no use. Somehow or other we've got to get it back.'

'Now listen,' said Winks. 'A wand will never hit its owner, you know that. Well, what about being very naughty in class this afternoon and having to go up to Mister Grim to be punished – and your wand will refuse to cane you, of course – and surely you can easily get it back then, and do a bit of magic to get yourselves free?'

'Oooh, yes,' said Chinky, looking very cheerful. 'That's an awfully good idea of yours, Winks. I'd forgotten that a wand never turns against its owner. I'll be very naughty – and then we'll see what happens.'

They all went in to afternoon school feeling rather excited. What would happen? It would certainly be fun to see Chinky being very naughty, to begin with – and even greater fun to see the wand refusing to punish him!

Chinky began by yawning very loudly indeed. Mister Grim heard him and tapped hard on his desk with the wand – crack! crack!

'Chinky? You are most impolite. Stand up during the rest of the class instead of sitting.'

Chinky stood – but he stood with his back to Mister Grim.

Mister Grim glared. 'Bad pixie! You are being impolite again. Stand round the other way!'

Chinky immediately stood on his hands and waved his feet in the air. All the brownies laughed and clapped.

86

Mister Grim looked as black as thunder. 'Come here!' he cried, and Chinky began to walk towards him on his hands. He really looked very funny indeed. Winks laughed till the tears rolled down his cheeks.

But Mister Grim didn't try to cane him that time. He told him to go and stand in the corner – the right way up.

So Chinky stood in the corner the right way up, turning every now and then to grin at the others. Mister Grim began firing questions at the class. 'Hands up those who know why brownies have long beards. Hands up those who know the magic word for "disappear." Hands up those who know why green smoke always comes out of chimneys of witches' houses. Hands up . . .'

He didn't even wait for anyone to answer so the brownies just shot up their hands at each question and then put them down again and waited for the next. Peter and Mollie thought it was the silliest class they had ever attended!

'And now – can anyone ask me a question *I* can't answer?' said Mister Grim. 'Aha! It would take a clever brownie to do that! Be careful – because if I *can* answer it, you'll have to come up and be punished. Now, who will ask me a question I can't answer?'

The brownies had all been caught by this trick before, so nobody put up his hand.

Mister Grim pounced on poor Winks. 'You, brownie! Can't you think of a question?'

'Yes, sir,' said Winks at once. 'I'd like to know why gooseberries wear whiskers. Do they belong to the brownie family?'

Everybody roared at this ridiculous question. Except Mister Grim. He looked as grim as his name. He rapped with his stick on the desk.

'Come up here, Winks. I will not have you upsetting the class like this with your silly remarks.' And Winks went up, grinning. He got three strokes of the wand, but it didn't hurt him, of course, as he had still got the spell in his hands that prevented the stick from hurting him.

'I've got a question; I've got a question!' suddenly called out Chinky, seeing a chance to get his wand.

'What is it?' said Mister Grim, frowning.

'Mister Grim, why do horses wear hooves instead of feet?' cried Chinky.

'Come up here,' said Mister Grim sternly. 'That's another silly question.'

Chinky went. 'Hold out your hand,' said Mister Grim. Chinky held it out. Mister Grim brought down the wand as hard as he could – but, dear me, he missed Chinky's hand altogether. The wand simply slipped to one side and didn't touch Chinky's hand at all.

Mister Grim tried again – and again – and again – but each time the wand slid away from Chinky's outstretched hand and hit the desk instead. It was very puzzling indeed for Mister Grim.

The brownies were all laughing. So were Peter and Mollie. Mister Grim's face was so comical to watch as he tried to hit Chinky's hand and couldn't.

'I shall break this stick in two!' he cried suddenly in a rage.

That gave Chinky a shock. 'No,' he shouted. 'No, you mustn't do that! You mustn't!'

'Why not?' said Mister Grim, and he put both hands on the wand as if to break it.

Peter, Mollie and Chinky watched in despair, waiting for the crack.

But the wand wasn't going to let itself be broken! It slid out of Mister Grim's big hands and shot over to Chinky, who caught it as it came.

'Ha!' shouted Chinky in delight. 'I've got it again – my lovely wand – I've got it!'

'What! Is it a wand?' cried Mister Grim in astonishment. 'I didn't know that. Give it back to me!'

He snatched at it, but Chinky was skipping down the room, waving it.

'I'll give you all a half-holiday! Yes, I will! See my wand waving to give you all a half-holiday! Go into the garden and play, all of you!'

The brownies didn't wait. They rushed out of the room at top speed, shouting and laughing. Soon only Peter, Mollie and Chinky were left with Mister Grim. Winks was peeping round the door.

'How DARE you treat me like this!' shouted Mister Grim, marching towards Chinky. 'I'll – '

'Go back, go back!' chanted Chinky, and waved his wand at Mister Grim, whose feet at once took him six steps backwards, much to his surprise. 'You see, I've got magic in my wand,' cried the pixie. 'Aha! I may have powerful magic, Mister Grim, so be careful!'

'Come on, Chinky,' whispered Peter. 'Let's go and find the Wishing-Chair and fly off.'

'But I want my doll Rosebud before we go,' said Mollie. 'And have you forgotten your engine and all the other toys, Peter? We must take those with us. Mister Grim, give us our toys!'

'Certainly not,' said Mister Grim, and he shook a large key at them. 'See this key? It's the key of the storeroom, which I've locked. You can't get your toys and you never shall!'

'We'll see about that,' said Chinky. 'We'll just see about that, Mister Grim!'

XIII

HOME, WISHING-CHAIR, HOME!

Mister Grim stared angrily at Chinky, who was still waving his wand to keep the teacher from coming any nearer to him.

'You can't get your toys, so make up your mind about that,' he said. 'And stop waving that ridiculous wand. Its magic will soon run out.'

Chinky himself was a bit afraid that it would. It was a very new wand and hadn't very powerful magic in it yet. 'I think we'd better go before the wand's magic wears out,' he said in a low voice to Peter and Mollie.

They darted out of the door and Mister Grim followed. But just outside the door he ran into a crowd of brownies that popped up from nowhere quite suddenly, and over he went! When he got up the children and Chinky were nowhere to be seen.

He began to run down the garden again, but once more he tripped over a mass of brownies. They weren't a bit afraid of him now because Chinky had taken his stick – the wand!

Chinky and the others raced to find the Wishing-Chair. Where was the bush they had hidden it in? Ah, there it was! They ran to the bush – but, oh dear, the chair wasn't there!

'One of the brownies must have found it and taken it,' said Chinky. Just then Winks ran up and pulled at his arm.

'I found your Wishing-Chair and hid it in the shed,' he said. 'I was afraid Mister Grim might see it if he walked round the garden. Come along – I'll show you where it is.'

He took the three to an old broken-down shed. The roof had fallen in at one end. There were no windows to the shed, so it was very dark inside. Chinky groped his way in – and immediately fell over the Wishing-Chair. He felt the legs anxiously to see if the chair still had its wings. Yes – thank goodness – it had!

The wings waved gently as they felt Chinky's anxious hands. The chair creaked softly. Chinky knew it was glad to have him again.

'Wishing-Chair, we must go quickly,' said Chinky, and he climbed on to the seat. 'Come on, Peter and Mollie – quickly, before Mister Grim comes!'

'What about Winks? Aren't we going to take him, too?' said Mollie.

'Oh – would you really?' said Winks, in delight. 'You really are very kind. I hate this school. I've been trying to escape for ages.'

He was just about to squeeze in the chair with the others when somebody appeared at the doorway. It was Mister Grim!

'So here you are!' he said, peering in. 'All complete with a Wishing-Chair, too! I might have guessed that was how you came. Well, I'm going to lock this door, so you won't be able to fly out – and there are no windows at all!'

Winks leapt off the chair and ran to him. He tried to take the key from Mister Grim's hand, and the two struggled at the door.

'Fly out where the roof has fallen in, fly out there!' suddenly shouted Winks. 'The chair can just squeeze through it!'

And the chair rose up into the air and flew to where the roof had fallen in! It got stuck half-way through, but Peter broke away a bit more roof and the chair suddenly shot through and out into the open air.

'Oh, poor Winks – we've left him there,' cried Mollie, almost in tears. 'We can't leave him!'

'Go on, Chair, fly off with them!' shouted Winks from below in the shed. 'Don't mind me! Escape while you can.'

The chair flew out of hearing. Chinky and Peter were very silent. Mollie wiped her eyes with her hanky. 'I think you two should have taken the chair down and tried to help Winks,' she said. 'It was wrong of you to leave him.'

'We'll go back for him,' said Chinky, taking Mollie's hand. 'But, dear Mollie, you see we had *you* to think of, and both Peter and I know we have to look after you, because you're a girl. We had to think of you – didn't we, Peter?'

'Of course,' said Peter. 'You're my sister, Mollie, and you know that brothers must always look after their sisters. I couldn't possibly risk taking you down into danger again just then, when I knew Mister Grim was so angry. We'll go back for Winks, don't worry.'

'And what about our toys, too?' said Mollie, with a sniff. 'I think it's very nice of you both to want to take care of me like this – but I do feel so sorry for Winks, and it's dreadful to have to leave Rosebud behind, too.'

'And my engine,' said Peter, gloomily, 'and the skittles and soldiers.'

'We'll get them all back,' said Chinky, comfortingly. 'You wait and see.'

The chair took them back to the playroom, flapping its wings strongly. They really were beautiful big wings. Mollie was glad they were, because now that she and Peter had grown heavier she felt that the chair really did need to be stronger.

They arrived at the playroom and flew in at the door. The chair gave a creaking sort of sigh and set itself down in its place. Its wings at once vanished.

'There! Its wings have gone already,' said Mollie, ready to cry again. 'So now we can't go and rescue Winks to-day.'

'Well – that's a pity,' said Chinky. 'We shall just have to wait till its wings grow again. Anyway, it will give us time to make a plan for getting back our toys, too. That will be difficult, you know, because if the storeroom is locked and Mister Grim keeps the key on his key-ring, and carries it about with him, I don't see at present how we can rescue the toys.'

Mother's voice was heard calling down the garden. 'Children! It's past tea-time – and you didn't come in to dinner either. Where are you?'

'Oh, dear – now we shall have to go,' said Mollie. 'And we haven't planned anything. Chinky, come and tell us AT ONCE if the chair grows its wings again – and do, do try to think of a good plan.'

'Come and see me again to-night if you can,' called Chinky. 'I may have a visitor here who will help us.'

Mother called again, rather impatiently. The children fled. Fortunately, Mother seemed to think they had had a picnic lunch down in the playroom, and she didn't ask any difficult questions.

'I was sorry to send you out of the room this morning,' she said. 'Especially as I expect you were not really naughty, but just nervous, and so dropped the biscuits and the coffee. Never mind – I expect you were glad not to have to stay with my visitors!'

'We were rather,' said Mollie, honestly, 'and I expect *you* were glad we kept out of your way to-day, Mother, really.'

'Now have your tea,' said Mother.

The children wished that Chinky was with them. He had had to go without his dinner at Mister Grim's school, so he must be very hungry. Perhaps he would go out to tea with one of his pixie friends in the garden, and have a good meal.

'Now, Daddy and I are going out to-night,' said Mother, when they had finished. 'Put yourselves to bed at the right time, half an hour after your supper, and don't lie awake waiting for us, because we shall be very late.'

'Right, Mother,' said Peter, at once making up his mind to go down to the playroom after his supper, just before they went to bed. Chinky's visitor might be there, and it would be fun to see him. Chinky's visitors were always interesting, and sometimes very exciting.

Mother put on her lovely evening frock, and then she

and Daddy said good-bye and went. The children did some jobs that Mother had asked them to do, and then found that it was suppertime. Jane brought them in bananas cut into small slices, scattered with sugar, and covered with creamy milk.

'Oooh!' said Mollie. 'This is one of my favourite suppers.'

After supper they slipped down to the playroom. Chinky wasn't there. There was a note left on the table, though.

'Gone to have supper with Tickles. Felt very hungry after having no dinner. Be back later. Can you come and meet my visitor at half-past nine if you're not asleep? VERY IMPORTANT.
'Love from Chinky.'

'I know, Peter,' said Mollie, 'let's go to bed now, then we can slip out for half an hour and meet Chinky's visitor without feeling guilty. We simply must meet him if it's important.'

So they put themselves to bed half an hour earlier than usual.

Both children went to sleep – but Peter awoke at half-past nine because he had set the alarm clock for that time and put it under his pillow. When the alarm went off, muffled by the pillow, he awoke at once. He slipped on his dressing-gown and went to wake Mollie.

'Come on!' he whispered. 'It's half-past nine. Buck up!'

Mollie put on her dressing-gown, too, and the two of

them slipped out of the garden door and down to the playroom. They peeped in at the door. Yes – Chinky's visitor was there – but, dear me, what a very, very surprising one!

XIV

MISTER CUBBS'S STRANGE ARMY

Chinky saw the children peeping in. He got up from the sofa and called them. 'Hallo! I'm so glad you've come. Come along in. I've got an old friend here, and I want you to meet him.'

The old friend stood up – and what do you think he was? He was a tall teddy bear, so old that his hair had turned grey! He was not as tall as they were, but a bit taller than Chinky.

'This is Mister Cubbs, the ruler of Teddy Bear Village,' said Chinky. The teddy bear bowed politely, and shook hands. Everyone sat down, the children and Chinky on the sofa and the teddy bear in the Wishing-Chair.

'I hope you don't mind my sitting in your Wishing-Chair,' he said, politely, to the children. 'But it is really such a treat and a privilege. I have never even *seen* one before.'

'Not at all. We're very pleased,' said Peter. 'I only wish it would grow its wings, then it could take you for a short ride. It feels funny at first, but it's lovely when you get used to it.'

'I've been telling Mister Cubbs about your toys that Mister Grim has got, and won't give you back,' said Chinky.

'I think Mister Grim should be forced to give them up to you,' said Mister Cubbs earnestly. 'I propose that I raise a little army from Toyland and march on the school.'

Peter and Mollie gazed at him in wonder and astonishment. It all sounded like a dream to them – but a very exciting and interesting dream. An army from Toyland! Good gracious – whoever heard of such a thing?

'Mister Cubbs has very great influence in Toyland,' explained Chinky. 'As I told you, he is head of Teddy Bear Village and very much respected and admired. In fact, he has now ruled over it for nearly a hundred years.'

'Are you really a hundred years old!' asked Mollie, amazed.

'One hundred and fifty-three, to be exact,' said Mister Cubbs, with a polite little bow. 'I became head when I was fifty-four.'

'Is it difficult to be head of Teddy Bear Village?' asked Peter.

'Well, no – not really, so long as you are very firm with the *young* teddies,' said Mister Cubbs. 'They are rather wild, you know. Now, what I suggest is this. I will send to the wooden soldiers, the clockwork animals and the sailor dolls – and also my teddies, of course, and tell them to meet me at a certain place. They will make a very fine army.'

'And you'll march on the school, I suppose?' said Chinky. 'And when you have defeated Mister Grim you will rescue Rosebud, the doll, and the other toys?'

'Exactly,' said Mister Cubbs.

'Can we come, too?' said Peter, excited. 'I'd simply love to see all this.'

'If only the Wishing-Chair would grow its wings when your army is on the march, we could hover above the battle and watch,' said Mollie. 'But it never does grow its wings exactly when we want it to.'

'I'll send you word when we mean to march,' said the teddy bear. 'It will probably be to-morrow evening. Well, I must go now. Thank you for a very pleasant evening, Mister Chinky.'

He shook hands with all three of them and went out of the door.

'Isn't he nice?' said Chinky. 'He's a very old friend of my Great-Aunt Quick-Fingers, you know, and I've often met him at her house. I thought I'd tell him about Rosebud and the other toys, and how Mister Grim wouldn't give them back. I guessed he would help.'

The playroom clock struck ten. 'We must get back,' said Mollie, with a sigh. 'We only meant to come for half an hour. It's been lovely, Chinky. I do think we're lucky, having you for a friend, and meeting all your friends and having such an interesting time.'

They went back to bed, hoping that the Wishing-Chair would grow its wings the next night if the teddy bear gathered together his curious little army.

They couldn't go down to the playroom till after tea, because Mother took them to see their granny. They raced down as soon as they could and were met by a very excited Chinky.

'I'm so glad you've come. The Wishing-Chair has grown little buds of wings already – they'll sprout properly in a minute! And the teddy bear has sent to say that his army is on the march!'

'Oh – *what* a bit of luck!' cried the children, and ran to the chair. Just as they got to it the knoblike buds on its legs burst open – and out spread the lovely green and yellow wings again! They began to flap at once and made quite a wind.

'Come on,' said Peter, sitting in the chair. 'Let's go! And, Chinky, don't let's forget to take Winks away from that horrid school, if we can. He can live with you here in the playroom if he hasn't got a home to go to.'

Mollie got in and Chinky sat on the back of the chair. Out of the door they flew at top speed.

The Wishing-Chair was told to go to Mister Grim's. 'But *don't* go down into the grounds,' commanded Chinky. 'Just hover about somewhere so that we can see what's going on, and can dart down if we need to.'

It wasn't really very long before the chair was hovering over the front gate of Mister Grim's school. Not far off were all the brownies, marching up and down in the big school yard, doing drill with Mister Grim.

Then the marching brownies suddenly caught sight of the Wishing-Chair hovering in the air, and they set up a great shout.

'Look! They've come back! Hurrah for Chinky and Peter and Mollie!'

Mister Grim stared up, too. He looked really furious, and, to the children's dismay, he bent down and picked up a big stone. It came whizzing through the air at them, but the Wishing-Chair did a little leap to one side and the stone passed harmlessly by.

Then Chinky gave the others a nudge. 'Here comes the army! DO look!'

The children looked – and, dear me, up the lane marched the strangest little army the children had ever imagined. First came the grey-haired teddy bear, swinging a little sword. Then came a row of wooden soldiers, beating drums. Then another row blowing trumpets. After them came a whole collection of clockwork animals.

'There's a jumping kangaroo!' cried Chinky in glee. 'And a dancing bear!'

'And a running dog – and a walking elephant!' said Mollie in delight.

'And look – a pig that turns head-over-heels, and a duck that waddles!' shouted Peter, almost falling out of the chair in his excitement. 'And behind them all are the sailor dolls. Don't they look smart!'

The strange army came to the gate. The clockwork kangaroo jumped right over it to the other side. He undid the gate and opened it for the army to walk through.

The brownies saw the toys before Mister Grim did and shouted in joy. They ran to meet them. 'Who are you? Where have you come from?' they called. 'Can we play with you? We never have any toys here!'

> 'We've come for Mister Grim,
> We don't like Mister Grim,
> We've come to capture him,
> We've come for Mister Grim!'

chanted all the toys.

Mister Grim stared at them as if he couldn't believe his eyes. 'After him!' shouted the teddy bear, and after him they went! He turned to run – but the jumping kangaroo got between his legs and tripped him up, and there he was, bumping his nose on the ground, yelling for mercy!

The toys swarmed all over him in delight.

'Don't pull my hair! Don't cut off my beautiful beard,' begged Mister Grim. The teddy bear seemed just about to saw the long beard off with his sword! The children and Chinky saw it all from their seat up in the Wishing-Chair and were just as excited as the toys and the brownies.

'I'll leave you your beard on one condition,' said the teddy bear, solemnly. 'Go and get the toys you have imprisoned here and bring them out to us.'

Mister Grim got up, looking very frightened, and went indoors.

He came out with all the toys. Mollie gave a scream of delight when she saw Rosebud.

'He's even got the teapot that grew wings, too,' said Peter, pleased. The chair flew down to Mister Grim, and the children took all their toys from him. Mollie cuddled Rosebud happily.

'Thank you,' she said to the grey-haired teddy bear. 'You and your army have done very, very well. Do please bring any of them to see us whenever you can.'

The brownies crowded round the chair. 'Take us back with you, take us back.'

'We've only room for one of you, and that's Winks,' said Chinky, firmly. 'Come on, Winks.'

Up got Winks, grinning all over his little brownie

face. The Wishing-Chair rose up in the air. 'Good-bye, good-bye!' shouted Chinky and the others. 'Let us know if Mister Grim behaves too badly to you and we'll send the army once again! Good-bye!'

Off they went, with all the toys and brownies waving madly. Mister Grim didn't wave. He looked very down in the mouth indeed – but nobody was sorry for him, not even Mollie!

XV

OFF TO THE LAND OF GOODIES!

The summer days went on and on. The Wishing-Chair seemed to have had enough of adventures for a time, and stayed quietly in its corner, without sprouting so much as one wing.

One day Chinky came tapping at the children's window. They came to it at once.

'Has the Wishing-Chair grown its wings again?' asked Peter, in excitement. Chinky shook his head.

'No. I haven't come to tell you that. I've just come to show you this.'

He pushed a piece of paper into their hands. This is what it said:

'DEAR COUSIN CHINKY,

'You haven't been to see my new house yet, so do come. I expect you have heard that I have moved to the Land of Goodies. It's simply lovely. Do come and see me soon. I have a biscuit tree growing in my garden, just coming into fruit, and a jelly plant growing round my front door.
'Yours ever,
'PIPKIN.'

* ★ ★ ★

'Well! Does your cousin *really* live there?' said Mollie, in wonder. 'How lucky you are, Chinky. Now you can go and eat as many goodies as you like. I only wish we could come too.'

'I came to ask if you'd like to go with me,' said Chinky. 'My cousin Pipkin won't mind. He's a very nice fellow, though I always thought he was a bit greedy. I expect that's why he bought a house in the Land of Goodies really – so that he could always have lots of things to eat. Why, if you pass a hedge you'll probably see that it's growing bars of chocolate.'

This sounded so exciting that the children felt they wanted to go at once.

'We can't,' said Chinky. 'We'll have to wait for the Wishing-Chair to grow its wings again. The Land of Goodies is too far unless we go by Wishing-Chair.'

'How disappointing!' said Mollie. 'I feel awfully hungry even at the thought of going. What about Winks, Chinky? Is he coming, too?'

Winks had come back with them to the playroom, and had stayed a night with Chinky, and then gone to tell his people that he wasn't going back to Mister Grim's again. He meant to bring back some of his things with him, and spend some of the time with Chinky in the playroom and some with his other friends. He was very pleased indeed at being free.

'Winks can come if he's back in time,' said Chinky. 'I don't know where he is at the moment. He's really rather naughty, you know, although he's nice, and very good fun. I hear that he met my Cousin Sleep-Alone

106

the other evening and, as soon as poor old Sleep-Alone was fast asleep in a little shed in the middle of a field, Winks took along two donkeys that had lost themselves and told them to cuddle up to Sleep-Alone.'

'Oh, dear – what happened?' said Mollie.

'Well, Sleep-Alone woke up, of course, and tried to throw the donkeys out,' said Chinky, 'but one of them gave him such a kick with its hind legs that he flew into the clouds, got caught on a big one, and hung there for a long time.'

'Well, it would certainly be a good place to sleep alone in,' said Mollie. 'What a monkey Winks is!'

'Yes. I'm not surprised really that his family sent him to Mister Grim's school,' said Chinky. 'Well, will you come with me to the Land of Goodies, then?'

'Of *course*,' said the children. 'You needn't ask us that again.'

The next day was rainy. The children went down to the playroom as usual, but Mother made them take a big umbrella to walk under. 'It really is such a downpour,' she said.

They shook the raindrops off the umbrella as soon as they reached the playroom door. Chinky's voice came to them, raised in joy. 'Is that you, Mollie and Peter? The Wishing-Chair has *just* grown its wings.'

'Oh, good!' cried Mollie, and ran in. Sure enough the chair was already waving its green and yellow wings.

'But it's pouring with rain,' said Peter, looking in at the door as he struggled to put down the big umbrella. 'We shall get soaked if we go miles through this rain.'

'We'll take the umbrella,' said Mollie. 'It will cover all three of us easily.'

'*Four* of us,' said Winks, and he popped out of the cupboard and grinned at them. 'I've come back for a day or two. I hid in the cupboard in case it was your mother or somebody coming.'

'Oh, Winks, I'm so glad you're coming, too,' said Mollie. 'Can we go now, this very minute, Chinky?'

'I don't see why not,' said Chinky. 'Don't put down that umbrella, Peter; we'll come now and you can hold it over us as we fly.'

So very soon all four were sitting in the Wishing-Chair, flying through the rain. Peter held the big umbrella over them, and although their legs got a bit wet, the rest of them was quite dry.

'It's quite a long journey, so I hope the chair will fly fast,' said Chinky. 'It will be a bit dull because the rain clouds stop us from seeing anything.'

The chair suddenly began to rise high. It went right through the purple-grey clouds, higher and higher and higher – and then at last it was through the very last of them, and the children found themselves far above the topmost clouds, full in the blazing sun!

'Well,' said Peter, trying to shut the umbrella, 'what a brainy idea of yours, Wishing-Chair. Now we shall soon be warm and dry again. Blow this umbrella! I simply *can't* shut it.'

So it had to remain open; and, as it happened, it was a very good thing it did, because Winks tried to catch a swallow going past at sixty miles an hour, and overbalanced out of the chair! He clutched at the umbrella as he fell and down he went, with the umbrella acting just like a parachute!

'Very clever of you, Winks!' said Chinky, as the chair swooped down and hovered by the umbrella for Winks to climb on to the seat again. 'I hope you only do this sort of thing when there's an open umbrella to catch hold of!'

Winks looked rather pale. He sat panting on the seat. 'I got a fright,' he said. 'I really did.'

'Well, don't be frightened if you do fall,' said Mollie. 'Do what Chinky did when he once fell! He changed himself into a large snow-flake and fell gently to earth! He hadn't even a bruise when he changed back to himself again.'

'Very clever. I must remember that,' said Winks. 'I say, doesn't this Wishing-Chair fly fast?'

It certainly did. It flew even faster than the swallows, and passed over miles and miles of country, which lay spread out like a coloured map far below. The children caught glimpses of it through openings in the clouds.

'What's your cousin Pipkin like?' asked Mollie.

'Well, he was a bit plump,' said Chinky. 'And I expect he's plumper still now that he lives in the Land of Goodies. He's very generous and kind, though he's rather greedy, too. He could easily beat Mollie at eating ice-creams.'

'Could he really?' said Mollie. 'Oh, look, Chinky – we're going downwards. Are we there?'

They went down and down through layers of clouds. When they came below them they found that the rain had stopped. Chinky peered down.

'Yes – we're there. Now just remember this, all of you – you can eat whatever is growing on bushes, hedges, or trees, but you mustn't eat anybody's house.'

Peter and Mollie stared at him in wonder. *'Eat* anybody's house! Are the houses made of eatable things, then?'

'Good gracious, yes,' said Chinky. 'Everything is eatable in the Land of Goodies – even the chimneys! They are usually made of marzipan.'

The Wishing-Chair landed on the ground. The children jumped off quickly, anxious to see this wonderful land. They looked around.

Mollie's eyes grew wide. 'Look – look, Peter – there's a bush growing currant buns. It is really. And look, there's a hedge with a funny-looking fruit – it's bars of chocolate!'

'And look at that house!' cried Peter. 'It's all decorated with icing sugar – isn't it pretty? And it's got little silver balls here and there in its walls – and all down its front door too.'

'Look at these funny flowers in the grass!' cried Mollie. 'I do believe they are jam tarts! Chinky, can I pick one?'

'Pick a whole bunch if you like,' said Chinky. 'They're growing wild.'

Mollie picked two. 'One's got a yellow middle – it's lemon curd – and the other's got a red middle – it's raspberry jam,' she said, tasting them.

'Better come and find my cousin Pipkin,' said Chinky. 'We're not supposed to come to the Land of

Goodies except by invitation, so we'd better find him, so that he can say we are his guests. We don't want to be turned out before we've picked a nice bunch of jam tarts, currant buns and chocolate biscuits!'

Chinky asked a passer-by where his cousin Pipkin lived. Luckily, it was very near. They hurried along till they came to a kind of bungalow. It was round and its roof was quite flat.

'Why, it's built the shape of a cake!' cried Mollie. 'And look, it's got cherries sticking out of the walls – and aren't those nuts on the roof – sticking up like they do in some cakes? Oh, Chinky, I believe your cousin lives in a cakehouse!'

'Well, he won't need to do much shopping then,' said Chinky, with a grin. 'He can just stay indoors and nibble at his walls!'

They went in at a gate that looked as if it were made of barley sugar. Chinky knocked at the door. It was opened by a very, very fat pixie indeed! He fell on Chinky in delight, almost knocked him over, and kissed him soundly on his cheek.

'Cousin Chinky! You've come to see me after all!' he cried. 'And who are these nice people with you?'

'Mollie and Peter and Winks,' said Chinky.

'Glad to meet you,' said Pipkin. 'Now – how would you like to see my Biscuit Tree to begin with? And after that we'll go for a nice hungry walk, and see what we can find!'

XVI

AN AFTERNOON WITH
COUSIN PIPKIN

Pipkin took them to see his Biscuit Tree. This was really marvellous. It had buds that opened out into brown biscuits – chocolate ones! There they hung on the tree, looking most delicious.

'Pick as many as you like,' said Pipkin, generously. 'It goes on flowering for months.'

'Aren't you lucky to have a Chocolate Biscuit Tree,' said Mollie, picking two or three biscuits and eating them.

'Well – it's not so good when the sun is really hot,' said Pipkin. 'The chocolate melts then, you know. It was most annoying the other afternoon. It was very hot and I sat down under my Biscuit Tree for shade – and I fell asleep. The sun melted the chocolate on the biscuits and it all dripped over me, from top to bottom. I *was* a sight when I got up!'

Everyone laughed. They ate a lot of the biscuits and then Mollie remembered something else.

'You said in your letter to Chinky that you had a jelly plant,' said Mollie. 'Could we see that, too?'

Pipkin led the way round to his front door. Then the children saw something they had not noticed when they had first arrived. A climbing plant trailed over the door.

It had curious big, flat flowers, shaped like white plates.

'The middle of the white flowers is full of coloured jelly!' cried Mollie. 'Gracious – you want to walk about with spoons and forks hanging at your belt in this land!'

'Well, we do, usually,' said Pipkin. 'I'll get you a spoon each – then you can taste the jelly in my jelly plant.'

It was really lovely jelly. 'I should like to eat two or three,' said Mollie, 'but I do so want to leave room for something else. Can we go for a walk now, Pipkin?'

'Certainly,' said Pipkin. So off they went, each carrying a spoon. It was a most exciting walk. They picked bunches of boiled sweets growing on a hedge like grapes, they came to a stream that ran ginger-beer instead of water and they actually found meat-pies growing on a bush.

The ginger-beer was lovely, but as they had no glasses they had to lie down and lap like dogs. 'I should have remembered to bring one or two enamel mugs,' said Pipkin. 'We shall pass a lemonade stream soon.'

'Is any ice-cream growing anywhere?' asked Mollie longingly.

'Oh, yes,' said Pipkin. 'But you'll have to go down into the cool valley for that. It's too hot here in the sun – the ice-cream melts as soon as it comes into flower.'

'Where's the valley?' said Mollie. 'Oh – down there. I'm going there, then.'

Mollie found a sturdy-stemmed plant with flat green leaves, in the middle of which grew pink, brown or yellow buds, shaped like cornets.

'Ice-creams!' cried Mollie, and picked one. 'Oooh! This is a vanilla one. I shall pick a pink flower next and that will be strawberry.'

'I've got a chocolate ice,' said Peter.

Pipkin and Chinky ate as many as the others. Chinky could quite well see why his cousin had grown so fat. Anyone would, in the Land of Goodies. He felt rather fat himself!

'Now let's go to the village,' said Pipkin. 'I'm sure you'd all like to see the food in the shops there, really delicious.'

'Is there tomato soup?' asked Peter; it was his very favourite soup.

'I'll take you to the soup shop,' said Pipkin, and he did. It was a most exciting shop. It had a row of taps in it, all marked with names – such as tomato, potato, chicken, onion, pea – and you chose which you wanted to turn, and out came soup – tomato, chicken, or whatever you wanted!

'There isn't the soup *I* like best,' said Winks, sadly. 'I like pepper soup.'

'You don't!' said Chinky. 'It would be terribly, terribly hot.'

'Well, I like it – and there isn't any,' said Winks.

'There's a tap over there without any name,' said Pipkin. 'It will produce whatever soup you want that isn't here.'

He took a soup-plate and went to the tap without a name. 'Pepper soup,' he said, and a stream of hot soup came out, red in colour.

'There you are, *red* pepper soup,' he said, and handed

it to Winks. 'Now we'll see if it really is your favourite soup or not!'

''Course it is!' said Winks, and took a large spoonful. But, oh dear, oh dear, how he choked and how he spluttered! He had to be banged on the back, and had to be given a drink of cold water.

'It serves you right for saying what isn't true,' Mollie said to Winks. 'You didn't like pepper soup, so you shouldn't have asked for any.'

'I was just being funny,' said poor Winks.

'Well, *we* thought it was all very funny, especially when you took that spoonful,' said Peter. 'Now – can I get you a little mustard soup, Winks?'

But Winks had had enough of soups. 'Let's leave this soup shop,' he said. 'What's in the next one?'

The next one was a baker's shop. There were iced cakes of all shapes and colours set in rows upon rows. How delicious they looked!

'Wouldn't you each like to take one home with you?' said Pipkin. 'You don't have to pay for them, you know.'

That was one of the nice things about the Land of Goodies. Nobody paid anyone anything. Mollie looked at the cakes. There was a blue one there, with yellow trimmings of icing sugar. Mollie had never seen a blue cake before.

'Can I have this one, do you think?' she said.

The baker looked at her. He was as plump as Pipkin and had a little wife as plump as himself. Their dark eyes looked like currants in their round little faces.

'Yes, you can have that,' said the baker. 'What is your name, please?'

'Mollie,' said Mollie. 'Why do you want to know?'

'Well, it's to be *your* cake, isn't it?' said the baker. He dabbed the cake and suddenly in the very middle of the icing came the letters MOLLIE – Mollie! Now it really was Mollie's cake.

Peter had one with his name, and Pipkin had another. Chinky chose a pretty pink cake and his name came up in white icing sugar.

Winks' name came up spelt wrongly. The letters were WINXS, and Peter pointed out that that was not the right way to spell his name. Winks hadn't noticed. He was a very bad speller. But Peter noticed it, and Winks chose another cake on which his name appeared spelt rightly. It was all very strange indeed.

'Well, Pipkin, thank you very much for a most interesting and delicious afternoon,' said Chinky, when they each had a cake to take home. 'How I'm going to eat this cake I really don't know. Actually I don't feel as if I could ever eat *any*thing again.'

They came to Pipkin's house and said good-bye to him. Then they went off to find their Wishing-Chair. Winks lagged behind, nibbling his cake. The others hurried on. They knew exactly where they had left the chair.

Suddenly they heard Chinky give a loud cry of anger. 'Look! Winks is doing JUST what I said nobody was to do! He's breaking off bits of gateposts to chew – and look, he's taken a bit of window-sill – it's made of gingerbread! And now he's throwing currant buns at that marzipan chimney to try to break it off!'

So he was! Poor Winks – he simply couldn't change from a bad brownie to a good one all at once. He was tired of being good and now he was being thoroughly naughty.

Crash! Down came the chimney, and Winks ran to it to break off bits of marzipan. And round the corner came two policemen! They had heard the crash and come to see what it was. When they saw Winks they blew their whistles loudly and ran up to him.

'Well – he's really got himself into trouble again now,' said Chinky. 'Isn't he silly?'

Winks was struggling hard with the two policemen. He called out to Chinky. 'Save me, Chinky, save me! Mollie, Peter, come and help!'

'Oho!' said the bigger policeman of the two. 'Are they

your friends? We'll catch them, too! No doubt they are as bad as you.'

'Quick! We must get in the Wishing-Chair and go!' said Chinky. 'Winks will always get into trouble wherever he goes – but there's no need for us to as well. Where's the Wishing-Chair?'

They found it where they had left it, hidden well away under a bush. They climbed in, with Chinky at the back, just as the big policeman came pounding up.

'Hey! What's all this?' he called. 'Is that chair yours?'

'YES!' shouted Chinky. 'It is. Home, Chair, home. Good-bye, Winks. Say you're sorry for what you've done and maybe you'll be set free.'

Off went the chair, high into the air, leaving the big policeman gaping in surprise. He had never seen a Wishing-Chair before. They were soon out of sight.

That night, when the three of them were playing Snap in the playroom, the door opened cautiously – and who should come in but Winks! The others exclaimed in surprise.

'Winks! You didn't get put into prison, then?'

'Yes,' said Winks. 'But the walls were made of chocolate cake – so I just ate my way through and got out easily. But, oh dear – I feel as if I never want to taste chocolate cake again! What is for supper?'

'CHOCOLATE CAKE,' roared everyone in delight, and Winks fled out into the night. No – he simply could not face chocolate cake again.

XVII

A MOST ALARMING TALE

For a week Chinky didn't see the children because they had gone to the seaside. They gave him all kinds of advice before they went.

'Now you see that you keep an eye on the Wishing-Chair for us, won't you?' said Peter. 'And if it grows its wings, don't you go on adventures without us. And DON'T let Winks have the chair at all. I like Winks, and he's good fun, but he's dreadfully naughty. I shouldn't be a bit surprised if he isn't sent back to Mister Grim's school again some day.'

'I know. I caught him practising magic with my wand last night,' said Chinky. 'He was trying to change the teapot into a rabbit. Silly thing to do.'

'Yes, very,' said Mollie. 'You can't pour tea out of a rabbit. Now you be sure to keep an eye on Winks, Chinky.'

'And don't sleep with the door or window open at night, in case the chair grows its wings when you're asleep and flies off by itself,' said Peter.

'Oh dear – it's so hot now,' said poor Chinky. 'It's dreadful to have to sleep with the doors and windows shut. I've been tying the chair to my leg, so that if it does try to fly off, it will tug at my leg and wake

119

me. Isn't that all right? I thought it was a very good idea.'

'Yes, it is,' said Peter. 'Well, so long as you remember to tie your leg and the chair's leg together at night, you can sleep with the door and windows open.'

'But watch that nobody slips in to steal the chair,' said Mollie.

Chinky began to look very worried. 'I'm beginning to feel you'd better not go away,' he said. 'Anyway, don't I always look after the chair at night for you? Nothing has ever happened to it yet!'

The others laughed. 'We're being fussy, aren't we!' they said. 'Good-bye, Chinky, dear. A week will soon go, so don't be too lonely. I expect Winks will be popping in and out to see you.'

The children had a lovely week at the seaside and came back browner than ever. As soon as Mother would let them they rushed down to the playroom to see Chinky.

He wasn't there, so they looked for a note. There wasn't one. 'Well, he's probably just gone out for a few minutes to see a friend,' said Peter. 'We'll hang up the seaweed we've brought, and tidy up the room.'

So they spent a happy ten minutes nailing up the long fronds of seaweed they had brought back, and tidying up their playroom, which seemed to have got very untidy whilst they had been away.

'It's funny Chinky hasn't kept it tidier than this,' said Mollie, pulling the rugs straight, and putting a chair upright.

Then she suddenly gave a cry. '*Peter!* Where's the Wishing-Chair? It isn't here!'

120

Peter looked round, startled. 'Well! Fancy us not noticing that as soon as we came in! Where is it?'

'I suppose Chinky's gone off in it,' said Mollie. 'He might have left a note! I suppose he's at his mother's.'

'He'll soon be back then,' said Peter, going to the door and looking out. 'He knew this was the day we were coming home.'

But Chinky didn't come, and by the time teatime came the children felt rather worried. Surely Chinky would have been back to tea on the day they came home? He always liked to spend every minute with them that he could, especially now that they had to go to boarding-school and leave him for months at a time.

They had brought their tea down to the playroom. They were sitting having it, rather solemnly, when a small mischievous face looked round the door. It was Winks.

'Hallo!' he said, but he didn't smile. He looked very grave and walked in quietly.

'Where's Chinky?' asked Mollie at once.

'And where's the Wishing-Chair?' said Peter.

'An awful thing happened two nights ago,' said Winks. 'I hardly like to tell you.'

This was most alarming. The children stared at Winks in dismay. 'For goodness' sake tell us,' said Mollie.

'Well,' said Winks, 'I was staying here with Chinky that night. I was to sleep on that rug on the floor with a cushion, and Chinky was to sleep on the sofa as usual. When we were tired we got ready for bed.'

'Go on,' said Peter, impatiently. 'I want to know what's happened to Chinky.'

'I went to sleep,' said Winks, 'and I suppose Chinky did, too. I suddenly woke up to hear a terrible noise going on – Chinky shouting and yelling, and furniture being upset and goodness knows what. I put on the light, and what do you think had happened? Why, you know Chinky always ties a rope from the chair to his foot, don't you – well, the chair grew its wings that night and we didn't wake – so it tried to fly out of the door all by itself, and –'

'The rope pulled on Chinky's foot and woke him!' said Peter.

'Yes, the chair pulled him right off the sofa,' said Winks. 'He must have landed with an awful bump on the floor, and I suppose he thought someone had pulled him off and there was an enemy attacking him – so he was fighting the furniture and the rugs and shouting and yelling – and all the time the chair was tugging at his foot, trying to fly off!'

'Gracious!' said Mollie. 'What happened in the end?'

'Well, when I put the light on I saw the chair struggling to get out of the door, and it was dragging Chinky along,' said Winks. 'I ran to stop the chair, but it rose into the air, dragged poor Chinky out into the garden, and flew up into the sky!'

'What about Chinky?' asked Mollie in a trembling voice.

'Oh, Mollie – poor, poor Chinky had to go, too, hanging upside-down by one foot,' said Winks blinking away tears. 'I couldn't do anything about it, though I did try to catch hold of Chinky. But he was too high up by that time.'

'This is awful,' said Mollie. 'Whatever are we to do? Has the chair gone to his mother's, do you think?'

'No. I thought of that,' said Winks. 'I went next day to see, but Chinky's mother said she hadn't seen either Chinky *or* the chair. She's very worried.'

'But *why* didn't the chair go to Chinkey's mother?' wondered Peter. 'Chinky would have been sure to yell out to it to go there.'

'Well, I think the chair was frightened,' said Winks. 'It didn't know it had got Chinky by the foot, you see. It couldn't understand all the yelling and struggling. It just shot off into the night, terrified.'

'This is awfully bad news,' said Mollie. 'Both Chinky *and* the chair gone. And we don't know where. How can we find out?'

'I don't know,' said Winks, who looked very tired. 'I've been all over the place, asking and asking.'

'Poor Winks,' said Mollie. 'You do look very tired. I suppose you've been worried to death about Chinky.'

'Yes, I have,' said Winks. 'You see, I've been teasing him rather a lot – and I hid his wand and made him cross – and I broke a cup – and now I feel awfully sorry I was such a nuisance to him.'

'You're really not very good at times, Winks,' said Peter, sternly. 'You ought to be careful, in case you get sent back to Mister Grim.'

'Yes, I know,' said Winks.

'The awful part is, even when we do find out, if ever

123

we do, we haven't got the Wishing-Chair to fly off in to rescue him,' said Peter, gloomily.

'Shall we go and ask Mr. Spells if he can help us?' said Mollie, suddenly. 'He's awfully clever. He might think of some way of finding out where Chinky's gone.'

'Yes – that's a very good idea,' said Peter. 'You've heard about Mr. Spells, haven't you, Winks? Shall we go straight away now? I think I remember the way. We have to go to the Village of Pin first, and then take the bus, and then a boat.'

'Yes,' said Winks, cheering up. 'I feel much better since I've talked to you.'

They set off. Down the garden they went, and through the gap in the hedge. Into the field, and across to find the dark patch of grass. It was still there. They all sat down in it and Mollie felt about for the little knob that set the magic going.

She found it and pressed it. Down shot the ring of grass, much too fast, and they all tumbled off in a heap below. 'Gracious!' said Winks. 'You might have warned me what was going to happen. I nearly died of fright when the earth fell away beneath me!'

'Come on,' said Peter. 'We have to go down this passage now – past all these doors. We really *must* find Mr. Spells as soon as possible.'

They went on down the twisting passage, which was still lighted clearly by some light nobody could see. Winks wanted to stop and read the names on each door.

'"Dame Handy-Pandy",' he said. 'Whoever is she? And this name says "Mr. Piggle-Pie." Oh, let's knock and see what he's like.'

'Winks! Come along at once,' said Mollie. 'We're in a hurry!'

'Wait!' cried Winks. 'Look at this door! Look at the name. Hey, Mollie. Peter – it says "MRS. SPELLS!" Do you think she's anything to do with *Mr.* Spells? Let's find out.'

And he banged hard at the little green door. 'RATTA-TATTA-TAT!' Oh, Winks – now what have you done?

XVIII

MR. SPELLS' MOTHER

RATTA-TATTA-TAT!

The echo of Winks' knocking at Mrs. Spells' door filled the underground passage and made the children jump. They turned round angrily.

'Winks! You shouldn't do that!'

'But I tell you, it says *"MRS.* Spells" on this name-plate,' began Winks. Just then the door opened and a black cat stood politely there, with a little apron round its tubby waist.

'If you've brought the papers, please don't knock so loudly again,' said the cat, politely but crossly. 'We were in the middle of a spell, and you made my mistress upset half of it. Now we've made a spell to make things small instead of big. It's most annoying.' He slammed the door, almost hitting Winks' nose. The children came running up, Peter calling out breathlessly:

'I say! I do believe that was old Cinders, Mr. Spells' cat! He had such enormous green eyes – like green traffic lights shining out!'

'Was it really?' said Mollie. 'Well, let's ask him if he is. Why, Mr. Spells might be here himself! It would save us quite a long journey.'

126

'Dare we knock again?' said Peter. 'That cat was really very cross.'

'I'm not afraid of a cross cat!' said Winks boldly, and he lifted the knocker and knocked again. He also found a bell and rang that, too.

'RATTA-TATTA-TAT! JINGLE-JANGLE-JING!'

Mr. Piggle-Pie's door flew open and a cross voice called, 'Who's making that row? Just wait till I get dressed and I'll come and chase you!'

'That must have been Mr. Piggle-Pie,' said Winks. 'Bother! He's shut his door again. Now I shan't know what he's like!'

Then Mrs. Spells' door flew open, and the cat appeared again. But this time it behaved much more like a real cat. It spat at Winks and scratched him on the hand.

It was just about to shut the door again when Peter called out, 'I say, aren't you Cinders?'

The cat stared at him. 'Yes, I'm Cinders. Oh, I remember you. You're the boy who came with a girl to rescue Chinky – and I helped my master do a spell to wake him up. What are you doing here, hammering at our door?'

'Well, we were really on our way to see Mr. Spells,' said Peter. 'But Winks here noticed the name "Mrs. Spells" on the door, and he knocked. He thought she might be some relation to Mr. Spells.'

'She is. She's his mother,' said Cinders. 'I came here to help the old lady with a new spell – the one you spoilt by making her jump. My master is coming to call for me in a few minutes.'

127

'Oh, *is* he?' cried Peter joyfully. 'Then do you think we might stay and see him – we do so badly want his help.'

'Well, come in, then,' said the cat. 'I don't know about this brownie though – Winks, do you call him? Banging and ringing like that. You wait till Mr. Piggle-Pie is dressed and comes after him. He'll get such a spanking.'

'I don't want to stay out in the passage,' said Winks, nervously. 'I'll be very good and quiet and helpful if you'll let me come in.'

'Who is it standing gossiping at the door?' suddenly called an annoyed voice. 'Tell them either to go or to come in.'

'You'd better come in and wait for Mr. Spells,' said Cinders. So they all trooped in and Cinders shut the door. Winks was quite glad to be out of the passage, away from a possibly furious Mr. Piggle-Pie.

The cat led them into a remarkably big room, with three windows. The children were so astonished to see what the windows looked out on that they quite forgot their manners for the moment, and didn't greet the bent old lady who sat in a chair in the middle of the room.

One window looked out on the sea! Yes, the sea, as blue as could be! Another looked out on a sunny hillside. The third looked out on an ordinary backyard, where washing was blowing in the wind. Most extraordinary.

'Well!' said rather a peevish voice, 'have the children of to-day no manners at all? Can't you even say how do you do to an old lady?'

128

'Oh, dear,' said Mollie, ashamed of herself. 'Please, Mrs. Spells, I'm so sorry – do forgive us – but it did seem so extraordinary seeing three windows like this – in an underground room – and one looking out on the sea, too. Why, I thought the sea was miles and miles away!'

'Things aren't always what they seem,' said Mrs. Spells. 'What is miles away for you, may be quite near for me. Now, what was all this noise about at my front door? When I was younger I would have turned you all into pattering mice and given you to Cinders, for making a noise of that sort in a respectable place like this!'

'Madam,' said the cat, seeing that the old lady was working herself up into a temper, 'Madam, these children know Mr. Spells, your son.'

The old lady beamed at once. 'Oh, do you know my son? Why didn't you tell me that at once? Cinders, some strawberryade, please, with strawberry ice, and some strawberry biscuits.'

This sounded exciting – and when it came, beautifully arranged on a large silver tray by Cinders, it was just as exciting as it sounded!

It was a pink drink made of strawberry juice. In it were pieces of ice shaped like strawberries, and the biscuit had tiny sugar strawberries in the middle!

'This is lovely,' said Peter. 'Thank you very much.'

There came the sound of a key in the door. 'Ah – my son, Mr. Spells!' said Mrs. Spells. 'Here he is!'

And there he was again, just the same as before, tall and commanding, but this time dressed in a long green

129

cloak that shimmered like water. He looked very surprised indeed to see the visitors.

'Why – I've seen you before!' he said to the children. 'How are you? Quite well, I hope. And let me see – have I seen this brownie before? Yes – I have. Aren't you the bad fellow who turned all his grandmother's pigs blue? Isn't your name Winks?'

'Yes, Mr. Spells, sir,' said Winks.

'I hope you got spanked for that,' said Mr. Spells. 'I had a terrible job turning the pigs back to their right colour again. I believe they've still got blue tails.'

Winks wished the floor would open and swallow him up, but it didn't. Mr. Spells turned to Peter.

'Well, have you come visiting my dear old mother?' he said.

Peter explained how it was they were in his mother's room. Then he told the enchanter about poor Chinky and the chair.

'Good gracious!' said Mr. Spells. 'We must certainly find out where that chair has gone. If it falls into the hands of some rogue he can use it for all kinds of wrong purposes. And Chinky, too – what a silly thing to do, to tie his foot to the chair! Why didn't he tie the chair to the doorhandle, or something like that?'

'We didn't think of that,' said Peter. 'Can you help us to find out where the chair is, and Chinky, too, Mr. Spells?'

'Of course,' said Mr. Spells. 'Now, let me think for a moment. This happened at night, you say – and the chair, as usual, flew up into the sky?'

'Yes,' said everyone.

'Well, then – who was about that night in the sky, who might possibly have seen the chair and Chinky?' said Mr. Spells thoughtfully.

'Hoot, the owl,' said the old lady at once.

'Quite right, Mother,' said Mr. Spells. 'Splendid idea. We'll call Hoot, the owl, and see if he knows anything about this. He's a very wise and observant bird, you know,' he said, turning to the children. 'Never misses anything that goes on at night.'

'Shall we go and ask him if he knows anything then?' said Mollie. 'Where does he live?'

'Oh, we'll get him here,' said Mr. Spells 'That's the easiest way. I'll go and call him.'

He went to the window that looked out on the sunny hillside. He clapped his hands three times and muttered a word so magic that Winks trembled in his shoes. And a very curious thing happened. The sunny hillside went dark – as dark as night – and behind the trees shone a little moon! It was all very peculiar, especially as the sun still shone out in the backyard and on the sea that could be seen from the other windows!

'I must make it dark, or the owl won't come,' explained Mr. Spells. 'Now I'll call him.'

He put his hands up to his mouth, placed his thumbs carefully together, and blew gently – and to the children's delight and surprise, the hoot of an owl came from his closed hands. 'Ooo-ooooooo-oooh! Ooo-ooo-ooh!'

An answering hoot came from outside the window. A dark shadow passed across the room. Then a big owl flew silently down and perched on Mr. Spells' shoulder.

131

He caressed the big-eyed creature, whilst Cinders looked on rather jealously.

'Hoot,' said Mr. Spells. 'Listen carefully. Two nights ago a Wishing-Chair flew off into the sky, and hanging to it by a rope tied to his foot was a pixie called Chinky. Did you see anything of this?'

'Oooooooo-ooo-ooo! Oooooo-oo! Ooooh! Ooooo-oo-oo-oo-oo-oo-oo-ooooooooooh!' answered the owl, hooting softly into Mr. Spells' ear.

'Thank you, Hoot,' said Mr. Spells, looking grave. 'You may go.'

The owl flew off silently. Mr. Spells waited a moment and then muttered another magic word. The moonlit hillside grew lighter and lighter – and, hey presto, it was the sun behind the trees now and not the moon – daylight was everywhere!

'What did the owl tell you?' asked Peter.

'Oh – I forgot you couldn't understand,' said Mr. Spells. 'Well, he saw the chair – and Chinky, too, dangling by his foot. He followed them out of curiosity – and he says they flew near the Wandering Castle, where Giant Twisty lives, and the giant must have seen them and captured them. He saw no more of them after that.'

This was very bad news indeed. 'Oh, dear – whatever are we going to do, then?' said Peter at last. 'Poor little Chinky!'

'I must help you,' said Mr. Spells. 'I can't let Twisty own that chair. Sit down. We must think of a plan!'

XIX

AWAY ON ANOTHER ADVENTURE

'We can't do anything this evening,' said Mr. Spells. 'That's quite certain. Anyway, the first thing to do is to find out where the Wandering Castle is.'

'Don't you know?' said Mollie, in surprise, as she thought Mr. Spells knew everything.

'I know where it was last year, and the year before, and even last month,' said Mr. Spells, 'but I don't know where it is now. It may have wandered anywhere.'

'Oh – does it move about?' asked Peter in amazement.

'Good gracious, yes! It's always wandering,' said the enchanter. 'One day it may be here, the next it's somewhere else. Giant Twisty finds that very useful because he's always getting into trouble because of his bad ways, and it's very convenient to have a castle that can slip away in the night.'

'It's going to be very difficult to find, isn't it?' said Mollie. 'I mean, even if we find out where it is now, it may not be there when we get there.'

'True. But there's a chance it may rest in the same place for some weeks,' said Mr. Spells. '*Winks*, what are you doing?'

Winks jumped. 'Just – just stirring this stuff in the pot,' he said.

'Look at your hands!' thundered Mr. Spells. 'You've been dipping them in – and now see what you've done! Meddlesome little brownie!'

Winks looked at his hands. Oh, dear, they were bright blue! He stared at them in horror.

'Now you know what your grandmother's pigs must have felt like when you turned them blue,' said the enchanter. 'Well, keep your blue hands. Every time you look at them you can say to yourself, "I must not meddle. I must not meddle."'

Winks put his hands into his pockets, looking very doleful.

'Well, children,' said Mr. Spells, 'I think you'd better leave things to me to-night. I'll do my best to find out where the Wandering Castle happens to be at the moment and we will make a good plan to get back the chair and Chinky. Can you come along early to-morrow morning?'

'Yes. We'll ask Mother to let us go out for the day,' said Peter. 'Come on, Mollie. Thank you, Mr. Spells, for your help. Good-bye, Mrs. Spells. Good-bye, Cinders.'

'You can go out of this door if you like,' said the enchanter, and the children suddenly saw a small silver door gleaming in the wall near the window that looked out on the hillside. They were sure it hadn't been there before. Cinders opened it for them.

He bowed politely to the children, but dug a claw into Winks, who yelled and shot outside in a hurry. Winks shook a bright blue fist at the cat.

'Where are we?' said Peter, as they walked down the

hillside, now filling with shadows as the sun sank low. 'Goodness – why, there's our garden!'

So it was, just nearby. How very extraordinary. 'If only people knew how near their gardens are to curious and wonderful places, how surprised they would be!' said Mollie, walking in at their side-gate, and going to the playroom. 'Well, we can take that short cut to-morrow. I do wonder how it is that the sea is outside that other window. I just simply can't understand that!'

They said good-bye to Winks, who had tried in vain to wash the blue off his hands under the garden-tap. Then off they went to ask their mother if they could have the whole day to themselves to-morrow. She said, Yes, of course they could! It would do them good to go into the country in the lovely summer weather they were having now.

'Well, I don't know what Mother would say if she knew we were going to hunt for Giant Twisty in his Wandering Castle!' said Peter. 'I suppose she just wouldn't believe it.'

The next day the children had breakfast very early indeed, and then set off down the garden to collect Winks. His hands were still as blue as ever, so he had put on a pair of gloves.

'Oh – you've borrowed them from my biggest doll, Winks,' said Mollie. 'You might have asked permission first. I should have said, "No, certainly you can't have them."'

'Yes. I felt sure you wouldn't let me,' said Winks. 'That's why I didn't ask you. I'll take great care of them, Mollie, I really will. Your doll doesn't mind a bit.'

They went out of the garden gate and looked round. Where was that short cut now? They couldn't find it at all! But Winks spotted it.

'I've better eyes for strange things than you have,' he said. 'I can see a little shining path in the grass that you can't see. Follow me.'

'Well, you must be right,' said Peter, as Winks led them straight over the grass to the same trees on the same sunny hillside as they had seen the day before. 'And there's the little silver door!'

Cinders opened it as they came near. Winks shot in so quickly that he hadn't time to scratch the brownie, though he did try!

Mr. Spells was there, surrounded by papers and old books of all kinds. 'My mother is still asleep in bed,' he said. 'I'm glad you're early. We can start off straight away.'

'Oh – have you found out where the Wandering Castle is?' asked Mollie, in delight. 'Did your magic books tell you?'

'They helped,' said Mr. Spells. 'And Cinders and I did a little Find-Out Spell we know. Wandering Castle is now on the island belonging to Giant Small-One, Twisty's brother.'

'Giant Small-One – that's a funny name,' said Mollie.

'Not really,' said Mr. Spells. 'He's small for a giant, that's all. Well, we'd better start!'

'But how can we get to an island?' said Peter. 'We haven't a Wishing-Chair to fly over the sea!'

'That doesn't matter,' said Mr. Spells. 'Cinders has been getting my ship ready.'

He pointed to the window that so surprisingly looked out on the sea. The children stared in wonder and delight. A most beautiful ship rocked gently on the calm blue sea, a picture of loveliness with its big, white sails. Mollie cried out in joy. 'Oh – what a beauty! And it's called *The Mollie!*'

'Just a little compliment to you,' said Mr. Spells, smiling. 'Also it's supposed to be lucky to sail in a ship bearing one of the passengers' names. Well – shall we set off? The wind is just right.'

Cinders opened the window. Just outside was a stone ledge, with steps leading down to a tiny jetty. Cinders went first and helped Mollie down.

They all stepped aboard the beautiful white sailed ship. Mr. Spells took the tiller.

'Blow, wind, blow.
And on we will go
Over the waters blue,'

he sang, and the white ship leapt forward like a bird.

'Is that a spell you sang?' said Mollie.

'Oh, no – just a little song,' said Mr. Spells. And he began to sing again, whilst the ship sailed lightly over the blue waters. The children and Winks enjoyed it very much. Mollie trailed her hand in the water.

'Did we bring any food?' asked Mollie, suddenly. 'I'm hungry!'

'No,' said Mr. Spells, and everyone at once looked rather gloomy. 'Enchanters don't need to,' he went on. 'I always carry a spell in my pocket that I use when I need any food.'

137

Soon they were all eating and drinking, as the ship sped on and on.

For two hours the ship sailed on – then Cinders gave a shout. 'Land ahoy! It's the island, Mr. Spells, sir.'

'Aha!' said the enchanter. 'Now we must be a bit careful.' They all looked hard at the island that was rapidly coming nearer as the ship sped over the water. It didn't look very big. It was crowded with tall buildings, some of them looking like palaces, some like castles.

'Which is the Wandering Castle, I wonder?' said Mollie.

'Can't possibly tell,' said Mr. Spells. 'Now here we go towards this little jetty. We'll land there. You'll have to watch out a bit, because several giants live here and you don't want to be trodden on like ants.'

Mollie didn't like the sound of this much. She was determined to keep very close to Mr. Spells. Cinders was left with the ship, much to Winks' relief. They all set off up an extremely wide street.

'We shall be all right if we keep to the narrow pavements that run beside the walls of the building,' said Mr. Spells, guiding them to one. 'There are plenty of small folk living here, as well as giants.'

So there were – pixies and brownies and goblins and elves – but there were also giants, and Mollie suddenly saw a most enormous foot, followed by another one, walking down the street! She shrank close to Mr. Spells.

When the giant came by the children tried to see up to the top of him, but he was too tall. 'That's a large-sized giant,' said Mr. Spells. 'I know him – nice fellow called Too-Big. Here's a smaller one.'

It was exciting and extraordinary to see giants walking about. Mr. Spells guided them to a palace not quite so tall as some of the buildings.

'This is where Giant Small-One lives – the giant the island belongs to,' he said. 'Come along – we will ask him whereabouts his brother's Wandering Castle is. Don't be afraid. I am much more powerful than he is and he knows it.'

They went up a long, long flight of steps. At the top was a big open door, leading into a vast hall. At the end of the hall sat a giant – but he was such a small one that he wasn't more than twice the size of the enchanter himself!

'Advance, Mr. Spells, and pay your respects to Giant Small-One,' boomed an enormous voice from somewhere.

And Mr. Spells boldly went forward. Now to find out what they all wanted to know!

XX

WANDERING CASTLE AT LAST

Mr. Spells made a small bow. 'Greetings, Giant Small-One,' he said. 'I see you have not yet found a spell to make you Tall-One instead of Small-One. I come to ask you a question. We want to find your brother, Giant Twisty. Is Wandering Castle on your island?'

'I believe so,' said the voice of Giant Small-One, rather a feeble voice for a giant. 'Go to High Hill and you will see it there. Why does Mr. Spells, grand enchanter, want my brother?'

'That is my own business,' said Mr. Spells. The children thought he was very bold indeed to speak to a giant like that.

'Pray stay to a meal,' said Small-One, and he clapped his big hands, making a noise like guns cracking. 'I have few guests as important as you.'

'Thank you, no,' said Mr. Spells. 'Our business is urgent. We will go.'

He walked back to the children and Winks, and they made their way to the door. But it was shut! They couldn't open such a big door themselves, so they had to go all the way back to Small-One and ask for a servant to open the door.

It took a long time to find a servant, which was

140

strange, considering how many there had been in the hall a few minutes before. 'He is delaying us,' said Mr. Spells angrily. 'He wants to get a message to his brother, before we reach him, to warn him that we are on his track!'

At last a servant was found, the door was opened and they all trooped down the endless steps. They made their way down the street, came into a wide lane, lined with hedges as high as trees, and then found a sign-post that said 'To High Hill.'

'There's High Hill,' said Peter, pointing across the fields to a very tall hill. 'There are quite a lot of buildings on it. I wonder which is Wandering Castle?'

They came to High Hill at last and toiled up it. They met a small pixie running down, and Mr. Spells hailed her.

'Hey, little pixie! Where's Wandering Castle?'

'Let me see, now – I saw it yesterday,' said the little pixie. 'Yes, I remember now. It's in the Silver Buttercup Field, sir.'

'*Silver* Buttercups!' said Mollie, astonished. 'I've never heard of those. I don't think I should like them. The golden ones are just right.'

'I agree with you,' said Mr. Spells, guiding them round a big house. 'But some enchanters are very silly – always trying out novelties, you know. Well, here we are – here is Silver Buttercup Field.'

So it was. Silvery buttercups nodded in a great shimmering carpet. 'Beautiful, but washed-out looking,' said Mr. Spells. 'The thing is – where's Wandering Castle? It's certainly not here! It's wandered away again.

Small-One got a message to his brother in time – whilst we were trying to get that door open. Well, where has it wandered to now?'

'Please, sir, I know!' said a small goblin, running up. 'It's gone to Loneliness! I don't know if you know that country, sir. It's over the sea to the east – a very, very lonely place, where nobody ever goes if they can help it. It is going to hide itself there till you've given up looking for Twisty and his castle.'

'How do you know all this?' demanded Mr. Spells.

'Because I was lying resting in these buttercups when a servant from Giant Small-One came running up to warn Twisty that you were after him,' said the goblin. 'And I heard Twisty say where he was going.'

'Right. Thank you very much,' said Mr. Spells. 'Come along, children – back to the ship. We must sail off to Loneliness at once. Twisty could easily hide himself in that strange, desolate land without anyone finding him for years.'

'Oh, dear – we really must find him, because of Chinky,' said Mollie. They went back to the ship. Cinders was so pleased to see them back so soon that he quite forgot to try and scratch Winks as he got on board.

They set off again, the wind filling the sails and making the ship fly like a bird. She rocked up and down lightly as she went, and the children began to feel very sleepy.

They fell asleep. Mr. Spells awoke them after a time. 'Mollie! Peter! We're here. Wake up, both of you.'

They sat up in the ship. It was moored to a small

pier. Mollie looked out on the land of Loneliness. It was a gloomy, desolate place, with enormous trees growing in thick masses. 'There are forests and forests of those,' said Mr. Spells, looking as gloomy as Loneliness looked. 'How we shall ever know where the Wandering Castle is, I can't imagine!'

They landed, and walked towards the nearest forest of trees. Just as they got there they heard a voice shouting furiously.

'No peace anywhere! None at all! I come here, where nobody ever goes – and what comes walking almost on top of me but a castle! A CASTLE! Just when I thought I was going to sleep alone in peace!'

And out of the trees burst Chinky's cousin, Sleep-Alone! He was just as surprised to see the children and Winks and Mr. Spells as they were to see him.

'Sleep-Alone! Oh, Sleep-Alone, you're just about the *only* person who would come here!' cried Peter. 'Where is that castle you've been complaining about? It's Giant Twisty's, and he's got Chinky a prisoner there.'

'Good thing, too,' grumbled Sleep-Alone. 'Mischievous creature, always coming and disturbing me at night!'

'Listen, Sleep-Alone,' said Mr. Spells. 'If you will lead us to that castle, we plan to rescue Chinky and the Wishing-Chair – and we will turn the wicked Twisty out of his castle. Then it will be empty, in the middle of the land of Loneliness. And *you* shall have it for your own! Think of being alone there, with no one to wake you at night, no one to bother your!'

Sleep-Alone listened to all this in delight. What, have a large empty castle all to himself, with a thousand rooms to sleep in – lost in the middle of a forest in the land of Loneliness? Wonderful!

'I'll show you where it is,' he said eagerly.

They followed him. He darted in and out of the trees, following no path that they could see – and then at last they saw Wandering Castle! It stood there, rocking a little in the wind, for it had no true foundations as other buildings have. It was tall and dark and gloomy – and it hadn't a single window of any kind!

'There you are!' said Sleep-Alone. 'A very fine castle, too – only one door – and no windows. Just the place for me!'

Mr. Spells looked at the castle in silence. One door – and no windows. A very difficult place to escape from if they got inside. But they must get inside. There was no doubt about that.

'Stay here by the door, Sleep-Alone,' said Mr. Spells at last. 'We're going in.' He went up the broad steps to the great studded door.

The door opened. A giant stood there, a cross-eyed fellow, with a twisted smile on his face.

'Come in,' he said. 'So you've found me, have you? Well, I'm not going to deny that I've got the Wishing-Chair – yes, and Chinky, too – and now I'll have you as well.'

To the children's surprise, Mr. Spells didn't run away. He stepped inside and the children and Winks went, too, all feeling rather scared. Twisty laughed.

'This is easier than I thought!' he said. 'How are you going to get out again, Mr. Spells? There is now no door – and, as I dare say you have seen, there are no windows at all!'

The children turned and looked behind them. The door had vanished. They were indeed prisoners. But Mr. Spells didn't seem at all disturbed.

'Where is Chinky?' he said.

'Follow me,' said Twisty, and he went down a long dark passage and through a door. He crossed the room beyond the door, and came to another one. The door to this was locked and bolted. He opened it.

Inside was Chinky, sitting miserably in the Wishing-Chair! He leapt up in the greatest joy when he saw the others. Mollie ran to him and flung her arms round him.

'Chinky! You're safe! Oh, Chinky, we've come to rescue you!'

Peter slapped Chinky on the back and Winks pumped his hand up and down, yelling, 'Chinky, good old Chinky!'

In the middle of all this there came the sound of the door being slammed and bolted. Then they heard Twisty laughing loudly.

'Easy! Too easy for words! You can't get out, Mr. Spells, however powerful you are. This door has a Keep-Shut Spell in it that I bought from an old witch years ago. And it's the only way out! You can go free if you give me some spells I've wanted for years.'

'You'll never get them from me, Twisty,' called Mr. Spells. 'Never!'

'Mr. Spells! You *are* going to get us out of here, aren't you?' begged Mollie.

'Sh! Don't get alarmed,' said Mr. Spells. 'I am going to do a spell on us all. Yes, and on the Wishing-Chair, too. Now, where's my chalk?'

He found a white chalk in his pocket and a blue one, too. He drew first a white circle and then a blue one inside it. He made the children, Chinky and Winks sit down in the middle of it.

Then he got inside the circle himself, and sat down in the Wishing-Chair.

'I'm going to say very magic words,' he said. 'Shut your eyes, please – and don't be surprised at whatever happens!'

XXI

A VERY EXCITING TIME

The children, Chinky and Winks shut their eyes. Mr. Spells began to mutter some magic words under his breath – then he spoke some aloud and then he suddenly shouted three spell-words at the top of his voice, making everyone jump violently.

There was a silence. Then Mr. Spells spoke in his ordinary voice. 'You can open your eyes now. The spell is done.'

They opened their eyes and looked round them in wonder. They were in the very biggest room they had ever seen in their lives. The floor stretched endlessly away from them. The walls seemed miles away. Not far from them was a colossal wooden pillar – or what looked like one. The ceiling seemed to have disappeared or else was so far away that they couldn't see it. Certainly there was no sky above them, so probably the ceiling was still there!

'What's that enormous wooden post?' said Peter in wonder. 'It wasn't here just now.'

'It's the leg of the table,' said Mr. Spells surprisingly.

'What do you mean?' said Peter. 'It's much too big for that – look, that's the wooden pillar I mean – over there. And where are the chalk circles gone?'

'We're still standing in the middle of them,' said Mr. Spells with a laugh. 'Do you mean to say you don't know what has happened?'

'No,' said Peter. 'I feel funny, you know – but except that we appear to be in quite a different place now I don't know what's happened.'

'*I* do,' said Chinky. 'You've used a very powerful Go-Small spell, Mr. Spells, haven't you? Goodness, I was awfully afraid you weren't going to stop the spell soon enough – I thought we were going to shrink to nothing. How big are we?'

'Smaller than mice,' said Mr. Spells. 'I wanted to make us small enough to creep under the door, you see.'

'How clever of you!' said Mollie joyfully. 'I see what has happened now – why the ceiling seems so far away, and why that table-leg looks like a great pillar – and why we can't see the chalk circles – we'd have to walk a long way to get to them now!'

'Quite right,' said Mr. Spells. 'Now I think we'd better make a move, in case the giant comes back and guesses what I've done. I'm glad the spell went so well – sometimes a powerful spell like that makes loud noises, and I've known it to make lightning come round the circle.'

'Gracious!' said Peter. 'I wish it had. I'd have enjoyed our own private little storm!'

'Now the thing is – where's the door gone?' said Chinky. 'We've gone so small that the room is simply enormous, and the wall where the door is seems miles away. We'd better begin walking right round the walls till we come to the door!'

But Mr. Spells knew where the door was. Carrying the Wishing-Chair, which had gone small, too, he led them for what seemed miles over the floor, and they at last came to where the door was fitted into the wall. A draught blew at them as they came near to the enormous door.

'That's the draught blowing under the bottom of the door,' explained Mr. Spells. 'Now – I'm going to squeeze under first to see that everything is safe. Be ready to follow me when you hear me call.'

He disappeared under the door, bending himself double. Soon they heard his voice. 'Yes – come along – it's all right.'

One by one they squeezed under the door, and found themselves in what they supposed must be the room outside – but now, of course, it seemed a very vast dark place indeed. 'Shall I make us our right size again – or shall I keep us small?' wondered Mr. Spells. 'On the whole, I think I'll keep us small.'

He led them across the room and down a passage, making them all keep very close to the bottom of the wall. It was a very good thing he did, too, because round the corner they heard the sound of tremendous footsteps that shook the floor and made it tremble – the giant coming along the passage!

In a trice Mr. Spells pulled them all into what appeared to be some kind of mouse-hole – it seemed as large as a cave to the children! They crouched there till the thundering footsteps had gone by. Then out they went as fast as they could.

'I want to find the front door if I can,' said Mr. Spells.

'We can easily slip under that. It must be at the end of this passage.'

But before they reached it a thunderous noise made them all jump nearly out of their skins.

BANG-BANG-THUD-RAT-TAT-TAT!

'What is it?' cried Mollie, and caught hold of Mr. Spells. 'What can it be?'

Mr. Spells laughed. 'I think I can guess what it is,' he said. 'It's Chinky's cousin, Sleep-Alone. He's got tired of waiting for the castle, and he's knocking at the door to see what's happened! Oh dear – now I don't know *what* will happen!'

Plenty happened. When the knocker banged again on the door, an answering roar came from inside the castle, and Twisty the giant came pounding along the passage in a fine temper.

'Who's that knocking at my door? How dare you make this noise!'

The door was swung open and a wind blew down the passage at once, almost blowing the five tiny people over. Sleep-Alone stood outside, a small figure compared with the giant, but seeming like a giant now to the tiny children!

'Quick!' said Mr. Spells, 'they are going to have a quarrel. Now's our chance to escape out of the door – but keep away from their feet. We're so small that neither of them will notice us.'

The children ran with Chinky and Winks out of the door, keeping well to the side. But they couldn't possibly go any further than the top step because the drop down to the second step seemed like a cliff to them!

'I'll have to take a chance now and change us back to our right size,' said Mr. Spells. 'Otherwise we'll have to stand on this top step and sooner or later be trampled on. Shut your eyes, please, take hands, and keep together. I haven't got time to draw chalk circles, so this spell will happen very quickly. As soon as you're the right size, run down the steps as quickly as ever you can, and go to that tree over there. I'll bring the Wishing-Chair, and we'll soon be off and away!'

'What about Sleep-Alone?' said Chinky. 'We promised he could have the castle.'

'He'll look after that all right,' said Mr. Spells, with a laugh. 'Sleep-Alone is bolder than I thought he was! Now – eyes shut, please, and hold hands hard.'

They all obeyed. Mr. Spells said the words that undid the Go-Small spell, and allowed them to shoot up to their right size again – but, as he had said, it happened very suddenly indeed, and all five of them gasped, felt giddy and fell over.

'Quick – get up – he's seen us!' shouted Mr. Spells. He picked up the Wishing-Chair which had also gone back to its right size, and ran down the steps with it. Everyone followed.

Sleep-Alone and the giant had been having a real rough and tumble. The giant was stronger and bigger than Sleep-Alone – but Chinky's cousin had got in so many sly jabs and punches that the giant had completely lost his temper.

He lashed out at Sleep-Alone, who ducked – but the blow just caught him on the top of his head. He stumbled – and that would have been the end of him if

151

the giant hadn't, at that very moment, caught sight of the five prisoners tearing down his steps!

He was so tremendously astonished that he forgot all about Sleep-Alone and simply stood there, staring out of his saucer-like eyes!

Then, with a bellow, he was after them. 'How did you escape?' he roared. 'Come back – or I'll throw you all up to the moon!'

Mr. Spells put down the Wishing-Chair. He sat in it quickly and pulled Peter and Mollie on his knee. Winks and Chinky sat on the back. 'Home, Chair,' ordered Mr. Spells, and at once the obedient Wishing-Chair rose into the air.

The giant made a grab at it, but the chair dodged, and Mr. Spells hit the giant smartly on his outstretched hand. The giant yelped.

'Good-bye!' called Chinky, waving his hand.

Meanwhile what had happened to Sleep-Alone? Plenty! When he saw the giant rushing after the others, he stood and stared for a moment. Then he grinned. Then he hopped into Wandering Castle and shut the door very quietly.

And when Twisty turned round to go back and finish his quarrel with Sleep-Alone, there was no castle there! It had gone on its wanderings again!

'Oh dear – I wish we could stay and see the giant looking for his castle,' said Mollie. 'What a shock he's having! His prisoners all escaping, the Wishing-Chair gone – and his castle wandering away in the forest with Sleep-Alone in charge. Won't your cousin be thrilled to have such a fine place to sleep in, Chinky?'

152

The Wishing-Chair didn't go back to the playroom – it went to Mrs. Spells' room.

They went in to see Mrs. Spells, and told her their extraordinary adventures. To their surprise, Cinders was there and produced some excellent fruit buns that Mrs. Spells said he had just made. He really was a most remarkable cat.

Mollie glanced out of the window that looked out on the sea. 'Oh, look! she cried, 'there's our ship! *The Mollie!* I wondered what would happen to her. She's come back, Mr. Spells.'

'Cinders brought her back,' said Mrs. Spells. 'He knew the ship wouldn't be needed again.'

'It was a grand adventure,' said Mollie. 'I was scared at times, you know – but somehow I knew everything would be all right with Mr. Spells there. Thank you, Mr. Spells, for being such a good friend.'

'Delighted,' said the enchanter. 'Now it's time you went home.'

The children went to find the Wishing-Chair, which was still in the back yard. They climbed into it with Winks and Chinky.

'Take us home, Chair!' cried Peter – and up into the air it rose, flapping its big wings – and in five minutes' time they were all back in the playroom once more.

XXII

WINKS AND CHINKY ARE SILLY

The Wishing-Chair seemed tired with all its adventures. It stood in its place for ten whole days and didn't grow its wings.

'We've only got a week and two days left before we go back to school,' said Mollie, who was a bit worried. 'I do hope we have another adventure before we have to say good-bye to you, Chinky. Where's Winks?'

'I don't know. He was here last night, looking very mysterious,' said Chinky. 'You know, the way he looks when he's up to some kind of mischief. I just hope he won't get into trouble.'

'You know he lost my doll's gloves on the last adventure? He says he dropped them into the sea,' said Mollie. 'Now his hands show up again – that awful blue colour!'

'I know. The things he loses!' said Chinky. 'He came in without his shoes the other day, and said he'd lost them. I said: "Well, where did you take them off, Winks?" And he said he'd lost them without even taking them off. How could anyone do that?'

'Sh! Here he is!' said Mollie. 'Oh, *Winks!* Your hands aren't blue any more! They're the right colour! How did you manage that?'

'Aha-ha-ha!' said Winks. 'I've got a secret.'

'What is it?' asked Chinky at once.

'Well, it won't be a secret if I tell it,' said Winks annoyingly.

'Have you been to see Mr. Spells?' said Mollie.

'No. I went to see Witch Wendle,' said Winks. 'I borrowed her wand – it's got very good magic in it.'

'Do you mean to say old Witch Wendle lent you her wand?' said Chinky disbelievingly. 'Why, it was only last week you told me you put her chimney pot upside down so that her smoke blew down into her kitchen. I don't believe you!'

'All right, then – but here's the wand, see?' said Winks, and he suddenly produced the wand from under his coat. It was a small, neat wand, not long and slender like Chinky's. He waved it about.

Mollie and Peter stared in surprise – and Chinky jumped up in alarm.

'WINKS! You took it without asking? I know you did. Witch Wendle would never lend her wand to you – why, look, it's absolutely *full* of magic!'

So it was. All wands glitter and shine and gleam and shimmer when they are full of magic, and this one was quite dazzling.

'I just borrowed it for a little while,' said Winks. 'The witch has gone to call on her sister. She won't miss it. I'll take it back soon. I wished my hands the right colour again – wasn't I pleased when they came all right!'

'You're a very bad, naughty brownie,' said Chinky. 'You ought to go back to Mister Grim's school. I've a good mind to make you go back!'

155

'Don't you talk like that to me, or I shall lose my temper,' said Winks, crossly, and he poked the wand at Chinky.

'Stop it,' said Chinky. 'You should never poke people with wands. Surely you know that? And let me tell you this – I shall talk to you how I like. You take that wand back to Witch Wendle AT ONCE!'

'I don't like you, Chinky,' said Winks, looking suddenly cross. 'I shall wish for a Maggle-mig to chase you!'

He waved his wand in the air – and goodness gracious, whatever was this extraordinary creature running in at the door?

It was rather like a small giraffe, but it had feathers, and it wore shoes on its four feet. It galloped round the room after Chinky. The children fled to a cupboard. If this was a Maggle-mig, they didn't like it! Winks sat down on the sofa and roared with laughter. Chinky was furious.

He rushed to the toy cupboard and felt about for his wand. He waved it in the air. 'Maggle-mig, change to a Snickeroo and chase Winks!' he cried. And at once the little giraffe-like creature changed to a thing like a small crocodile with horns. It ran at Winks, who leapt off the sofa in a hurry.

Winks waved his wand at the Snickeroo and it ran into the fireplace and completely vanished. Winks pointed the wand at Chinky.

'Horrid Chinky! Grow a long nose!'

And poor Chinky did! It was so long that he almost fell over it! Winks took hold of it and pulled it.

Chinky hit out at Winks with his own wand. 'Grow a tail!' he yelled.

And, hey presto! Winks grew a tail – one like a cow's, with a tuft at the end. It swung to and fro, and Winks looked down at it in alarm. He tried to run away from the swinging tail, but you can't leave a tail that's growing on you, of course, and the tail followed him, swinging to and fro.

'Ha, ha!' said Chinky. 'A brownie with a tail!'

Winks was crying now. He picked up his wand, which he had dropped. He and Chinky hit out at each other at the same moment.

'I'll change you into a puff of smoke!' shouted Winks.

'I'll change you into a horrid smell!' cried Chinky.

And then they both disappeared! Mollie and Peter stared in the utmost dismay. A little puff of green smoke blew across the room and disappeared out of the door. A horrid smell drifted about the room for a few minutes and then that went, too.

Mollie burst into tears. 'Now look what's happened!' she sobbed. 'We've lost both Chinky and Winks.'

Peter saw that the two wands were on the floor. He picked up Chinky's and put it into the toy cupboard. Then he picked up the one Winks had taken from Witch Wendle's and looked at it. Mollie gave a cry.

'Don't meddle with it, Peter. Don't!'

'I'm not going to,' said Peter. 'I'm just wondering what to do about all this. It's very serious. I think we ought to take this wand back to Witch Wendle.'

'Oh, let's take it back quickly then,' said Mollie. 'And perhaps if we do she'll tell us what to do about Chinky and Winks. How shall we find the way?'

'We might ask Mr. Spells,' began Peter, and then

157

suddenly stopped in delight. He pointed behind Mollie.

She turned and saw that the Wishing-Chair was growing its wings again! The buds on its four legs burst into feathers, and soon the big green and yellow wings were waving gently in the air.

'Oh! *What* a bit of luck!' cried Mollie. 'Now we can get in the Wishing-Chair and just tell it to go to Witch Wendle's!'

Peter sat in the chair and pulled Mollie down beside him. He had the witch's wand in his hand.

'Wishing-Chair, we want to go to Witch Wendle's,' he said. 'Go at once!'

The chair rose into the air, and made for the door. Out it went and up into the cloudy sky. It made for an opening in the clouds and shot through it. Now the children were in the sunshine above.

They flew for a long way, and then Mollie shouted in surprise, and pointed. 'Look! What's that? It's a castle in the clouds!'

Both children stared. It was a very surprising sight indeed. A big purple cloud loomed ahead, thick and gloomy. Set in its depths was what looked exactly like a castle, with towers and turrets. The chair flew straight to the cloud and stopped. It hovered just above the cloud, and the children couldn't get down.

'Go lower, Chair!' cried Peter. But the chair didn't. A head popped out of a window of the castle.

'Wait! I'll get you cloud-shoes! If you walk on the cloud without them you'll fall.'

The head disappeared. Then out of the castle came

Witch Wendle, a bright star glinting at the top of her pointed hat. She carried what looked like snowshoes, big flat things, to fasten to their feet.

'Here you are!' she said. 'Put these on your feet and you will be able to walk easily on the clouds. That's why your Wishing-Chair wouldn't land – it knew it would be dangerous for you without cloud-shoes.'

'Oh, thank you,' said Mollie. She liked Witch Wendle very much, because her face smiled and her eyes twinkled. The children put on the cloud-shoes and then stepped down on the cloud. Ah, they could get along quite well now – it felt rather as if they were sliding on very, very soft snow.

'What a strange home you have, set high in the clouds,' said Peter.

'Oh, people often build these,' said the witch. 'Have you never heard of people building castles in the air? Well, this is one of them. They don't last very long, but they are very comfortable. I've had this one about two months now.'

She led the way to her curious castle. 'We've come to bring you your wand,' said Peter. 'I must tell you all that happened.'

So he did, and the witch listened in silence. 'That tiresome Winks!' she said. 'He should never have left Mister Grim's school.'

'What can we do about Chinky and Winks,' said Mollie, 'now that they are a puff of smoke and a horrid smell? Where have they gone?'

'To the Land of Spells,' said the witch. 'We'll have to get your Wishing-Chair to go there – come along!

159

XXIII

WHAT HAPPENED IN THE LAND OF SPELLS

The witch led the way to where the Wishing-Chair stood waiting patiently on the edge of the cloud, its wings flapping gently.

'That's a really wonderful chair of yours,' she said. 'I only wish I had one like it!'

They all sat in it. 'To the Land of Spells!' commanded the witch, and the chair at once rose into the air. It left the cloud and the curious castle built in the air, and flew steadily to the north.

'I'm very glad to have back my wand,' said Witch Wendle. 'Luckily it is only my third best one. If it had been my best one, the magic would have been so powerful that it would have shrivelled Winks up as soon as he touched it.'

Mollie and Peter at once made up their minds that they would never, never touch any wand belonging to a witch or wizard. Goodness – what a blessing that it had been the witch's third best wand and not her best one!

The chair flew on for a long while and the witch pointed out the interesting places they passed – the Village of Stupids, the Country of No-Goods, the Land of Try-Again, and all kinds of places the children had never heard of before. They stared down at them in interest.

'What's the Land of Spells like?' asked Mollie.

'It's a strange land, really,' said the witch. 'All kinds of spells wander about, and bump into you – Invisible Spells to make you invisible, Tall Spells to make you tall, Laughter Spells to make you laugh – they've only got to touch you to affect you at once.'

'Oh dear,' said Mollie in alarm. 'I don't like the sound of that at all.'

'You needn't worry,' said Witch Wendle. 'They only affect you whilst they bump into you – as soon as they drift away you're all right again. We shall have to look for a puff of smoke and detect a horrid smell – then we shall know we've got Winks and Chinky and I must do my best to put them right for you.'

The chair flew rapidly downwards, and landed in a very peculiar place. It was full of a blue-green mist and queer sounds went on all the time – sounds of rumbling, sounds of music, of bells, and of the wind blowing strongly.

They got off the chair. 'Now take hands,' said the witch. 'And keep together, please. You're all right so long as you're with me, because I am a mistress of all spells – but don't slip away for goodness' sake, or you may get changed into a white butterfly or a blue beetle, and I would find it difficult to know you again.'

Mollie and Peter held hands very hard indeed, and Mollie took the witch's hand, too. And then all kinds of extraordinary things began to happen.

A little trail of yellow bubbles bumped into Mollie –

and, to Peter's great alarm, Mollie's neck grew alarmingly long, and shot up almost as tall as a tree! She was very alarmed, too.

'It's all right,' said Witch Wendle. 'It will pass as soon as the trail of bubbles goes.'

She was right. When the bubbles flew off in another direction. Mollie's neck came down to its right size! 'You did look queer, Mollie,' said Peter. 'Don't do *that* again!'

It was queer to think of spells wandering about like this. Mollie began to look out for them and try to dodge them. She dodged a silvery mist, but it wound itself round Witch Wendle – and she at once disappeared completely.

'Where's she gone?' cried Peter in fright.

'I've still got hold of her hand,' said Mollie. 'I think she's only invisible – but she's here all right.'

'Yes, I'm here,' said the witch's voice. As soon as the silvery mist cleared away she became visible again and smiled down at the children. 'I didn't see that spell coming or I would have dodged it,' she said. 'Oh dear – here's an annoying one coming!'

Something that looked like a little shower of white snowflakes came dropping down on them. The witch changed into a big white bear, Peter changed into a white goat and Mollie into a white cat! That lasted about two minutes, and they were all very glad when they were back to their right shapes again.

They went wandering through the queer misty land, listening to the queer noises around, trying to dodge the spells that came near them. The witch put out her hand

and captured a tiny little spell floating through the air. It looked like a small white daisy.

'I've always wanted that spell,' she said to the children. 'It's a good spell – if you put it under a baby's pillow it makes a child grow up as pretty as a flower.'

Suddenly Peter stopped and sniffed. 'Pooh! What a smell of bad fish!' he said. 'I'm sure that must be Winks. Can you smell a horrid smell, Witch Wendle?'

'I should think I *can*,' said the witch. She took a small bottle out of her pocket and uncorked it.

'Come here to me, you bad little smell,
Into this bottle you'll fit very well!'

she sang. And the children saw a very faint purplish streak streaming into the bottle. The witch corked it up.

'Well, we've got Winks all right,' she said. 'Now for Chinky. Look – here comes a puff of green smoke. Would that be him?'

'Yes!' said Peter. 'I'm sure it is. He and Winks would be certain to keep together.'

The witch took a small pair of bellows from under her long, flowing cloak and held them out to the puff of green smoke, which was hovering near. She opened the bellows and drew in the puff of smoke! She hung the bellows on her belt again.

'And now we've got Chinky,' she said. 'Good! We'd better get back home now, and see what we can do with them. It's so easy to change people into bad smells and green smoke – any beginner can do that – but it takes a

163

powerful witch or wizard to change them back to their own shapes again.'

They walked back to find the Wishing-Chair, still bumping into curious spells every now and again. Mollie walked into a Too-Big spell and immediately towered over the witch and Peter. But she went back to her own size almost at once.

The witch bumped into a train of bright bubbles that burst as they touched her. When they looked at her they saw that she had changed into a beautiful young girl, and they were amazed. But she was soon her old self again.

'That was a nice spell,' she said with a sigh. 'I should like to have caught that spell and kept it. Ah, is that the Wishing-Chair?'

'Yes – but there's only half of it!' said Mollie, in surprise. 'Oh, I see – it's just been touched by an invisible spell – it's coming all right again now.'

Soon they were sitting in the chair. 'To the children's playroom,' commanded the witch. 'And hurry! The puff of smoke in the bellows is trying to get out. We'll lose Chinky for ever if he puffs himself out, and gets lost on the wind.'

'Oh dear!' said Mollie. 'Do hurry, Wishing-Chair!'

The Wishing-Chair hurried so much that the witch lost her hat in the wind and the chair had to go back for it. But at last they were flying down to the playroom, and in at the door. Thank goodness!

The witch got carefully out of the chair. She took the bellows from her waist. 'Is there a suit of Chinky's anywhere?' she asked. Mollie got Chinky's second-best one from the cupboard. 'Hold it up,' said the witch. 'That's right. Now watch!'

Mollie held up the little suit. The witch took the bellows and blew with them. Green smoke came from them and filled the little suit, billowing it out, and – would you believe it? – it was Chinky himself filling it out, growing arms and legs and head – and there he was standing before them in his second-best suit, looking rather scared after his curious stay in the Land of Spells!

Then it was Winks' turn. The witch asked for the teapot and took off the lid. She uncorked the bottle in which she had put the bad smell, and emptied it into the teapot. She put on the lid.

Then she lifted up the teapot and poured something out of the spout, singing as she did so:

'Teapot, teapot, pour for me
A brownie naughty as can be,
He's not as clever as he thinks,
That wicked, wilful little Winks!'

And before the children's astonished eyes the teapot poured out Winks! He came out in a kind of stream, which somehow built itself up into Winks himself!

When Winks saw Witch Wendle he went very red and tried to hide behind the sofa. She pulled him out, saying, 'Who stole my wand? Who changed Chinky into a puff of smoke?'

'Well, he changed me into a bad smell,' said Winks, beginning to sniff.

'He at least used his own wand to do it with,' said the

witch. 'Winks, I'm sending you back to Mister Grim's school. You've a lot to learn.'

Winks howled so loudly that Mollie felt very sorry for him.

'Please,' she said, 'could he just stay with us till we go back to boarding school? We might have another adventure, a nice one.'

'Very well,' said Witch Wendle. 'One week more. Don't sniff like that, Winks. You bring all your trouble on yourself.'

'I'm sorry, Witch Wendle,' wailed Winks.

'You'll be sorry till next time – then you will do something tiresome once more and be sorry all over again,' said the witch. 'I know you, Winks! Well, good-bye, children. I'm very pleased to have met you – and, by the way, may I sometimes borrow that Wishing-Chair of yours when you are at school? It would be such a treat for me to do my shopping in it sometimes.'

'Oh, yes, please do,' said Mollie at once. 'It would be a nice return for all your help. You'll have to go to Chinky's mother to borrow it when we're at school. He keeps it there.'

'Thank you,' said the witch, and off she went. Chinky turned to Winks. 'We were silly to quarrel like that,' he said. 'I'm sorry I turned you into a bad smell, Winks. Go and wash. I still think you smell a bit horrid.'

So he did – and it was two or three days before he smelt like a brownie again. You just can't meddle with spells, you know!

XXIV

THE ISLAND OF SURPRISES

'You know,' said Mollie to Chinky, 'we've only one more day before we go back to school. Mother has already sent off our trunks.'

'Oh dear,' said Chinky, sadly. 'The holidays have simply flown! I do wish you didn't have to go to school.'

'Well – we love being at home – but we really do love school, too,' said Peter. 'It's great fun, you know – and it's so nice being with scores of boys and girls who are our own age. I'm awfully glad we do go to boarding-school, really, though, of course, I'm sorry to say good-bye to Mother and Daddy and you and the garden and Jane and the Wishing-Chair, and everything.'

'We never went to the Land of Goodness Knows Where,' said Mollie. 'I'd like to go before we leave for school.'

'Wishing-Chair, you *might* grow your wings quickly,' said Peter, looking at the chair standing quietly in its place. 'You really might!'

And, dear me, for once in a way the chair was most obliging and began to grow them! Unfortunately the children didn't notice that it was actually doing what it was told, and they went out into the garden to play.

The next thing that happened was the chair flying out of the door of the playroom, its wings flapping strongly! Luckily Chinky caught sight of it, or goodness knows where it would have gone by itself. He felt the swish of the big wings, and looked up. The chair was just passing by his head!

He gave such a yell that Mollie and Peter jumped in fright. They turned, to see Chinky making a tremendous leap into the air after the chair. He caught one leg and held on. 'Help! Help!' he yelled to the children. 'Come and help me, or the chair will go off with me like this.'

However, the chair went down to the ground, and allowed Chinky to sit in it properly. Mollie and Peter ran up eagerly.

'Gracious! Whatever made us leave the playroom door open?' said Peter. 'The chair might have flown off anywhere and not come back. We shall really have to get a watch-dog for it.'

'It was lucky I just saw it,' said Chinky. 'Well now – shall we go to the Land of Goodness Knows Where or not? Is there anywhere else you'd like to go?'

The children couldn't think of anywhere else, so the chair was told to go there. It flew off in the right direction at once. It was a lovely, clear day, with hardly any cloud at all. The children and Chinky could see down below them very clearly indeed.

'Go lower, Chair,' said Chinky. 'We'd like to see the places we're flying over.' The chair obediently flew down lower still, and then Chinky gave a shout.

'Look – there's Winks! Isn't it Winks?'

It was. He, too, saw the chair and waved madly.

'Shall we take him with us?' said Chinky.

'Well – it's his last chance of coming with us for a long time,' said Mollie. 'We said we'd let him come with us once more, didn't we, before he goes back to Mister Grim's school. We'll take him.'

So they ordered the chair to go down to the ground to fetch Winks. He was simply delighted. He clambered on to it at once. 'Did you come to fetch me?' he said. 'How nice of you.'

'Well, actually we weren't fetching you,' said Chinky. 'The chair suddenly grew its wings, flew out into the garden, and I just managed to grab it in time. It was a bit of luck, catching sight of you like that. Winks, you must try and be good to-day – don't spoil our last adventure by being silly or naughty, please. We're going to the Land of Goodness Knows Where.'

'That's a silly land,' said Winks. 'Why don't you go somewhere more exciting – the Land of Birthdays or the Land of Treats, or the Village of Parties – somewhere like that.'

They were just passing over a big blue lake. They came to an island in the middle of it, and as they flew over it a surprising thing happened. Fireworks went off with a bang, and coloured stars burst and fell all round the chair. It was startled and wobbled dangerously, almost upsetting the children.

'Gracious!' said Mollie. 'What a surprise! What island is that?'

'Oh!' cried Chinky, in great excitement, 'I do believe it's the Island of Surprises! Isn't it, Winks? I really think it is.'

'Yes,' said Winks, peering down. 'It is! Look out, here comes another rocket or something. My word – what a lovely shower of coloured stars!'

'Can't we go to this island?' said Mollie. 'Chinky, let's go.'

'Right,' said Chinky. 'Mind you, the surprises may not all be nice ones – but if you're willing to risk that, we'll go.'

'Of course we'll go!' said Winks. 'Chair, go down to the island at once, please.'

Down went the chair, dodging another rocket. It landed on a patch of green grass, which at once changed into a sheet of water! The chair almost sank, but just managed to get itself out in time, and flew to a little paved courtyard.

'First surprise,' said Chinky, with a grin. 'We shall have to be careful here, you know. Winks, you mustn't be an idiot on this island – you'll get some unpleasant shocks if you are.'

'Can we leave the chair here?' said Mollie doubtfully. 'It would be a horrid surprise if we found it gone when we came back for it.'

The chair creaked and flew towards Mollie. 'It says it's not going to leave us!' said Chinky, with a grin. 'Very wise of it. Right, Chair, you follow us like a dog, and we'll all be very pleased.'

So the chair followed them closely.

The first really nice surprise came when they saw a table set out in the sunshine, with empty dishes and plates in a row. The children, Chinky and Winks stopped to look at them. 'Is there going to be a party or something?' said Peter.

A small goblin came up and sat himself down on the form by the table. He stared earnestly at the plate and dish in front of him. And, hey presto, on the dish came a large chocolate pudding, and on his plate came a big ice-cream to match. He began to eat, beaming all over his ugly little face.

'Oooh,' said Winks at once, and sat down at the table. So did the others. They all stared hard at their dishes and plates.

Mollie got a pile of sausages on her dish and some fried onions on her plate. Peter got a big trifle on his dish and a jug of cream on his plate. Chinky got strawberries on his dish and found his plate swimming in sugar and cream to go with them.

They looked to see what Winks had got. That bad little brownie, of course, had been tricky as usual. He had put *two* plates and *two* dishes in front of him!

But he wasn't looking at all pleased! On one dish had appeared a wonderful-looking pie – but when he cut the crust there was nothing in the pie. On the other dish had appeared a chocolate cake – and, as we know, that was the one cake that poor Winks simply couldn't bear to eat.

On one plate had come some steaming cabbage and on the other two prunes. How the others laughed!

'A pie with nothing in it – a cake he hates – cabbage – and prunes! Oh, Winks, what a horrid surprise. It serves you right for being greedy!' cried Chinky.

Winks was cross. He stood sulkily whilst the others tucked into their exciting food. Mollie was sorry for him and offered him a sausage.

171

The next surprise was also a very nice one. They finished their meal and then suddenly heard the sound of loud music coming from round the corner. They hurried to see what it was.

It was a roundabout! There it stood, decorated with flags that waved in the wind, going round and round, the music playing gaily. How lovely!

'How much is it to go for a ride on this roundabout,' asked Chinky, feeling in his pocket.

'Oh, nothing!' said the pixie in charge of it. 'It's just a nice surprise for you. Get on when it stops.'

When the roundabout stopped, the children saw that there were all kinds of animals and birds to ride, and each of them went up and down as well as round and round. The brownies, goblins and pixies who had had their turns got off, and the children, Chinky and Winks looked to see which animal or bird they would choose to ride.

'I'll have this pony,' said Mollie, who loved horses and always wanted one of her own. She climbed on to a dear little black pony.

'I'll have this camel,' said Peter. 'It's got two humps, and I'll ride between them!'

Chinky chose a snow-white gull with outstretched wings that flapped as the roundabout went round. Winks chose a big goldfish. Its fins and tail moved in a very life-like manner. Winks cut himself a little stick from the hedge nearby. 'Just to make my fish swim well on the roundabout,' he said to the others as he climbed on.

'No whipping allowed!' shouted the pixie in charge. 'Hey, you – no whipping allowed!'

The roundabout started off again. The music blared gaily, the animals, fish and birds went round and round, up and down, flapping their wings and fins, nodding their heads and waving tails – all very exciting indeed.

And Winks was disobedient – he whipped his goldfish with his stick! 'Gee up!' he cried.

Then he got such a shock. The goldfish suddenly shot right off the roundabout through the air and disappeared! The roundabout slowed down and came to a stop. The pixie in charge looked very angry.

'He whipped his goldfish and I told him not to. Now I've lost the goldfish, and my master will be very angry with me.'

'Oh *dear*!' said Mollie, getting off her pony. 'I'm so very sorry. Winks did promise to be good. Where has he gone, do you think?'

Then there suddenly came the sound of a terrific splash, and a loud wail came on the air. 'That's Winks,' cried Peter, beginning to run. 'Whatever has happened to him?'

XXV

HOME AGAIN – AND GOODBYE!

The yells went on and on and on. 'Help me! I'm drowning! Help, help, HELP!'

The children and Chinky tore round the corner. The sea lay in front of them, blue and calm. The goldfish was swimming about in it, looking enormous. Winks was splashing and struggling in the water, and every time he tried to wade out, the goldfish bumped him with his nose and sent him under.

There was a crowd of little people yelling with laughter. Peter waded in and pulled Winks out. The goldfish flapped out, too, and lay on the beach. It didn't seem to mind leaving the water at all – but then, as Mollie said, it wasn't a *real*, *live* fish. It was just a roundabout one.

'Winks, we're not a bit sorry for you,' said Peter. 'As usual, you brought your trouble on yourself. Now, just pick up that fish and take it back to the roundabout.'

The fish was big but not heavy. Winks groaned and put it on his shoulder. It flapped its fins and made itself as difficult to carry as it possibly could. Winks staggered back to the roundabout with it.

But the roundabout was gone. It had completely disappeared.

'Well,' said Winks, dumping the fish on the ground at once. 'I'm not carrying this fish any longer, then.'

But the others made him. 'We might meet the pixie in charge of the roundabout,' said Peter. 'And you could give it him back then. He was very upset at losing it.'

So Winks had to stagger along carrying the goldfish. Still, as Peter said, if he was going to make trouble, he could jolly well carry his own troubles!

It certainly was an Island of Surprises. There was a surprise round almost every corner! For one thing, there was a wonderful Balloon Tree. It had buds that blew up into balloons. Under the tree sat a brownie with a ball of string. You could choose your own balloon, pick it off the tree, and then get the neck tied with string by the brownie. They all chose balloons at once.

Winks stayed behind and they had to go back and fetch him. He had done a very surprising thing. He had picked six of the biggest balloons and had got enough string from the brownie to tie each of them to the big goldfish. And just as Chinky and the children reached the Balloon Tree again they saw Winks set the goldfish free in the wind – and the breeze took hold of the balloons and carried goldfish and all high up in the air.

'Oh, Winks!' said Mollie. 'Now look what you've done!'

Winks grinned. 'Just a little surprise for the goldfish,' he said. 'Thank goodness I've got rid of him.'

Well, what can you do with a brownie like that? The others gave him up in despair and walked on again. The Wishing-Chair followed them closely, as if it was a bit afraid of the Island of Surprises.

Round the next corner was another surprise. There

were a dozen small motor cars that seemed to go by magic. 'Come and race, come and race!' chanted a little goblin. 'The winner can choose his own prize!'

The prizes were as exciting as the little cars. There was a purse that always had money in it no matter how many times you took it out.

There was a little clock that didn't strike the hour, but called them out in a dear little voice. 'It is now twelve o'clock!' And there was a teapot that would pour out any drink you liked to mention.

'Ooooh – do let's try a race!' cried Winks, and he leapt into a fine blue car. 'I want one of those prizes!'

They all chose cars. The goblin set them in a row and showed them how to work them. 'Just press hard on these buttons, first with one foot and then with the other,' he said. 'Now – are you ready – one, two, three, GO!'

And off they went. Winks bumped into Chinky and both cars fell over. Mollie's foot slipped off one button and her car stopped for a moment or two. But Peter shot ahead and won the race, whilst all the little folk cheered and clapped.

'Choose your prize,' said the goblin. Peter chose a little dish with a lid. It was a wonderful dish. Every time you lifted the lid there was some titbit there – a sausage or a bar of chocolate or an orange, or an ice-cream – something like that. Peter thought it would be very useful indeed to keep in the playroom.

They had a wonderful time that day. Once the surprise was not very nice. They went to sit down for a rest on some dear little rocking chairs. The chairs at once began to rock as soon as everyone was sitting in them – and they rocked so violently that everyone was thrown roughly out on the ground.

The goblin in charge laughed till the tears ran down his cheeks. '*Not* a very pleasant surprise,' said Mollie, picking herself up and running after her balloon, which was blowing away. 'Funny to watch, I dare say – but not funny to do!'

They kept having titbits out of the Titbit Dish, but Mollie wished there were more ice-creams. So it was a lovely surprise when they came to a big public fountain, which had a tap labelled: 'Ice-cream Tap. TURN AND SAY WHAT KIND.'

Mollie turned it at once. 'Chocolate ice-cream,' she said, and out came a stream of chocolate cream that ran into a small cornet underneath and froze at once.

'Oh, look!' cried Peter. They had come to the little field, and in it were big white swans waiting to take people for flights in the air.

'Shall we have a fly?' said Peter. 'Do you think the Wishing-Chair will be jealous if we do?'

'I think one of us had better stay down on the ground with the chair, whilst the others are having a turn at flying on the birds,' said Mollie. 'Just in *case* it flies off in a huff, you know.'

So Mollie sat in the Wishing-Chair whilst the others chose swans and rose up in the air on the backs of the beautiful white birds.

When it was Winks' turn to sit in the Wishing-Chair and stay with it, whilst the others rode on the swans, he thought he would get the chair to chase the swans and make them fly faster!

And up went the Wishing-Chair into the air and began to chase the swans, bumping into their tails and creaking at them in a most alarming manner. One swan was so startled that it turned almost upside down trying to get away from the Wishing-Chair – and the rider on its back fell headlong to the ground.

It was a witch! Fortunately she had her broomstick with her and she managed to get on that as she fell.

She was so angry with Winks! She called the Wishing-Chair to the ground at once and scolded Winks so hard that he tried to hide under the chair in a fright. Mollie, Peter and Chinky flew down at once, angry, too, because of his mischievous trick.

'Ha, Chinky!' said the angry witch, 'is this brownie a friend of yours? Who is he?'

'He's Winks,' said Chinky.

'What – Winks, who turned his grandmother's pigs blue?' cried the witch. 'I thought he was at Mister Grim's school. Well – it's time he was back there. Swan, come here!'

A big white swan flew down to her. The witch picked up Winks as if he were a feather and sat him firmly down on the swan's back.

'Now,' she said to the swan, 'take Winks to Mister Grim's school and deliver him to Mister Grim himself.'

'Oh, no, oh, no!' wailed Winks. 'Mollie, Peter, don't let me go.'

'You'll have to, Winks,' said Mollie. 'You really are too naughty for anything. Try to be good this term, and perhaps you'll be allowed to spend your next holidays with Chinky and us. Good-bye.'

'But I shan't get enough to eat! I always have to go without my dinner!' wailed Winks.

Peter couldn't help feeling sorry for him. 'Here – take the Titbit Dish,' he said, and pushed it into Winks' hands. 'You'll always have something nice to eat, then.'

Winks' tears dried up at once. He beamed. 'Oh, *thank you*, Peter – how wonderful! Now I don't mind going back a bit! I'll be as good as anything. I'll see you all next holidays. Good-bye!'

And off he went on the swan, back to Mister Grim's school for Brownies, hugging the Titbit Dish in joy.

'He's very, very naughty, and I can't help thinking that Mister Grim's school is the only place for him,' said Mollie. 'But I do like him very much, all the same.'

179

'Look, the sun's going down,' said Chinky suddenly. 'We must go. They say the Island of Surprises always disappears at sunset, and we don't want to disappear with it. Quick – it's disappearing already!'

So it was! Parts of it began to look misty and dream-like. The children and Chinky went to the Wishing-Chair at once. 'Home, Wishing-Chair,' said Mollie. 'Quick, before we all disappear with the Island. That witch has vanished already!'

And home to the playroom they went. They heard Mother ringing the bell for bedtime just as they arrived.

'Oh dear – our very last adventure these holidays, I'm afraid,' said Mollie. 'Chinky, you'll take the chair to your mother's won't you, and take great care of it for us? You know the date we come back home from school. Be here in time to welcome us!'

'We'll slip in and say a last good-bye before we leave for school,' promised Peter. 'Don't be lonely without us, Chinky, will you? And couldn't you go and see Winks once or twice at school – in the Wishing-Chair – just to cheer him up?'

'I'll see if my mother will let me,' said Chinky. 'She doesn't like Winks, you know. Anyway, he will be quite happy with the Titbit Dish, Peter. It *was* nice of you to give it to him.'

'Good-bye, Wishing-Chair,' said Mollie, patting it. 'You've taken us on some wonderful adventures this time. Be ready to take us again next holidays, won't you?'

The chair creaked loudly, as if it, too, were saying good-bye. The bedtime bell rang again, this time quite impatiently.

'We must go!' said Mollie, and she gave Chinky a hug. 'We *are* lucky to have you and a Wishing-Chair, we really are! Good-bye!'

Good-bye, too, Mollie, Peter, Chinky, Winks and the Wishing-Chair. We'll see you all again some day, we hope!

Enid Blyton™

THE ADVENTURES OF THE
WISHING-CHAIR

'Oh dear!' said Peter. 'I do wish we were safely home!'
And then the most extraordinary thing of all happened!
The chair they were in began to creak and groan, and
suddenly it rose up in the air, with the two children in it!

Once Mollie and Peter hace discovered the Wishing-Chair, their lives are full of adventure. It takes them to all sorts of magical places, from the giant's castle where they rescue Chinky the pixie, to the amzing party at Magician Greatheart's castle.

Enid Blyton™

WISHING-CHAIR
MORE
STORIES

Mollie and Peter and Chinky the pixie have more amazing
adventures on their Wishing-Chair. They find gold at the
end of the rainbow, they meet brownies and they visit the
Land of Wishes. Best of all they get to help Santa Claus
deliver presents for Christmas!

The third magic Enid Blyton Wishing-Chair adventure.

Enid Blyton™

THE ENCHANTED WOOD

'Up the Faraway Tree,
Jo, Bessie and me!'

Jo, Bessie and Frannie move to the country and find an Enchanted Wood right on their doorstep! And in the wood stands the magic Faraway Tree where the Saucepan Man, Moon-Face and Silky the fairy live.

Together they visit the strange lands which lie at the top of the tree, and have the most exciting adventures – and narrow escapes.

Enid Blyton™

THE MAGIC FARAWAY TREE

*'Oh, do let's take our lunch up into the
Land of Topsy-Turvy. Oh, do, do!'*

Rick thought it would be dull in the country with Joe,
Beth and Frannie. But that was before he found the
magic Faraway Tree!

The four children have the most extraordinary
adventures with the Saucepan Man, Moon-Face and
Silky the fairy. They only have to climb through the
cloud at the top of the huge tree tobe in the Land
of Spells, or Land of Topsy-Turvy, or even the Land of
Do-As-You-Please!

Enid Blyton™

THE FOLK OF THE FARAWAY TREE

Joe, Beth and Frannie are fed up when they hear that Connie is coming to stay – she's so stuck-up and bossy. But they don't let her stop them from having exciting adventures with their friends Silky the fairy, Moon-Face and Saucepan Man.

Together they climb through the cloud at the top of the tree and visit all sorts of strange places, like the Land of Secrets and the Land of Treats – and Connie learns to behave herself!